WARNINGS FROM
THE FAR SOUTH

WARNINGS FROM
THE FAR SOUTH

*Democracy versus Dictatorship in
Uruguay, Argentina, and Chile*

William Columbus Davis

 PRAEGER

Westport, Connecticut
London

Library of Congress Cataloging-in-Publication Data

Davis, William Columbus.
    Warnings from the far south : democracy versus dictatorship in
Uruguay, Argentina, and Chile / William Columbus Davis.
      p.   cm.
    Includes bibliographical references (p.   ) and index.
    ISBN 0–275–95021–2 (alk. paper)
    1. Uruguay—Politics and government—20th century. 2. Argentina—
Politics and government—20th century. 3. Chile—Politics and
government—20th century. 4. Democracy—South America—
History—20th century. 5. Authoritarianism—South America—
History—20th century. I. Title.
F2217.D38   1995
320.98'09'045—dc20   95–7017

British Library Cataloguing in Publication Data is available.

Library of Congress Catalog Card Number: 95–7017
ISBN: 0–275–95021–2

First published in 1995

Praeger Publishers, 88 Post Road West, Westport, CT 06881
An imprint of Greenwood Publishing Group, Inc.

Printed in the United States of America

The paper used in this book complies with the
Permanent Paper Standard issued by the National
Information Standards Organization (Z39.48–1984).

10 9 8 7 6 5 4 3 2 1

To
Dorothy

Contents

Preface

An account of the dramatic developments in the Far South during the last half century is more than just a recent history of Uruguay, Argentina, and Chile. It is an amazing story of three of the most advanced Latin American republics and the problems their people brought upon themselves in trying to improve their lives and acquire larger shares of the world's resources. It is a revelation that should be of great interest and significance not only to residents of these three countries but also to those of the United States and other parts of the globe. The misguided efforts, colossal blunders, and recent solutions of Uruguayans, Argentines, and Chileans provide striking examples and clear warnings to all persons engaged in climbing the ladder of success. If only they would heed!

My keen interest and close association with the Far South and other parts of Latin America go back to 1940, when I began studies at Harvard University leading to a Ph.D. in Latin American History. Since then, through many visits and daily information from the news media and additional sources, I have followed developments in Uruguay, Argentina, and Chile as well as the other Latin American states. The data in this volume have been gathered from various news accounts, personal observations, and interviews with many people in the Far South.

I am indebted to all civilian and military officials and other residents of Uruguay, Argentina, and Chile who have contributed information that has been useful in the writing of this book. I wish to express my appreciation to the U.S. foreign service and military officers stationed in these countries during my visits there who in different ways aided this study. I am especially grateful to my former students, Ambassador George W. Landau for very valuable assistance and information while he was in Chile, and Ambassador Thomas J. Dodd for significant information on Uruguay during his tour of duty there. Most of all I am indebted and thankful to my wife, Dr. Dorothy

Fleetwood Davis, for her invaluable encouragement and assistance in many ways leading to the completion of *Warnings from the Far South: Democracy versus Dictatorship in Uruguay, Argentina, and Chile.*

William Columbus Davis
McLean, Virginia
November, 1994

Chapter 1

The Far South and Latin American Environment

DIVERSITY

The Latin American republics are NOT ALIKE. On the contrary, they ARE ALL DIFFERENT. And some are more different than others.

In many respects the three most exceptional are those of the Far South—Uruguay, Argentina, and Chile. They have been endowed with numerous advantages and few of the disadvantages found in other parts of Latin America. For many years, in an environment characterized by militarism, dictatorships, and instability, they stood out from most Latin American countries for their long records of democracy, political stability, and personal freedoms. With excellent lands and climate, they developed prosperous economies that effectively utilized the natural resources. Culturally they are outstanding for high levels of literacy and individual achievements in literature and the arts. Socially they are unusual for racial homogeneity, large middle classes, and progressive social legislation. Altogether they have been unique in Latin America and in many respects have compared favorably with the most advanced nations of the world.

But in recent decades Uruguay, Argentina, and Chile have been outstanding for another reason—the troubles they brought on themselves. Because their people abused their advantages—particularly the freedoms and democratic political systems—these states evolved into Latin America's real problem countries. In the 1970s they became noted for military dictatorships and abuses of human rights, as well as fantastic economic difficulties. The fact that they are in Latin America should not becloud the significance of what happened here and the applicability of these experiences to other parts of the globe.

Among the relatively few people in the United States who give any thought to Latin America, there is a strong tendency to be overly critical of what they see—or think they see—there. Especially is this true with respect to Latin American political developments. Revolts and dictatorships, often over-played and misinterpreted, make headlines in the U.S. news media, while little is said about the reasons behind them; and the impressive progress along many lines that takes place from day to day usually goes unnoticed.

Also people in the United States tend to believe *our* concept of democracy to be the only desirable form of government for other countries, including those in Latin America. In doing so we overlook great contrasts in their back-ground and environment as compared with what we have experienced in this country. We likewise often forget that situations can look quite different from another point of view. Although there are significant differences be-tween political systems of the Latin American republics and the United States, there are many similarities—more than most people in this country care to recognize. It is often just a matter of degree. Particularly is this true regarding the republics of the Far South.

Then there is the erroneous belief that Latin America is one big area all the components of which are much alike. Frequently it is viewed as a com-posite of some of the so-called banana republics. Actually there are twenty different countries, not including several non-Hispanic colonies and newly independent states in the Caribbean region, which are not really part of Latin America. It is important to remember that while there are certain common characteristics that apply in varying degrees to most of them, each country is distinctly different from every other one. They vary in size from big Brazil with more than 3 million square miles to El Salvador with slightly over 8,000, from Brazil's 155 million people to Panama's 2.5 million. Their contrasting racial compositions include the virtually all-white populations of Argentina, Uruguay, and Costa Rica; the African inhabitants of Haiti, Brazil, and others; and the numerous Indians of Peru, Bolivia, Ecuador, Guatemala, and Mexico. Together these countries cover approximately 7.75 million square miles and embrace more than 450 million people—well over half the total inhabitants of the Western Hemisphere.

In order to evaluate fairly the political situation in any Latin American republic, one must be aware of the factors that retard or aid development there. Most of these countries have faced serious handicaps, with the ele-ments retarding orderly political life far outweighing those favoring it. With this fact in mind, we should look briefly at the general background and some of these problems, remembering that they do not apply equally to all states and that Uruguay, Argentina, and Chile are exceptional cases.

TRADITION

Probably the most important of all influences shaping the course of polit-ical events in Latin American countries is tradition. In any part of the world the way people live and are governed is largely a matter of tradition—how they have done it for many years or centuries. And tradition changes very slowly.

The Latin American republics have inherited traditions of dictatorship in one form or another. In both Spain and Portugal, before the conquest of America and throughout most of the colonial period, more and more power was being gathered into the hands of the crown, creating virtually an absolute monarchy. In pre-Conquest America dictatorial governments were also to be found among many—but not all—of the Indian tribes. Actually there have been significant contrasts between different groups of Spanish people—the more economically progressive and democratic inhabitants of northern Spain, for example, as compared with those of Andalucía. Likewise, in America there were striking differences between such aborigines as the Incas of Peru, with their tradition of one-man rule and strict regimentation, and the liberty-loving Araucanians of Chile. The proportion of such diverse groups in the makeup of any modern Latin American republic has influenced its political development. In this respect Uruguay, Argentina, and Chile have been very fortunate.

Added to this diversity is a lack of political experience during the colonial era. Under the Spanish and Portuguese systems there was little opportunity for people in America to participate in government. Laws were made in Spain to be handed down and applied in the Spanish colonies. Most of the high officials came from Spain, served a few years, and went back to Europe. With rare exceptions, the colonists could gain political experience through service only at the municipal level. Portuguese rule of Brazil was similar in theory although more relaxed in practice.

These colonists achieved independence in the early nineteenth century, when the trend of the times was toward democracy. Falling in line with this trend, most of them tried to set up so-called republics, actually contrary to the advice of many of their most outstanding leaders of the independence movements. They attempted something for which they were unprepared, and in the process of trying to make work systems of government they knew little about, for which they had no tradition, they have stumbled and fallen many times.

Some of the Latin American republics have done much better than others largely because they had certain advantages the others did not have. For one thing, the Spanish colonial system was not applied the same in all of Spain's American colonies. Those considered of less importance to the crown, such as Chile and the Uruguayan-Argentine area, were ruled less forcefully; thus there was opportunity for a greater degree of self-government and political experience. This and several other favorable factors have enabled these countries to progress more rapidly and firmly up the democratic ladder than some of their neighbors. Brazil also profited by the more relaxed Portuguese rule and the fact that it began independent life as a constitutional monarchy, which gave it time to evolve gradually into a republic.

The prominent role of the Roman Catholic Church is also very significant. Due to the close tie between church and state, the church was much involved in politics. This continued after the colonies gained independence, and only slowly has the church been stripped of its political influence. In some Latin American states its political power is still very strong. Although from time to time members of the clergy—particularly the lower clergy—have broken with tradition, and some have even become revolutionary leaders, throughout the colonial period and since independence most of the church hierarchy have been aligned with the conservative, aristocratic class. In a few of the republics, however, this alignment has changed rather dramatically within recent years.

CORRUPTION

There have been many honest, dedicated public servants—the number varies considerably from one country to another, but unfortunately political corruption is well established. While trying to promote honest government in America, Spain unwittingly contributed to dishonesty by introducing, in the mid-sixteenth century, the sale of public offices in the colonies—all except the highest ones. This measure was taken as a means of raising additional revenue for the Spanish crown—but what were the results? A man buying a public office sought to gain from it everything he could, and such behavior became the accepted practice. Frequently offices so acquired could be passed down through several generations, and a few families often obtained control over a certain area.

The colonies also were subjected to overregulation—too many laws made from too great a distance. Virtually all legal restrictions for the colonies, even minute municipal ordinances, were formulated in the mother country, usually by men unfamiliar with colonial conditions. Unrealistic colonial laws and attempts to restrict trade actually promoted smuggling, encouraged violations of unpopular decrees, and contributed to bribery of public officials. In such ways under the Spanish and Portuguese systems a tradition of corruption developed.

Today corruption still plagues Latin America. The colonial tradition lives on. Low salaries of public officials, commonly justified by the assumption that an office holder is going to supplement his income, is also a contributing factor. Indeed, in Latin America there are two kinds of graft—"legitimate" and "illegitimate." It is generally assumed that a public official is going to accept graft—that he is going to use his office for whatever pecuniary gain he can. He is thought by many to be foolish if he does not do so. If he oversteps the accepted bounds, however, and acquires too much, it is considered illegitimate. The bounds vary in degree from one republic to another and from place to place within a given country. Some of the most pernicious corruption has been among port authorities—an interesting carryover from colonial smuggling. There are certain Latin American states today in which the overall level of honesty in government is considerably higher than in others. It is largely a matter of custom and what the public will tolerate.

This spirit of corruption together with unrealistic forms of government and the rewards available in public office have resulted in many dishonest elections. Even if they are allowed to vote freely, it is not necessarily the way people cast their ballots but the way the votes are counted and recorded that determines the outcome. Latin American politicians have employed all the tricks of the trade. Upon being asked why he was so sure his party was going to win a forthcoming election, a provincial governor replied, "It is in the bag," as he pointed to bags containing the identification booklets (necessary in order to vote) that he had filched from many of his constituents. There are numerous other tricks. But Latin Americans do not hold a monopoly on dishonest elections. One is quite naive if he thinks all U.S. elections are completely honest.

TOPOGRAPHY

A brief topographical map study will reveal serious physical handicaps that retard Latin American political development. Most of these countries lie within the tropical zone. They also contain some extremely rugged terrain. In most of this area, where climate depends so much on altitude, a majority of people live in the highlands. But the mountains, which provide cool temperatures, create transportation and communication barriers. A result has been isolated, often rebellious, communities that make control by a central government more difficult than it otherwise might be. Also inadequate transportation facilities have retarded economic development. Only slowly, partially, and at great cost have such problems been solved. On the other hand, in certain regions of Latin America geographical configuration has aided political unity. Especially is this true in Chile and Costa Rica, where populations are concentrated in relatively small, accessible central zones, and in Argentina and Uruguay, where the terrain facilitates communication throughout the country.

ETHNOLOGY

There are several ethnological influences that play significant roles in political affairs. First, we might look at racial composition. Here Uruguay, Argentina, Chile, and Costa Rica, with their rather homogeneous racial groups, have an advantage. On the other hand, in the countries with large aboriginal populations—Bolivia, Peru, Ecuador, Guatemala, and Mexico—many of the Indian people do not even speak the Spanish language. They cling to their own native tongue and way of life. They resist change and are, in effect, a nation within a nation. It is very difficult to bring them into the life of the country. In other republics there are diverse racial groups. In spite of any claims to the contrary that Latin Americans may make, here, as elsewhere in the world, wherever two or more races are present in large numbers, there is friction. This has been a source of political as well as economic and social problems.

Certain personal characteristics also exert influences on the political life of these countries. Latin people are more inclined to be emotional than are those of Northern European origin, and there is a strong tendency for Latins to think with the heart more than the head. Pride is also present to an extreme degree, especially among men of Spanish heritage. These factors have been influential in many disturbances that have occurred, including revolt. A man runs for public office and loses. It is very difficult for him to accept defeat gracefully; and if he thinks there is an opportunity to succeed, he may take the revolutionary road in an effort to save face. The history of unfair elections makes it easy for him to claim fraud and thereby justify turning to revolt to gain the office he seeks.

Individualism is another characteristic inherent in people of Latin background. It limits a person's ability to fit into and conform to a political system, and is partly responsible for the personal political parties that have been prevalent.

There is also the influence of family cohesion. Family unity is very strong—much more so than in the United States. In many respects this is good, but it has certain interesting and sometimes disturbing political effects. As the spoils system prevails in most of these countries, each new president has numerous opportunities to make appointments. In the United States there is normally much objection to a man in high public office appointing his relatives to important posts, but to most Latin Americans nepotism is an accepted practice—indeed a family duty. Thus, when a man gains the presidency of a Latin American country, it is expected that he will take care of his relatives with appointments to various good positions. Of course, such practice is not unheard of in the United States, but it is frowned upon.

A very significant Latin characteristic is paternalism. The head of the family is looked up to as its leader and he wields considerably more influence than is customary in the United States. The concept of one-man rule, therefore, is not only an inheritance from the absolute monarchy of colonial times but is basic in the structure of the family itself. Thus *caudillismo*—the tendency to look to the *caudillo*, the leader or boss—is deeply ingrained in the fabric of Latin American society, from the smallest unit, the family, through the various larger social and political units, to the head of state itself.

One of the greatest dangers to preservation of a democracy is the tendency of many people toward hero worship. This is a problem in the United States, but is even more serious in Latin America. It is one of the strongest forces working against democracy there.

CLASSES OF SOCIETY

The Spanish and Portuguese came to America as exploiters. They exploited the mineral wealth, the native Indians, and the Africans who were imported as laborers. This practice quickly led to a two-class society. Throughout the long colonial period in most of the colonies there were only two social classes—the wealthy, so-called landholding aristocracy and, far beneath them in power, wealth, and influence, the mass of people. In many of the independent republics this situation is still largely true, although in a few—particularly Uruguay, Argentina, Chile, and Costa Rica—there is a large middle class, which began to appear even in the colonial era. In a few other countries—especially Mexico, Venezuela, and Brazil—the middle class has been growing rapidly in recent years, but in most others it is still quite small.

This social arrangement has had profound political effects. In Spanish America independence brought only a change of masters from Spaniards to upper-class creoles (American-born colonists of Spanish ancestry). Neither there nor in Brazil did it transfer power to the middle or lower classes. In most of the republics, rule by the aristocracy has prevailed since the colonial period. In only a few has the middle class become powerful enough to gain control.

POPULATION EXPLOSION

In recent decades, of even more serious consequence than social class divisions has been the very rapid population growth and concentration of people in urban areas. With an overall annual increase of nearly 3 percent, until recently Latin America was the fastest growing major region of the world. During the last two decades this rate has declined. But the rate of increase has been far greater in some countries than others. In Argentina it has been only about 1.3 percent and in Uruguay under 1 percent. Overall figures, however, do not really tell the story. Cities have been growing at very rapid rates due to the great migration of people from rural areas. For example, within the past forty years the population of Mexico City (now apparently the world's largest metropolis) has increased about tenfold, Bogotá ninefold, Lima eightfold, Santiago fivefold. Thus Latin America is suffering from what may be termed urbanitis.

This situation presents momentous problems. One is the virtual impossibility of providing adequate housing and utilities. Even more serious from the political point of view is the restlessness of people who have crowded into cities seeking jobs that often do not exist. Another result of the population explosion is a greater proportion of young people. All these factors have tended to increase the political volatility of an already volatile population. On the other hand, movement of rural peasants to cities and their consequent exposure to a more advanced civilization and increased opportunities for economic improvement have enabled some of them to climb the ladder to middle-class status.

ILLITERACY

Illiteracy has been a serious problem throughout much of Latin America. Spain and Portugal gave to their colonies what they had in the field of education; but during the colonial period, education was for the privileged few—not the mass of people. At the time of independence the average level of literacy in Latin America was only about 5 to 10 percent. From this low starting point, there have been drastic improvements in several of the republics until today in some, particularly Uruguay, Argentina, Chile, and Costa Rica, literacy is comparable to that in the United States. A few others are only slightly behind. Some, however, are far below this level.

A largely literate electorate does not necessarily assure a country a stable, democratic government, but without at least a fairly high degree of literacy, this kind of government is virtually impossible. Not only do the people need to be literate, they need to be educated for democracy. This was recognized at an early date in a few parts of Latin America, notably in Chile. The Chileans began early in the nineteenth century to educate their people to govern themselves and worked at it rather consistently. This effort contributed significantly to Chile's long record of democracy down to the unfortunate events of the 1970s.

FRAMEWORK OF GOVERNMENT

With the achievement of independence in the early nineteenth century, political leaders in the new Latin American states set about drawing up frameworks of government. Constitution writing and rewriting have been going on ever since. Authors of Latin American constitutions have borrowed heavily from the U.S. Constitution, the Spanish Constitution of 1812, the French Constitution of 1793, and several U.S. state constitutions. They also have adopted ideas from one another. Such efforts have produced many impressive, idealistic documents. A significant weakness in most of them, however, is length. They tend to be too comprehensive and include many items that should be left to legislation, with the result that they are quickly outdated. As a constitution becomes obsolete, the tendency is to cast it aside and write a new one.

The general attitude toward the constitution is considerably different in a Latin American country from that in the United States. We tend to take our constitution very seriously as our framework of government and the law of the land. By contrast, Latin Americans often look upon their constitutions as theories of government composed of ideals toward which the country is working—principles that may be attained sometime in the future. Nevertheless, a Latin American constitution is a popular legal format with which even the most extreme dictatorship finds it convenient to cloak itself; and many a dictator, rather than abolishing the constitution after attaining power, has hastened to rewrite it to embrace principles compatible with his ideas of administration.

EXECUTIVE POWERS

Although the constitution may provide in theory for a democratic system of government with a division of powers, with rare exceptions even in the most democratic republics the executive is considerably more powerful than either the legislative or judicial branches. Outstanding exceptions were Chile and Uruguay before the 1970s. Unfamiliar with the principle of the separation of powers, Latin Americans have tended to operate on the theory that the legislative body and the courts should follow the lead of the chief executive. Thus not only does the congress tend to go along with what the president wishes, but he generally also has the power to issue executive decrees that have the force of law and are not usually questioned by the legislature. In times of crisis (imaginary or real), the president also normally has the right to declare a state of siege, although in some countries it must have legislative approval and there have been some cases of such approval being denied.

Actually, the president of the United States, especially in emergencies, has just as much—in some cases more—power than many so-called Latin American dictators. An important consideration is the degree to which he uses these powers. Again, as in so much else regarding government, it is largely a matter of tradition. In many Latin American countries, tradition enables the president to pursue a more dictatorial role than would be tolerated in the United States. But we should bear in mind that this varies greatly in the United States from one chief executive to another. It also varies from one Latin American republic to another and from one individual to another.

POLITICAL PARTIES

In Latin America political parties are not usually founded and maintained on isms but on men. In view of the tradition of *caudillismo*, this fact should not be surprising. Long-lived parties based on ideologies, such as the Institutional Revolutionary Party (PRI) in Mexico, the traditional Liberal and Conservative parties in Colombia, the Blanco and Colorado parties in Uruguay, the old-line parties in Chile, and a few others elsewhere are exceptional. For the most part, a party forms around a political leader and exists as long as he retains a position of leadership. When the leader passes from the scene, the party usually disappears or reforms. Thus Latin American political parties are generally personal affairs. In some countries this pattern together with the ease with which they may be formed and participate in government have led to a multiplicity of parties that tends to complicate the political system.

MILITARISM

A question frequently asked in the United States is why the military in Latin America is so influential politically. This influence is difficult for a U.S. native to understand. It is primarily an inheritance from the wars of independence and the political systems that followed. As has been pointed out, prior to independence there was little opportunity for civilian political leaders to develop in the colonies. The leaders who emerged from the 1810–1825 revolutionary era were for the most part military heroes—those who had led the fight for independence. Having been instrumental in freeing his country, such a leader often felt he should be rewarded with high public office, and he set about to obtain it by any means possible. Under the political systems that were created, elections could easily be controlled by the group in power, and usually were. Thus an election was not necessarily a fair test. Frequently the man who won the presidency of his country was the one who had a sufficient military force behind him, and he retained office as long as this force supported him effectively. He lost office when someone else appeared with a more impressive and loyal military backing.

This situation put the military as an institution in a position of control. Not only could the armed forces demand and obtain favors from the government, but many military officers became ambitious for power and did, throughout the nineteenth and into the twentieth century, gain power by such means. Some still do. The result was a great deal of political instability, with many cases of a president being forced out of office before his term expired.

In recent years there has been a considerable change in the complexion of the military in much of Latin America. This varies, of course, from one state to another. Whereas in the past the military was generally considered to be an instrument of the aristocracy and most of the commissioned officers came from this group, today more are coming from the middle and even lower classes of society. These origins are changing their political orientation. Also many have been influenced by contacts with the United States and other countries. For various reasons they are becoming more reform conscious. In several countries the military has been in the forefront in bringing reforms to benefit the mass of people.

Today, probably more than ever before, leaders of the armed services see themselves as protectors of the republic; and in recent decades, coups have occurred for this reason more than formerly. The military is the one force that is strong enough to preserve order and prevent the country from going too far to the left or actually losing its independence. At times it also serves as moderator between political parties and factions, and may be the only group to which people can turn to rid the state of an unpopular or dangerous government. In many Latin American republics there is a long history—indeed, a tradition—of military rule. But even in Uruguay, Argentina, Chile, and Brazil, where civilian control seemed well established and the armed forces had been carefully kept in the background, military government has appeared—brought about by popular disgust with elected officials and appeals to the military to set affairs in order.

REVOLT

To an outsider who hears of Latin America primarily during times of political disturbance, revolt or revolution might seem to be the customary way of life there. If one uses the term "revolution" in its true meaning of a profound, fundamental change in the life of a country, rather than just a change of rulers, there have been very few revolutions in Latin America. If, however, the term is used to mean a successful rebellion that overturns a government, there have been many revolutions. And, of course, revolts that did not succeed are far more numerous.

Latin American revolts fall into several categories. By no means are they all bloody affairs. The most prevalent form is what is known as a palace revolt. As the name indicates, it centers on the presidential palace. This may not involve anyone directly except the president, his immediate associates, and certain members of the armed forces. It may be simply a matter of one or more military officers informing the president that he is out of office. If he sees that he does not have sufficient force with which to resist, he may accept the ultimatum as a fait accompli. In such case the coup is a bloodless one. If, on the other hand, the president still has armed support, he probably will resist and this decision can lead to bloody clashes. Even under these circumstances, however, members of the general public need not be involved if they are careful to stay off the streets while shooting is going on. There have been cases in which the outcome of a revolt was arranged by telephone or radio communications between commanders of the various military units around the country.

A popular revolt, in contrast, is a people's uprising. Under these circumstances many civilians tend to become involved, and as they meet with armed resistance, there is likely to be much bloodshed. Civil war, a third type of revolt, may ensue when the people of a country become seriously divided over one or more important issues. A fourth, and peaceful, type of revolt that has been used successfully several times in recent decades is a general strike. If effectively organized, enough members of the professions, business, and labor join together in protest against the administration to bring professional and commercial activities within the country virtually to a standstill. Under these circumstances the president may be forced to resign. In recent decades strikes have been used quite effectively in Chile, El Salvador, and Guatemala.

RIGHT OF ASYLUM

There is a certain code of ethics between politicians and the military that normally protects the "outgoing" president and his associates who are overthrown by revolution, or other public leaders whose freedom is endangered. This is the right of asylum. Customarily those in danger of political persecution hurry into the most convenient embassy in the capital, which, being property of a foreign country, is considered a safe refuge. As long as they remain in the embassy compound, they are generally secure from arrest. It is customary that within a reasonable time the new administration will grant such individuals safe conduct out of the country. There have been some notable exceptions to this, including the case of Víctor Raúl Haya de la Torre, American Revolutionary Popular Alliance (APRA) leader in Peru, who, being pursued by political opponents, gained entrance into the Colombian embassy in Lima in 1949 and remained more than five years because the then Peruvian president, Manuel Odría, refused to grant him safe conduct.

SUBVERSION

Subversion has been a constant threat in most Latin American countries. This is not just foreign subversion. It is an old, domestic situation—a way of life among the "outs" since independence. There is a lack of loyal opposition among many Latin Americans. As a result, those out of power seek ways to seize power, and a normal pastime is plotting how to accomplish this aim, often by revolt.

Since World War I there has been a great deal of foreign-inspired subversion in Latin America. Except in the period just before and during World War II, when there were Nazi designs on certain parts of this region, such subversive efforts were directed and financed principally by the USSR until its disintegration. (Communist Chinese activities have been minimal by comparison.) Beginning in the early 1960s, Cuba served as a funnel through which large amounts of Soviet funds, equipment, and propaganda flowed into various Latin American countries. It also has been a primary training center for terrorist techniques. During the 1970s and early 1980s the Soviet Union was rather successful at a double game of appearing more respectable and extending its Latin American diplomatic and economic contacts while at the same time promoting subversive activities wherever feasible—often through its Cuban connection. This policy magnified the political problems in several republics. Most vulnerable have been some of the more democratic states where leftist administrations facilitated Marxist penetration. Especially disturbing have been various acts of terrorism, mainly centered in large cities. Both domestic and foreign-inspired subversion have created disorder, and such subversive groups have from time to time influenced Latin American governments to resort to unwise and disruptive policies.

FOREIGN INTERVENTION

In several Latin American republics foreign intervention occasionally has been influential—indeed, at times decisive—in determining the type of government or degree of political stability. Through much of the nineteenth century the internal political situation in Uruguay was disturbed by Argentine and Brazilian rivalry and influence there. Argentine meddling in Paraguay and Bolivia has on occasion furthered political instability. In the mid-nineteenth century Spanish intervention in Peru and the Dominican Republic and French intervention in Mexico contributed to political instability in those countries. In the twentieth century Soviet support perpetuated Fidel Castro's hold on Cuba and Sandinista control of Nicaragua. The United States, in efforts to promote democracy and political stability throughout Latin America and eliminate subversive elements deemed dangerous to hemisphere security, has on several occasions intervened either overtly or covertly, especially in Middle America. It has brought the demise of some "undesirable" governments simply by withholding diplomatic recognition. Physical intervention—overt in the Dominican Republic in 1965 and covert in support of Guatemalan rebels in 1954—was effective in preventing a probable Communist takeover in the former and in ousting a pro-Communist regime in Guatemala. By agreement, until relinquished by treaty revisions in 1934 and 1935 respectively, the United States had the right to intervene in Cuba and Panama for the purpose of preserving internal order. In both cases the intention and result were promotion of political stability. A number of other examples may be cited. In other words, there have been numerous instances where, for better or worse, certain Latin American republics have had limitations placed by foreign countries on their conduct of internal political affairs.

ECONOMY

Economic problems in Latin America are numerous and varied. One of the major handicaps to economic development in some of these countries is political instability; but economic difficulties often breed political instability. Indeed, in a few Latin American republics these two have developed into a vicious circle—political instability contributing to economic stagnation and the serious economic problems creating insurmountable political difficulties.

The traditional system of extensive landholdings with a resultant large landless class, lack of economic diversification, entrenched monopolies, and antiquated tax structures—all inherited from the colonial period—are not only economic matters but have political overtones as well. One of the most prominent recent political issues has been agrarian reform. In several of the republics serious attempts have been made to break up great estates and provide some land for the landless class. But landholding in Latin America is not merely an economic consideration. It is also social—a matter of prestige. Attempts at agrarian reform pit one class of society against another and liberal politicians against conservatives. Under these circumstances reform is difficult, and occasionally these clashes result in violence.

In attempting to promote economic growth, several Latin American governments have become excessively involved in industrial development of various kinds. The result has been government ownership not only of public utilities but also of many other types of enterprise from mining and manufacturing to banking and insurance. Unfortunately, government operation of industry is usually quite inefficient and costly, resulting in serious drain on the public treasury. In several Latin American states this has been a major reason for recent financial difficulties. It also has had the effect of discouraging private enterprise in some sectors of the economy. A resulting current trend is privatization, with several governments trying to dispose of their industries to private buyers.

The flight of local private capital to supposedly safer investments abroad is a phenomenon that long has plagued many Latin American countries. It is both a result of political instability and, by retarding economic development, a contributor to political instability.

Several Latin American states also have been victims of a nationalism versus realism struggle, which has been of serious proportions in some of them. On the one hand, Latin American political leaders plead for more foreign capital for various kinds of development. On the other hand, an extreme spirit of nationalism, often played upon by either patriotic or subversive elements, frequently has resulted in restrictions and even expropriation of foreign-owned industries that discourage the inflow of needed investments. Practices such as these in Uruguay, Argentina, and Chile have created unnecessary economic difficulties and brought disturbing political repercussions.

IRRESPONSIBILITY

Another problem in Latin America, as well as many other parts of the world, has been the large number of irresponsible individuals in positions of influence or control. Pressure groups play significant roles. The average university student in Latin America takes a great deal more interest in political affairs than does his counterpart in the United States. Student agitation is often loud and influential but too frequently in support of impractical objectives. This also has been true of Latin American labor organizations, extreme nationalists, and other groups. Often these have pressured a government into unwise policies. Of course, Latin America is not the only part of the world where such influences are prevalent.

Fiscal irresponsibility has been especially disturbing in several of the Latin American republics in recent decades. Politicians have been swayed more by political expediency than by financial realism, particularly in some of the countries where voter influence is quite effective. Many reforms are needed; many reforms are expected and demanded by the public. One of the greatest problems has been how to grant improvements and at the same time preserve the financial soundness of the government. This difficulty has been compounded by the traditional Latin American resistance to taxation. Several governments have gone so far in trying to provide welfare, public housing, schools, highways, economic development, and various other benefits, without sufficiently increasing tax revenue to pay for them, that they have virtually spent themselves into bankruptcy. Years of deficit financing have set off and perpetuated some of the world's most serious inflation, which in time has destroyed much of what the political leaders were trying to accomplish, as well as the systems of government themselves. Such destruction has been particularly true of Uruguay, Argentina, and Chile. These have been extreme cases of fiscal irresponsibility in recent years, but they are not the only ones. By contrast, in some states that generally have pursued sounder fiscal policies the overall development has been more impressive. Outstanding examples were Mexico and Venezuela; but in the early 1970s even Mexico succumbed to the lure of wild spending—with dire consequences. And more recently Venezuela took a fatal leap in that direction.

Time and again the United States, while practicing massive deficit financing itself, has advised against unsound fiscal policies in Latin America. The countries plagued by inflation are ones that have followed our example rather than our advice.

DEMOCRACY VERSUS DICTATORSHIP

A question often raised is why Latin Americans accept dictatorship. Aside from tradition, one reason is that many of these republics have had some sad experiences with other forms of government. At times the people have been faced with a choice between undesirable civilian incumbents in office or the military, as the only force capable of doing so, taking over and throwing the rascals out. Or it may be a choice between a rather democratic but unstable, ineffective government as against some form of dictatorship which, being more stable, can better preserve law and order and pursue a sound and progressive policy. Thus, as many Latin Americans see it, a dictatorship is not necessarily bad. It is not how democratic a Latin American government is that really counts. More important is how constructive it is.

UNDERSTANDING AND EVALUATING LATIN AMERICAN DEVELOPMENTS

Unfortunately, many people in the United States, including government officials, try to evaluate Latin American events by looking only on the surface at what has happened recently. This approach can be very misleading. It accounts in great measure for many errors in judgment that have appeared from time to time in our dealings with this part of the world. Only by knowing the past can one comprehend the present or predict the future. Really to understand the problems of any Latin American country, it is necessary to study its history as well as the area as a whole, to become acquainted with the people, their traditions, how they think, how they react to given situations. It is also necessary to recognize that each individual state has a combination of factors, different from the others, that has determined its course of political, economic, and social development.

SIGNIFICANCE OF THE FAR SOUTH

It already has been indicated that Uruguay, Argentina, and Chile are virtually in a class by themselves among Latin American nations. As the states that most closely resemble the United States, Canada, and Western Europe, their experiences and problems should be of wide and profound interest. For this reason, it is with these republics of the Far South—especially their recent and current developments—that the remainder of this volume is concerned.

Chapter 2

Uruguay: Lost Utopia

In early 1978 the Organization of American States (OAS) was considering a site for its annual general assembly of foreign ministers of the member countries. Uruguay, long known as the most extreme welfare state in the Western Hemisphere and an outstanding center of freedom and democracy, had offered to serve as host. But the OAS rejected Uruguay's offer—because of its recent alleged violations of human rights! Its current government, controlled by the military, had earned a reputation as one of the most oppressive in South America.

Uruguay, once ranked as one of the world's most advanced twentieth-century republics and often termed the "Switzerland of South America," has had the makings of a utopia. For many years it tried to become one—and almost succeeded. As one Uruguayan expressed to me in 1955, "We have such a wonderful country. Our only fear is that it might change."

By that time the unreality of the life this delightful, little state had been leading was becoming quite apparent, and the story of subsequent developments there is a sad one. Political experimentation had resulted in a very democratic system of government; but along with it, socialistic experiments had led to an extreme welfare state. The economic burdens of too much welfarism together with serious leftist guerrilla activities that developed amid the freedoms of the late 1960s and early 1970s were largely responsible for destroying the democracy that the country had enjoyed. From a near utopia, Uruguay degenerated into a state of political and economic chaos.

LOCATION AND PEOPLE

Uruguay, approximately 72,000 square miles in area and with a population in the 1990s of about 3 million, was literally born on a battlefield. Sandwiched between the South American giants, Argentina and Brazil, in colonial times it was claimed by both Spain and Portugal. After these imperial powers lost their South American possessions in early nineteenth century, it was fought over by Argentines and Brazilians. In 1828, due in considerable measure to British intervention, Uruguay became an independent republic with about twice as much territory as today. Nevertheless, throughout most of the nineteenth century Argentina and Brazil continued to interfere in its internal affairs and helped perpetuate its domestic political struggles. In 1851, in return for Brazil's assistance against the Argentine dictator Juan Manuel Rosas, Uruguay was pressured into relinquishing much northern territory and became confined to approximately its present size. During the twentieth century, however, there has been much less outside interference and Uruguayans have been relatively free to pursue their own course.

Because at the end of the colonial era Uruguay, Paraguay, Bolivia, and Argentina constituted the Spanish Viceroyalty of the Río de la Plata, with Buenos Aires as the capital, since independence Argentines have been obsessed with the belief that these three smaller states should be part of Argentina. Although not daring to take military action for fear of reprisals by other OAS members, several times during his dictatorship in Argentina Juan D. Perón tried in other ways to extend his influence (and he hoped his control) over Uruguay.

In other respects Uruguay has been very fortunate. Located between 30 and 35 degrees south latitude, it is the only country in Latin America lying completely within a temperate zone, and it enjoys an excellent climate at low altitudes, without extremes of heat or cold and with adequate rainfall throughout the year. It is not broken by high mountains, and the gently rolling terrain makes communication easy. This geography has facilitated the construction of extensive railroad and highway networks, which effectively tie the nation together. Although small in area, virtually all of Uruguay's territory is usable. Indeed, with the exceptions of Brazil, Argentina, Mexico, and Peru, all of which are much larger, this little state has more good, arable land than any other in Latin America.

As far as is known, Uruguay does not possess great mineral wealth. With an abundance of fine grazing land, it has been primarily a sheep and cattle country. Meat and wool have been its principal exports. With approximately 300 miles of beautiful beaches, it is also a playground that attracts many thousands of visitors each year, mainly from Argentina (about 90 percent) and Brazil, making tourism one of the most important industries.

In every Latin American country except Brazil and Ecuador the capital is the largest and most important city. Uruguay is the extreme example of this. About half its people live in and around Montevideo, which is far larger than any other place in the nation. It is not only the center of political and cultural life but also the chief port, focus of the communication networks, and the hub of finance, trade, and industry. Although showing signs of shabbiness in recent years because of the economic difficulties, Montevideo is one of the most attractive and substantial cities in South America. Unlike other large Latin American urban centers, it has virtually no slums. With fine beaches nearby, it profits considerably from the tourist trade. Because of its size, location, and many advantages, it plays the dominant role in national life. Political issues and struggles generally have revolved around the urban interests of Montevideo versus rural interests of the interior.

Uruguay also has been fortunate in its people. With a population almost completely European in background, it has very little racial diversity and virtually no ethnic problems. Here, as in Argentina, Indians were scarce and hostile. Their descendants have disappeared. There are only a few blacks. In the late nineteenth and early twentieth centuries Uruguay, like Argentina and Brazil, experienced waves of immigration from Europe. This influx has been the primary factor in determining its present almost entirely white composition. It was particularly fortunate in attracting many settlers from northern Spain as well as industrious Italians and some Germans and Swiss. With a large middle class, there has been emphasis on mass education, resulting in one of the highest levels of literacy in the world.

Politically the nineteenth century proved a turbulent era for Uruguay. Early in the independence period two principal political parties appeared—the Colorados (liberals), whose appeal has been mainly urban, and the Blancos (conservatives), later also known as Nacionalistas, whose strength has centered in the rural areas. The names by which these parties have been known came from the colors of their respective banners—red and white. The nineteenth century was a time of bitter strife between these two—struggles for power, military dictatorships, and very little of the democracy Uruguay came to know in the twentieth century. Remarkably, the turn of the century brought a turnabout in the political life of the nation.

THE BATLLE REVOLUTION

In various parts of the world there have been times when a revolutionary leader appeared, but the people were not ready for change. There have been other instances when the time was ripe, but there was no effective leader. Then there have been a few occasions when popular demand for reform and a capable leader appeared on the scene simultaneously. Under these circumstances, far-reaching transformations may result. Such was the situation in Uruguay in the early twentieth century. As a consequence, this South American state has experienced one of the few real revolutions in Latin America. It was a peaceful revolution, inspired and initially led by José Batlle y Ordóñez, the father of modern Uruguay.

The numerous recently arrived immigrants had no interest in nineteenth-century political quarrels. Most had come to the New World seeking a better life, and their principal desire was for an atmosphere of freedom, peace, and political stability within which to pursue their economic and social goals.

Likewise significant was the fact that in Uruguay the previous quarter century had witnessed a cultural awakening, particularly a greatly increased interest in education and the establishment of an effective public school system. The influence of this awakening was felt in a dramatic rise of literacy and the appearance of a new, literate electorate that could make itself felt and would demand sweeping improvements along many lines. Of special importance to the nation's future was the emerging popularity of socialism and welfarism and their promises of economic security and higher standards of living. Twentieth-century Uruguayans were destined to embrace these and other philosophies and undertake a search for utopia that transformed this country into a world-famous laboratory of social, economic, and political experiments.

Batlle was born in 1856. His father served a term as president of Uruguay in 1868–72, and the son grew up in this political environment and in the Colorado Party. He received a good education, studied law for a while, but abandoned it for his primary interest, journalism. By 1878 he had begun a journalistic career and spent the next several years in a crusade, through the columns of several newspapers, against political evils as he saw them, particularly Uruguayan dictatorships. In 1886 he founded *El Día*, which became the nation's most influential newspaper. With this publication as his mouthpiece, he spread his message and pointed Uruguay down paths toward political democracy and social welfare.

By 1887 he began a campaign to clean up and reorganize the Colorado Party, which, although it had long controlled the national government, was at that time viewed as seriously in need of rejuvenation. After serving in several prominent political capacities, including governor of a province, senator from Montevideo, and president of the Senate, in 1903 Batlle was elected president of the republic. (In those days the president was elected by the General Assembly.) The modern history of Uruguay begins with his election and was shaped by the far-reaching changes he initiated.

During the first part of this administration Batlle was engaged in putting down a Blanco revolt, and succeeding years were required to insure political tranquility. These events retarded his drive for political and social reform. Even so, he was able to begin expanding and improving the educational system, with the goal of free instruction at all levels. He also undertook a campaign to elevate the status of women, which succeeded during this term in the passage of a law legalizing divorce. Of primary concern to Batlle was the welfare of laboring classes, and during these years he started a long and vigorous drive for an eight-hour working day and other improvements.

Although urged to stand for reelection in 1907, Batlle refused because of his determination to uphold the constitutional provision prohibiting two successive terms. Instead he helped bring about the election of his friend Claudio Williman. He spent most of the next four years in Europe and thus allowed his successor a free hand in governing the country. Williman proved an able executive and succeeded in securing adoption of some of Batlle's proposed reforms, particularly in the field of education. In 1911 Batlle returned for a second term in the presidency.

Between 1911 and 1915 he forced through the General Assembly (congress) many of the social and economic reforms he had long advocated. During these years and later he was instrumental in laying the groundwork for what evolved into an elaborate welfare system that included minimum wages, very generous retirement annuities, accident and health insurance, free medical services, free public education from the lowest grades through the highest levels of the university, and various other social benefits. Changes in the system of justice abolished the death penalty and authorized probation and parole. Labor benefitted by the eight-hour day and forty-four-hour week, adopted before the end of Batlle's second term—the first such limitation on hours of labor in Latin America. Complete freedom was also accorded labor organizations.

Believing that the state should not be entirely dependent on private capital or foreign sources for its financial needs and economic development, that basic commodities should be available at reasonable prices, and that there was room for both public and private enterprise. Batlle launched the government into operation of certain industries. Initially this effort included reorganization and complete control of the Bank of the Republic and creation of state insurance and mortgage banks. The state also acquired from the foreign owners control of electric power facilities. Subsequently the government expanded its operations to embrace virtually all public utilities as well as a number of other industries.

Batlle was also very much concerned with the structure of government. He was disturbed over the political unrest and internal conflicts of the nineteenth century and felt that some way should be devised to avoid them. As he saw it, Uruguay's political troubles had been due primarily to concentration of too much power in the hands of the president, which in turn encouraged dictatorships. Also serious had been party rivalries that had led to civil wars. While touring Europe between his two presidential terms, Batlle had spent considerable time in Switzerland studying its system of government. He was very favorably impressed by the fact that this well-governed country did not have a president but a seven-man council that jointly performed the administrative functions. The presidency of the council rotated among its members, each of whom served in this capacity only a year and had no more authority than the others. Batlle saw in this system a possible solution to Uruguay's problem of administration.

In late 1912 he and the General Assembly set in motion the process of electing a constituent assembly to revise the constitution under which Uruguay had lived since 1830. A few months later he announced his proposal to abolish the presidency and substitute a nine-member executive council. This plan immediately encountered widespread opposition and led to a bitter battle extending over several years, which split the Colorado Party into two factions. But through the columns of *El Día* and in other ways, Batlle continually urged elimination of the single executive. By the end of his second term he had succeeded in making his executive council proposal the major issue in political reform.

After the constitutional convention began its sessions in early 1917, a compromise was reached whereby the presidency would not be abolished but restricted by dividing powers between the chief executive and a National Council of Administration. The president, formerly picked by the General Assembly, now would be elected by popular vote for a period of four years and be ineligible for immediate reelection. The council would consist of nine members, one-third chosen each two years for six-year terms. It was also provided that in each election for council members the party winning the most ballots would receive two of the seats and the one gaining the next largest vote would have the other seat. This arrangement was designed to appease the Blancos by assuring them at least three council members. Administrative duties were divided between the president and the council, with the president heading the ministries of foreign affairs, defense, and the interior, while the council controlled the departments of finance, education, public works, public welfare, industry, and labor. Under this compromise, however, no one person or group had ultimate responsibility for all branches of administration.

The new constitution was approved by popular referendum in November 1917 and became effective in early 1919. Among its other provisions were a bicameral congress with at least one-third of the seats held by the leading minority party, considerable local autonomy for territorial departments and municipalities throughout the country, secret ballot in all elections, and separation of church and state.

Although charges that Batlle was an atheist never have been proved, he and his wing of the Colorado Party were definitely anticlerical. Since independence, several Latin American countries have experienced bitter struggles over attempts—normally led by liberals—to eradicate the powerful political and economic influences of the Roman Catholic Church, which were inherited from the colonial era. Uruguay presents an extreme case of church suppression. The church never was as strong there as in most other parts of Spanish and Portuguese America. In contrast to conservative parties in some Latin American republics, the Blancos have refrained from taking a pro-church stand, and consequently after Uruguayan independence the established church did not have an effective political organization on which to lean for support. The Civic Union (Unión Cívica), founded in 1872, has existed as the official Catholic party, but it has been unable to compete effectively with the Colorados and Blancos. Prior to Batlle's time, the church's power and influence had been restricted in several respects. Such limitation also was imposed on the Catholic Church in some other Latin American states in mid- and late nineteenth century.

Constitutional separation of church and state in 1919 was only one of the steps taken in the twentieth century to curb church influence. The teaching of religion in public schools was banned by a 1909 law, and subsequently this ban was broadened to prohibit any mention or suggestion of religion in a classroom. In contrast to the 1830 Constitution, no reference to God appeared in the preamble of the 1917 document or in the oath of office it prescribed for the president, and these omissions have been perpetuated in subsequent constitutions. In Batlle's newspaper, *El Día*, any reference to God (*Dios*) traditionally has been printed with a lower case "d." Religious activities and holidays have been played down to the point where officially Christmas came to be designated only as "Family Day" and Holy Week became "Tourist Week."

The *batllista* anticlerical campaign has tended to weaken Catholic influence not only along political and economic lines but also as a religious institution. Although certainly not the only factor, it definitely has contributed to the alarming drift away from church affiliation in Uruguay. A result is fewer and smaller Catholic churches, in relation to population, than is customary in other parts of Latin America. Amid the complete freedom of religion existing there, Protestant denominations have found broad fields for penetration; but although they have established many churches and missions and won numerous converts, they have not succeeded in mounting a Christian crusade that has swept the nation and filled the religious void.

During periods of economic prosperity, it is relatively easy for a government to succeed and retain popular support among its constituency; but in times of economic distress, the political picture is likely to change quickly and radically. After inauguration of the constitutional reforms in 1919, *batllista* Colorados continued to dominate the national political scene. Under these circumstances, the new administrative system got off to a good start. Uruguay had prospered economically during World War I, and most of the 1920s was a period of prosperity and economic advancement. With these advantages, administrative problems were minimal.

The compromise national administrative arrangement inaugurated in 1919 contained a weakness that had appeared in Spanish colonial government, where executive power in a viceroyalty or captaincy general was divided between the viceroy or captain general, on the one hand, and a council, known as the *audiencia*, on the other. This division resulted in considerable friction. Baltasar Brum, a close associate of Batlle in his fight for the plural executive, became president in 1919. He was an outstanding statesman, and under his leadership the new system of government worked smoothly. Nevertheless, he recognized its inherent weakness; and during his presidential term he proposed that the presidency be abolished and all executive functions assumed by the National Council of Administration. But after the long and bitter fight that had resulted in this compromise, it was virtually impossible to arouse further interest in the matter at this time, and nothing came of Brum's proposal. Throughout the 1920s the system survived without serious difficulty. Economically Uruguay was prosperous; politically it was a leader in freedom and democracy.

But then came 1929. By the early 1930s the Great Depression had shaken the world and brought sudden, and often violent, changes of government in many countries. Uruguay was caught up in this turmoil; but there the results were less radical than in many other states of Latin America. Sharp declines in the prices of meat and wool along with other economic reverses brought not only lower wages or unemployment to many Uruguayans but serious financial problems for the government, whose costly welfare system was becoming increasingly burdensome.

Gabriel Terra, another Colorado, was inaugurated president in March 1931. Batlle had died in 1929; and as the depression tightened its grip on Uruguay and the economic effects became more disastrous, there was growing dissatisfaction with the form of government he had played a major role in creating. Criticism of Terra's policies mounted, and the General Assembly and the National Council of Administration grew more uncooperative. With the six Colorado and three Blanco members of the council quarreling among themselves and increasing friction between this body and the president, the inherent weakness of the administrative system was quite apparent.

Terra blamed the administrative council for hindering his efforts to restore prosperity, and in 1932 he expressed the opinion that either the president or the council should go. When an allegedly Communist-inspired uprising occurred in late March 1933, he called out troops to suppress it. The congress and council, which had been increasingly hostile toward Terra, condemned his handling of this situation. He retaliated by ordering the dissolution of both bodies and the arrest of many political opponents. This action brought not only the demise of the National Council of Administration but also the suicide of Baltasar Brum, who had been serving as its president.

For several months Terra governed by decree with the assistance of an eight-member advisory junta, appointed by himself, and a deliberative assembly chosen by the junta. Terra's administration following this coup d'état was termed a dictatorship, but it was a very mild one by Latin American standards. Freedom of speech continued and most other individual rights were respected. Terra announced that constitutional government would be restored as soon as a new constitution could be formulated and adopted. Within a few months a constitutional convention produced the necessary document, which was ratified by plebiscite in April 1934.

The new Constitution of 1934 largely reflected Terra's ideas. As should have been expected, it eliminated the National Council of Administration and returned Uruguay to a single chief executive. It inaugurated woman suffrage by granting the right to vote to all men and women over eighteen years of age. Theoretically it provided a modified form of parliamentary government by permitting the General Assembly to force the resignation of cabinet members by a vote of no confidence. In case of serious disagreement, the president could be compelled to resign by a two-thirds vote of the General Assembly in joint session; but if such a procedure should be undertaken and the required two-thirds not obtained, the president then could dissolve the congress and call new elections.

Two unusual—and unrealistic—features of this constitution were a provision that the president must select three of his nine cabinet members from the leading minority party and a stipulation that one-half of the thirty Senate seats would go to this party. Terra had gone overboard to please the Blancos; but in granting them an equal number of senators, he was producing a serious problem. The key figure now would be the vice president, an official created by this constitution, who, as presiding officer of the Senate, also had a voice and a vote. Before adjourning, the constitutional convention selected Terra president for another four years, even though its authority to do so was seriously questioned.

During his second term this constitution, although defective, worked reasonably well mainly because Terra disregarded it whenever it got in his way. When the congress proved uncooperative, he simply governed by decree. An abortive coup by part of the army in 1935 and subsequent revelation of a Communist conspiracy furnished excuses for Terra's strong-arm tactics. His methods were rather effective in helping alleviate some of the worst effects of the depression, and economic conditions did improve in the mid-1930s. Terra was able to please certain groups by providing low-cost housing, liberalizing old age pensions, and extending laws for the protection of labor. As a result of his commitment to socialism, these years also witnessed a further expansion of government with the creation of additional national industries. In an effort to protect the currency and balance of payments, the government restricted imports from a given country to the value of Uruguayan exports to that country. At this time Uruguay's currency remained strong, with the peso approximately equal to the U.S. dollar.

Before the end of 1937 economic conditions had improved considerably and there appeared to be no threats of further political disturbances. Under these circumstances, Terra announced that he would not be a candidate for reelection in 1938.

COMMUNIST MENACE

During the depression of the 1930s, the Communists for the first time appeared a menace in Uruguay. Diplomatic recognition of the Soviet Union in 1922 had permitted establishment of a Soviet legation in Montevideo. For more than a decade it was the only Soviet diplomatic contact in South America and served as Communist headquarters on that continent; and from there

Communist agents and literature were sent into all South American countries. Beginning in 1921, a Communist political party also operated legally. In keeping with the nation's democratic principles, the Communists generally were given complete freedom and their constitutional rights were carefully respected. Realizing the advantages of maintaining a legation in Montevideo, the Communists usually were cautious in their relations with the Uruguayan government and refrained from openly attacking it. In the 1930s, however, they overstepped their bounds and abused Uruguayan hospitality. An uprising in 1933 was attributed to them; and the scare over an alleged "Red" plot in 1935 caused Terra to terminate the relationship on the ground that the Soviets were financing and spreading Communist propaganda through their diplomatic representatives there. But due in part to pressure from the United States, which during World War II urged many Latin American countries to do so, Uruguay reestablished relations with the Soviet Union in 1943.

For many years Uruguayans tended to laugh at the suggestion that Communism posed a serious threat in their country. It was believed that their brand of socialism and the relatively high standard of living most Uruguayans enjoyed did not provide an atmosphere conducive to Communist success. Nevertheless, as a political party the Communists managed to survive, although they attracted only a small following. Their strength has been almost entirely in the cities, principally Montevideo. By capturing influential positions in labor organizations and student groups, they became a nuisance and often promoted labor unrest, including strikes and violence. Profiting by the Soviet Union's temporarily improved image during and right after World War II, the Uruguayan Communist Party gained some adherents; and in the elections of 1946, its candidates polled about 5 percent of the total vote. In subsequent years Communist influence as a disturbing factor increased.

Under the presidency of Gabriel Terra, a civilian, the Uruguayan government had temporarily become a dictatorship. Under his brother-in-law, Gen. Alfredo Baldomir, who was elected president in 1938, democracy was restored. Before his election, Baldomir had emphasized the need for democracy, and after his inauguration he appeared determined to govern in a democratic fashion. He tried to work closely with the General Assembly and even restored the National Council of Administration, which restricted his own authority. But the beginning of World War II in late 1939 brought difficulties.

The discovery of an alleged Nazi plot to seize Uruguay and transform it into a German colony caused Baldomir to begin improving the nation's military defenses and cooperate more effectively with the United States for protection. This policy aroused serious opposition from the Blancos, whose longtime leader, Luis Alberto de Herrera, was an outspoken critic of the United States. After the Blancos had used their powerful position in the government to block needed legislation, including authorization for an Export-Import Bank loan for defense purposes, Baldomir reverted temporarily to more dictatorial methods. In early 1942 he replaced the three Blancos in his cabinet with members of his own party. He also dismissed the congress and governed by decree. Later that year, when the political situation had improved, he felt safe in restoring democracy; and elections, which had been postponed a few months, were scheduled for November. By constitutional amendments, approved by the electorate at this time, the National Council of Administration was again abolished and proportional representation was restored in the Senate. Thus two of the most serious administrative handicaps were eliminated.

Baldomir's successor in the presidency, Juan José Amézaga, elected in 1942, strengthened the democratic process. During his term the principal threat appeared to be from Argentina, which succumbed to military dictatorship in 1943. After his subsequent rise to power, Juan D. Perón revived traditional Argentine designs on Uruguay, and there were rumors of possible armed aggression against this small neighbor. Although not daring to resort to military intervention, he did make an unsuccessful attempt, through economic pressure, to bring about a Blanco victory in Uruguay's 1946 elections. Traditionally the Blancos were pro-Argentine; and Herrera and his followers apparently were sympathetic to Argentine intervention, which they thought might bring them to power. Nevertheless, the Colorados continued in control of the presidency and both houses of the General Assembly, and the government remained quite democratic and free of foreign influence. In November 1946 Tomás Berreta, a *batllista* Colorado, was elected president, and Luis Batlle Berres, nephew of José Batlle y Ordóñez, was chosen vice president. Berreta, inaugurated in March 1947, died the following August, and Batlle completed the term as president.

Uruguay's unique system of elections, which permitted the holding of party primaries and general elections at the same time, has preserved the two major parties despite factional divisions in both. Inaugurated in the 1920s, the system especially aided the Colorados, who became badly split into factions. If the party agreed, each of several factions could list its candidates on a ballot under the party label (*lema*). The voter then cast his ballot for the candidates (or list) of his choice, but in doing so he also was voting for the party. The candidate for a certain office who won the most votes within his party was given the cumulative vote of all candidates for that office running under that party's label. Thus no matter how many factions might appear, the party's strength would be preserved. For example, even though the leading Blanco (Nationalist) candidate for president might gain more votes than any single Colorado candidate, the highest Colorado would win if the combined tally for himself and other Colorado candidates exceeded the total votes of all Blanco candidates. In such a manner, although there have been some minor parties, Uruguay preserved (until the military takeover) what really was a two-party political system.

GOVERNMENT BY EXECUTIVE COUNCIL

The 1950 election was especially significant because it brought to the presidency Andrés Martínez Trueba, another *batllista* Colorado. In his inaugural address the following March, he revived the original plan of Batlle y Ordóñez—to replace the office of president with an executive council. It was a rare occasion of a man advocating abolition of his own office. This idea now met with a more favorable response than previously. Herrera announced his support because he saw in it an opportunity for his Blanco Party to regain a meaningful voice in government. The *El Día* faction of the *batllista* Colorados, headed by the sons of José Batlle, supported this executive council proposal; but the Luis Batlle Berres faction and also the Civic Union, Socialists, and Communists opposed it. Over the next several months necessary constitutional revisions were prepared, and in December what became known as the 1951 Constitution was approved by a narrow margin in a nationwide plebiscite. It brought into existence a true executive council administration, not a compromise such as had been tried before.

Beginning March 1, 1952, Uruguay's chief executive would be a nine-man National Council of Government, the members to be chosen by popular vote for terms of four years and not eligible for immediate reelection. Six of the council seats would go to the party winning the most votes and the other three to the leading minority party. To provide for any likely vacancy, two alternates would be elected for each seat. The presidency of the council would rotate among the majority members, the top four serving one year each in order of succession determined by the number of votes he had polled. All administrative matters would be decided by majority vote, and theoretically the president of the council would serve only as the executive officer and have no more power than any other member. As the council president, however, normally he would represent the nation on ceremonial occasions.

The powers of the National Council of Government and its relationship with the General Assembly were the same as those held by the single executive. There was also a cabinet of nine members to head the various ministries, now to be chosen by the executive council. This arrangement differed from the Swiss system, where the council members also headed ministries. As under the preceding constitution, cabinet members could be dismissed by a General Assembly vote of no confidence; but the legislative body could not force the resignation of the executive council.

Members of the first National Council of Government, who took office in 1952, were appointed by the two leading parties for a period of three years. It was agreed that Martínez Trueba, whose office had been abolished in order to set up the council, would serve as president of this body for the remaining three years of the term for which he had been elected president of the nation. The first popularly elected council would be chosen in late 1954 and take office in March 1955. At this time also the chief executive (*intendente*) in each of Uruguay's nineteen departments would be replaced by a popularly elected executive council. This system actually provided the territorial departments only a moderate amount of local autonomy as the national government still retained control of most local affairs.

In the early and mid-1950s administration by executive council worked well. There appeared to be a maximum of cooperation among the members and a minimum of friction and time-consuming arguments, which opponents of the council had predicted. Of course, during the first three years the National Council of Government had as its president Martínez Trueba, who had been largely responsible for bringing it into existence. His skill as a leader and his dedication to the system played a major part in its success.

In the elections of November 1954, the Colorados won as expected. Now in this first popularly elected National Council two of Uruguay's leading political figures gained seats—Luis Batlle Berres and Luis Alberto de Herrera. As the majority member with the highest popular vote, Batlle served the first year (1955–56) as president of the council. But having previously been president of the nation and apparently hoping for reelection to such a position, he was not enthusiastic about the National Council of Government and had opposed its adoption in 1951. During his year as president of the council there were rumors that he might try to abolish it and restore the single executive, but this did not happen. Over these four years, however, there was a decline in enthusiasm for the council form of administration and its opponents became more vocal.

One of the issues on which Uruguayans voted in the 1958 elections was a constitutional amendment to abolish the National Council of Government and return to a single president. This proposal was defeated. But in these elections—for the first time in ninety-three years—the Blancos won control of the national government! Herrera, perennial candidate for president of Uruguay, who had been defeated six times, was ineligible to run for a National Council seat in 1958 as he had been a member during the previous four years. Realizing the council might be abolished and the single chief executive restored by the referendum at this time, he did appear on the ballot as a candidate for president of the republic. He won; but as the single executive amendment was defeated, he had no office. Now advanced in years, he died in early 1959, just before his party took over the council.

SOCIALISM, WELFARISM, INFLATION

Why did the Blancos win in 1958? By this time Uruguay's very democratic political system, which had resulted from experiments inaugurated by Batlle y Ordóñez and his associates, was being seriously threatened by the socialism and welfarism they and their successors had imposed upon the country. From a modest beginning, based on the theory that there was need and room for both public and private enterprise and that the national treasury would benefit from the profits, the state had gradually expanded its commercial operations until it came to dominate the economic life of the nation. Now the government was operating public utilities, including electric power, the telephone system, railroads, domestic airlines, and even the seaports. The principal oil refinery, the fishing industry, and the manufacture of alcohol, cement, and several other items were government monopolies. The state also owned various other commercial enterprises, including hotels, night clubs, gambling casinos, and the republic's largest bank. In an attempt to curb rising food prices, the government established retail outlets. These in turn led to protests and demonstrations by private shopkeepers who felt the pinch of government competition.

On the theory that private and state industries could compete, a government meat-packing plant had been established. In time, however, the inevitable happened—the government plant gradually encroached upon the private businesses and gained a monopoly of the domestic market. Left with only foreign markets and beset by labor difficulties, for which Uruguay's liberal laws were blamed, the two chief private packing houses, subsidiaries of the U.S.-owned Armour and Swift companies, found themselves so restricted that it was no longer economically feasible to remain in business. These plants closed in early 1958, throwing some 4,000 employees out of work and seriously curtailing Uruguay's exports. This event set off a twenty-four-hour general strike, in support of the Swift and Armour workers who had lost their jobs, which virtually paralyzed Montevideo.

To avoid the obvious pitfalls of political control, state economic enterprises were set up as autonomous corporations. Theoretically they operated independently; but no matter how independent in theory, they were still branches of the government and thus dumping grounds for job seekers with political pull. The members of their boards of directors, general managers, and other high officials were political appointees. In the absence of a civil service system, they might change with administrations every four years. For most other employees the prime qualification was political connection rather than industrial skill. Thus these government corporations generally were seriously overstaffed with incompetent personnel and became notorious for inefficiency and their drain on the public treasury. (Under Uruguay's labor laws, it was almost impossible to dismiss an incompetent employee.) State monopolies and state subsidies to virtually all industries, whether government or private, not only sapped the nation's financial resources but forced up the prices of Uruguayan products to where they could not compete effectively in the world market.

By the mid-1950s the state political and economic structure had become a great bureaucracy with nearly one-third of the working population on its payrolls. Government employees were so numerous that in some offices it was said they had to arrive early in the morning to find a seat! Getting a seat was essential so the occupant would not be too weary for his second job. As government employees worked only a thirty-hour week and salaries were very low, moonlighting was considered necessary.

The chief ambition of most workers was to be able to retire. This aim was encouraged by the very generous retirement benefits the government had created. As early as 1838 legislation was adopted providing pensions for public employees; but because of political instability, it was not applied effectively during the nineteenth century. Under Uruguay's twentieth-century social security system, however, a government or private industry employee could retire at full pay by the age of fifty after thirty years of service, and since he no longer would be subject to retirement fund deductions from his salary, would receive a larger income than when he was working. But there were serious problems. Because of the inefficiency with which the system operated, when a person retired, it often took several years to get on the pension rolls. And once he was on, he had no assurance that the government would meet its commitment on time.

Well before mid-century the numerous other social benefits of Uruguay's famous welfare state were fully developed, including free medical services and free public education at all levels. All of this welfarism helped provide what Uruguayans considered the good life, but it was very expensive and proved increasingly burdensome on the government.

After weathering the depression of the 1930s, the country was able to coast along for a while on a wave of economic prosperity provided by demands for Uruguayan products during World War II and the Korean War period. But by the mid-1950s this demand had subsided. Several years earlier Perón, in a futile attempt to gain economic concessions, had seriously damaged Uruguay's tourist industry by imposing restrictions on Argentine travel there. By withholding Argentine wheat, he stimulated large-scale grain production in Uruguay and it even became an exporter of wheat; but by 1955 there were difficulties in selling this wheat abroad. An even more decisive blow was the collapse of the wool market in 1957, due largely to the competition of synthetic fibers. In a vain effort to improve economic conditions, in 1957 the Colorado government began trading with the Soviet Union. The Blancos opposed this trade. The closing of the Armour and Swift packing houses in early 1958 proved a crowning disaster in this economic chaos. Although these plants reopened under worker management in November, by then it was too late to offset the loss in meat exports, which fell from an annual average of over $40 million to $15 million for 1958.

For many years Uruguay had been living beyond its means. Even during the prosperous era of the 1940s and early 1950s, year after year heavy borrowing and the issuance of increasing amounts of currency so depreciated the once stable peso that by July 1946 it had shrunk to approximately 2 pesos per U.S. dollar—half its value a decade earlier.

By 1952 Uruguay, where life had seemed so good and secure, was ex-

periencing social unrest, and through the next several years there were
strikes and other expressions of discontent. Some of these were promoted
by Communist-controlled labor unions. Peronist influence from Argentina
also was significant here as Perón tried to obtain some control over Uruguay
by penetrating its labor organizations. Really, however, the strikes and demonstrations were protests against the ever escalating cost of living, which,
although not freely admitted, was primarily a result of too much welfarism.
In January 1958 there was a taxpayers' revolt, inspired by drastic increases
in property and business taxes. Despite repeated fiscal deficits, although
apparently every other method of raising revenue had been tried, Uruguay
still had avoided an income tax, traditionally unpopular in Latin America.

The Blanco victory in late 1958 was a direct result of popular discontent
over economic problems, especially inflation. In previous years Colorado
governments had been unsuccessful in holding down living costs, expanding
production, relieving unemployment, or stopping currency depreciation. Actually the situation had grown much worse, especially during 1958, which
economically was a disastrous period in most Latin American states. In Uruguay this year brought a more drastic rise in the cost of living and a drop in
the free market value of the peso from 4.7 to 12 per U.S. dollar.

Faced with this predicament, the majority of Uruguayans refused to focus
blame for their plight on the system of government, as many politicians tried
to do. Instead, their reaction followed the pattern of voters in other countries
under adverse economic circumstances. They threw out the party that had
been in power so long and under whose leadership these problems had
arisen—a party that in recent years had appeared increasingly disorganized,
corrupt, and ineffective. They turned to the more conservative group whose
"save the peso" campaign had promised to end Uruguay's economic woes
by a program of austerity and common sense.

With a pledge to reduce spending and solve the nation's financial difficulties, the new National Council of Government assumed office on March
1, 1959, in a simple ceremony before a joint session of the General Assembly,
now also under Blanco control. Only a few hours earlier three factions of
this party had managed to put aside their bickering over personal rivalries
and political spoils long enough to join in a general agreement on policy.
One principal objective was to provide a sound currency. Another was to
stimulate economic production and increase exports by a free-market economy and abolition of exchange controls and subsidies. More efficient administration of government-owned business enterprises and the elaborate
welfare system was also a significant goal.

The new administration immediately found itself confronted by problems
from the past, including continuing unfavorable trade balances and deficits
in most government industries. With the cost of living rising at a 40 percent
annual rate, there were labor demonstrations and strikes in support of de-

mands for large wage increases. But there were also some serious new difficulties. In 1959 the worst floods of the century devastated parts of Uruguay and forced the country to turn to the United States for agricultural commodities it normally exported. This action increased the international trade deficit considerably. On the brighter side, however, was a return of the Argentine tourist trade, gradually lured back after the fall of Perón by an intensive Uruguayan advertising campaign and especially, after 1958, by the sharp decline in value of the Uruguayan peso, which provided vacation bargains to foreigners.

By three principal measures, the Blanco administration tackled the job of reconstructing the economy. Enactment of an exchange-reform bill abolished the multiple exchange rates, formally devalued the peso, and created a situation favorable to exports. Reorganization of the banking system tightened controls on credit. The adoption of a direct income tax for the first time in Uruguay was a desperate attempt to balance the budget by increasing revenue.

A short-term result in 1959 and 1960 was greater inflation. That led to industrial overexpansion, with the construction industry building too many expensive housing units and merchants overstocking in hope of ever rising prices. This situation together with the administration's tight money policy brought a recession in 1961. Especially hard hit were the construction business, where more than 35 percent of the workers lost their jobs, and the textile and clothing industry, both quite important in the nation's economy. Increased exports, decreased imports, and the now revived tourism enabled Uruguay to break even in international trade in 1961, but the recession continued and showed little sign of improving in the near future.

Significantly disturbing during this period were the Communists, who stepped up their efforts to provide chaos by creating and exploiting divisions among major sectors of the population. The accession of Fidel Castro to power in Cuba at the beginning of 1959 stimulated and facilitated the Soviet bloc propaganda campaign in Latin America. By 1960–61 this effort was quite serious in Uruguay, where the last two months of 1960 witnessed three Communist-led general strikes in which 90 percent of the labor unions participated. Communist agitators organized anti-United States demonstrations during Vice President Richard Nixon's visit to Montevideo in 1958 and while President Dwight Eisenhower was there in March 1960, as well as on numerous other occasions. Uruguay's conservative leaders also encountered trouble from the two Communist members in the General Assembly. In January 1961, after police had stormed Communist Party headquarters, arrested 139 people, and seized documents, the Cuban ambassador and the first secretary of the Soviet embassy were expelled from the country on charges of promoting street fights and pro-Castro demonstrations.

National, provincial, and municipal elections were held on November 25,

1962. By a margin of less than 8,000 out of a total 1,100,000 votes cast, the Blancos retained administrative control of the government. This was far less than their plurality of 100,000 four years earlier. But the results in congressional races were even more disturbing to the party in power. In both the Senate and Chamber of Deputies (also known as Chamber of Representatives) the Blancos won only one more seat than the Colorados. Of special interest was the extremely active campaign of the Communist front, running this year under the label "Fidel" (initials of Frente Izquierda de Liberación—Leftist Front of Liberation) in an attempt to attract admirers of the Cuban dictator. Although they received only slightly more than 3 percent of the total vote, which they had won in 1958, the Communists made a better showing than either the Catholic or Socialist parties. Particularly significant were their gains in the General Assembly, which gave them 1 seat in the Senate and 3 in the Chamber of Deputies. With a Senate lineup of 15 Blancos, 14 Colorados, 1 Communist, and 1 Catholic, and a Chamber of Deputies composed of 46 Blancos, 45 Colorados, 3 Communists, 3 Catholics, and 2 Socialists, it was obvious that the far Left could play a strategic role in the customary conflicts between the two major parties.

In the elections of 1962, as in 1958, Uruguayan voters considered—and rejected—a constitutional amendment to abolish the executive council and return to a single president. But amid the intensifying economic stresses of the next four years, this issue aroused increasing interest and agitation. Serious factional divisions within the Blanco Party, in both the congress and executive council, and disturbing rivalry with the Colorados handicapped efforts to deal with the nation's difficulties and provoked widespread dissatisfaction with the government's economic and social policies.

Believing that a growing population would bear the huge financial burden, for many years successive governments had expanded the social welfare programs as politicians found it more popular to increase benefits than to hold the line or retract. But a census taken in 1963 (the first since 1909) revealed the shocking fact that the population had not increased to 3.5 million, as had been thought, but was only 2.6 million with a rising percentage of elderly. With a work force of approximately 1 million, there were about 400,000 retirees entitled to pensions. Uruguay not only had Latin America's lowest birth rate, but many of its well-educated young people were being lured away by better employment opportunities in other countries.

As the government continued to live beyond its financial means and print more currency to pay its bills, an annual inflation of 45 percent in both 1963 and 1964 was followed by a cost of living surge of about 88 percent in 1965. During a three-week period in the middle of that year, the peso suffered a sharp drop on the free market from 26 down to 46 per U.S. dollar, and continued to slide after that. By this time Uruguay was experiencing its worst economic crisis in decades.

Rather than effectively face up to the harsh realities of the situation, an easier way out for politicians was to blame the administrative system and demand a change. Upon assuming the presidency of the National Council of Government on March 1, 1965, Washington Beltrán, leader of the moderate majority faction of the Blanco Party, proposed in a nationwide television and radio address that the single chief executive be restored. The following June he said he considered the council system a "complete failure." There were also other Blancos as well as some Colorado leaders calling for a referendum on reforming the structure of government. It should be noted that several of those, including Beltrán, who advocated a return to the single executive were hopeful of being elected to that office.

About this time politicians were disturbed and administrative problems increased by rumors that certain right-wing officers of Uruguay's traditionally nonpolitical military, encouraged by some leaders of Brazil's armed forces, were contemplating revolt unless the executive council would deal more effectively with economic problems as well as the Communist-led agitation among labor and student groups. Attempts by the government to impose wage restrictions in order to hold down inflation met with strong resistance, which Communists and other extremist agitators did not hesitate to exploit. Belatedly the National Council invoked a more stringent austerity program, but this measure provoked a wave of strikes that in December 1965 almost paralyzed the country. In 1965 there were more than 300 strikes by government employees alone. Only after administration leaders warned of possible military action to counter such disturbances and threatened to outlaw the Communist Party and break relations with Moscow did the strikes subside.

In September 1964 Uruguay, following the lead of all other Latin American republics except Mexico, had broken diplomatic and trade ties with Communist Cuba. In late 1965 the U.S. government, citing a study by the security committee of the Organization of American States, warned of increased Soviet subversive activities in Latin America, especially Uruguay. While apparently reluctant to expel Soviet representatives, in early 1966 the Uruguayan government did oust three members of the North Korean trade mission who had been actively spreading subversive propaganda there. Finally, in October, after other serious labor unrest, believed to be Communist led, and after warning the Soviets to stop meddling in Uruguay's internal affairs, the National Council of Government decided to expel four members of the large Soviet embassy staff.

In early 1966, with a substantial balance-of-payments surplus and a temporary easing of labor agitation, the situation appeared somewhat improved. Aided by a ban on new appointments and salary increases for government employees during an election year, the Blancos made some further efforts to bring order out of the chaos that now prevailed and did succeed in reducing inflation to approximately 50 percent for this year. But it was too little and too late to retain their control of the government.

By July 1966 the threat of a coup d'état appeared very real, encouraged by the new military regime in Argentina as well as the one in Brazil, both of which viewed with alarm Communist activities in the little neighbor between them. By mid-August more than 800,000 signatures appeared on petitions demanding elimination of the council system of government; and well before the November elections, polls indicated that at least 70 percent of the people favored returning to a single executive.

RETURN TO SINGLE EXECUTIVE

Colorados joined Blancos in supporting this change, but the appearance on the ballot of four rival plans was confusing and raised a serious question whether any one of them would receive the necessary support. Nevertheless, a bipartisan constitutional reform, backed by a majority of Blancos and Colorados, was approved.

Not content with merely changing the system of administration, Uruguayan voters, by a margin of over 100,000, also rejected the party that had been in power nearly eight years and turned again to the Colorados, who had governed for so long before the Blanco interlude. They elected president of the republic a sixty-five-year-old retired air force general, Oscar D. Gestido, who had been a minority member of the outgoing National Council.

The new system of government provided for a president elected for five years and ineligible for reelection, and a vice president, who would preside over the Senate and could be elected for a second five-year term. The president was given broad executive powers, but there were safeguards against abuses. A council of ministers, appointed by the president with Senate approval, had the right to pass on presidential decisions. The composition of the General Assembly remained as before, but the term for which members were elected was extended to five years to correspond with that of the president and vice president. As previously, a joint session of the congress could force the resignation of a cabinet member by a vote of censure. In case of disagreement over an important issue, the president could dissolve the congress but must call new congressional elections within sixty days. At the provincial and municipal levels the administrative councils were also replaced by single executives; and, with more limited autonomy, the government corporations would now be headed by individual directors, responsible to the president, instead of executive boards as under the council system.

With 16 out of 31 seats in the Senate and 50 of the 99 members of the Chamber of Deputies, the Colorados held very slim majorities in both houses of the General Assembly. Blanco representation was cut to 13 and 41 respectively. The Communist front, running again under the "Fidel" label, retained its 1 Senate seat and increased its membership in the Chamber of Deputies to 5. Because of serious divisions within the Colorado Party, the new president had no assurance of gaining approval of legislation he desired.

In an effort to prevent the passage of extravagant welfare bills for purely political reasons, the framers of this constitutional reform included a provision prohibiting the congress from introducing new social security programs. Henceforth, only the president was empowered to initiate salary increases for federal employees, establish social security rules, or fix prices.

Although in 1966 the government had managed to hold down wages and slash the inflation rate to 50 percent, President Gestido inherited a nightmare. In early 1967 the outgoing Blanco regime had approved 90 percent pay raises for federal workers. The new administration was saddled with the task of paying the bill. With strikes an almost daily occurrence, the new chief executive selected a cabinet of what he believed to be the best men, regardless of party politics, and set out to solve the nation's problems. "There is no magic formula to make things well, only mental honesty, hard work and routine and meticulous planning for the future," he stated at the time of his inauguration on March 1, 1967.[1] He said he did not intend to end the welfare state concept but hoped to make it more efficient. He announced plans for a series of wage and price controls as well as new taxes, and called upon all classes to make sacrifices.

Fearful of being classed with the military dictators of neighboring Argentina and Brazil, President Gestido hesitated to take advantage of the new, broad powers of his office. Instead he appeared colorless and politically inept and for several months allowed the country to drift into worse economic chaos. In answer to complaints that he was not forceful enough in dealing with the nation's problems, he replied, "I was not elected as a general, but as a president."[2]

By mid-October, after numerous strikes, riots in the streets of Montevideo, 107 percent inflation since the first of the year, and impending national bankruptcy, there was fear of a Communist coup, threat of a military takeover, and evidence that Brazil and Argentina were considering joint intervention. Through their domination of the National Convention of Workers (CNT), the Communists now exerted considerable influence over almost half the labor force. Brazilians were worried by the presence in Uruguay of activist exiles from the ousted João Goulart regime, while both Argentines and Brazilians feared a possible Communist seizure of the buffer state. They compared their position to that of the United States, which had intervened in the Dominican Republic to prevent a Communist government there.

Friendly discussion and persuasion had not worked, and now Gestido suddenly came to life and decided to get tough. He declared a limited state of siege for two weeks. Politically this was a shrewd maneuver because it brought the resignation of five members of his cabinet who had been opposing any effective reform program. He could not have fired them without incurring serious political consequences. Gestido devalued the peso from 99 down to 200 to the dollar, thus eliminating overnight the black market in foreign currency, where dollars had been selling for 170 pesos. He began curtailing government expenditures and issued $100 million in treasury bonds to finance deficits. Because of the great popularity of Uruguay's welfare system, it was very difficult for any government to impose restrictions that would cut back any of its benefits. For this reason the administration had rejected guidelines of the International Monetary Fund, which called for strict budget balancing that would reduce welfare expenditures. In October, however, Gestido decided he should adhere to the IMF guidelines and reestablish with this organization relations that had terminated several months earlier.

Within a few weeks the administration's drastic measures appeared to be getting favorable results. The devaluation of the currency improved Uruguay's balance of payments by promoting increased exports of wheat and wool. Labor difficulties subsided, enabling the government to lift special security controls. There were also important political repercussions, the most significant being support offered by the wing of the Colorado Party led by Jorge Battle Ibáñez, great nephew of José Batlle y Ordóñez and a presidential candidate in 1966, who until this time had consistently opposed the economic policies of the Gestido government. Unfortunately, as Gestido's new efforts began to take hold and a cautious optimism was spreading over the country, the president died of a heart attack on December 6, 1967. He was replaced by Jorge Pacheco Areco, the forty-seven-year-old vice president.

As president, Pacheco promised to continue, and even augment, Gestido's austerity policies. "I refuse to serve merely as Uruguay's undertaker," he stated. "I will be president!"[3]

With approximately 50 percent of the labor force now on public payrolls, he ordered government departments and the autonomous enterprises to reduce the number of employees and improve operating efficiency. He negotiated a $40 million aid agreement with the United States, as well as trade pacts with the Soviet Union and other eastern European countries. Subsequently he banned two left-wing Montevideo newspapers and jailed their editors for promoting disorderly demonstrations.

During 1967 the cost of living had risen 136 percent, and May 1968 brought another devaluation of the peso—from 200 down to 250 per dollar. Nevertheless, with well-stocked stores and apparently thriving industry, Montevideo still presented an illusion of prosperity. But the exodus of approximately 1,200 Uruguayans per month to other countries in search of better economic opportunities more accurately reflected the sad state of conditions at home.

In his efforts to decrease the size and cost of the bureaucracy, Pacheco faced serious opposition within his own Colorado Party as well as from political opponents. Patronage jobs for constituents were more important to many politicians than reduction of government expenditures. Despite the obvious need for less spending, labor unions continually demanded large wage increases. With union leadership almost entirely in Communist hands, the motives of such demands and frequent strikes usually were more political than economic.

By mid-1968, after several cabinet shakeups and charges of scandal among high officials, there seemed to be a general feeling that the administration's political problems were insurmountable and that the economic situation was bound to get worse. Amid growing labor unrest, in June Pacheco decreed a limited state of siege, price and wage freezes, and censorship of the press. These in turn prompted a general twenty-four-hour protest strike, in violation of government orders, which brought business virtually to a halt. By July there was increasing insurrection, in spite of several hundred arrests each day. In early August Uruguayans were beginning to witness disturbing activities of a new and very effective urban terrorist group—the Tupamaros.

TUPAMARO TERRORISM

The Movement of National Liberation, which took the name Tupamaro, was founded in 1962–63 by a leftist agitator, Raúl Sendic. The name was adapted from Tupac Amaru, a descendant of the royal Inca dynasty who, in 1780–81, led an unsuccessful uprising against Spanish authority in Peru. A law school dropout, Sendic had become a leader in the Socialist Party and subsequently was a union organizer among laborers on sugar beet farms in northern Uruguay. Having led in 1962 the first of what became an annual sugar workers' march on Montevideo to air their grievances, he remained in the capital and began gathering around him embittered, young radicals, most of them well educated and from upper-middle-class families, who were frustrated by the scarcity of career opportunities. From a few dedicated activists, this organization grew until by the early 1970s its total membership was estimated at about 3,000. Some of these were believed to hold significant positions in the government, banks, labor unions, and educational institutions.

The Tupamaros spoke vaguely of creating a socialist society; but, as has been true of many other subversive groups, their principal aim was to destroy existing institutions—without any realistic conception of what might follow. They believed the only way to do this was by force. Although their activities were frowned upon by Uruguay's Communist Party, which advocated a less violent road to power, the Tupamaros were supported by Castro and (after 1970) Chile's Marxist president, Salvador Allende. Some of their members received training in Cuba. Initially content to commit robberies and win followers by distributing money and food to the poor, they perfected the technique of urban guerrilla warfare to such a degree that in time they had one of the world's most sophisticated guerrilla operations. Their remarkable success was due in part to very effective intelligence sources among the military and police. They sought to discredit the government in every way possible; and by 1968 they were dealing massive shocks by stealing weapons and ammunition, robbing banks, bombing radio stations, and organizing various strikes and riots, which the government appeared powerless to stop.

On August 7 the Tupamaros began a long series of spectacular kidnappings by seizing Ulises Pereira Reverbel, close friend and adviser to President
Pacheco and head of the state telephone and electric service corporation.
According to a leaflet distributed by the kidnappers, this act was in reprisal
for his strong support of Pacheco's attempts to suppress strikes and student
violence. They termed it "a warning that nothing will remain unpunished
and that popular justice will be exercised through the most convenient channels."[4] Two of the assailants, identified by Pereira's chauffeur, were known
as Peking Communists. This time Pereira, who was released unharmed five
days later, fared much better than some of the subsequent Tupamaro kidnap
victims.

The search for Pereira included a police raid on the national university, in
violation of the institution's traditional autonomy, which in turn set off five
days of street fighting between students and police that resulted in numerous
injuries and the death of one student. This violence culminated in an antigovernment demonstration by more than 50,000 people and another twenty-
four-hour general strike, called by the National Convention of Workers in
support of the students. The next several weeks brought other general strikes
instigated by the CNT for the purpose of embarrassing the government.

Militant labor groups, generally under Communist leadership, and students, usually led by more extreme Marxists, demanded an end to President
Pacheco's price and wage freeze. Student grievances also included press
censorship, the breach of university autonomy, and alleged police brutality.
Pacheco's austerity program had succeeded temporarily in halting the spiraling inflation and even reversing it slightly, but the continued fighting
threatened to destroy everything by expanding into an all-out civil war. From
mid-August until late September there was a series of clashes between in-
surgents and police that escalated in intensity and casualties and reached a
climax on September 22, when the government closed the university and
secondary schools and called out the army to help stop the bloody conflicts.
This latest attempt to curb violence also included the expulsion of three
Soviet embassy officials.

By the end of the year, with summer weather and the return of over half
a million tourists, there was some relaxation of the strife of previous months.
During 1968 the cost of living had risen only 77 percent as compared with
136 percent in 1967. At the beginning of 1969 the peso still remained at 250
per dollar, the rate to which it had been devalued the previous May. Increased exports and severe restrictions on imports had produced a substantial balance of trade surplus. These actions together with Pacheco's other
austerity measures had brought temporary economic improvement. Nevertheless, as expressed in a riot by striking government employees in downtown Montevideo on January 21, there was continuing dissatisfaction. But
the overall situation moderated sufficiently that by March 15 Pacheco felt

justified in relinquishing the emergency powers he had assumed nine months earlier.

In late June, however, the president was faced with a new wave of strikes, riots, and terrorism and also a move in the General Assembly to impeach him. Beset by this crisis, on June 24 he again imposed a limited state of siege. In a clash with congressional members over his decree ordering striking bank employees into the army if they did not return to work immediately, the legislators backed down when it became clear that Pacheco, supported by the army, might dissolve the legislative body. By now many politicians were worried and the possibility of a military coup was being seriously discussed.

While not daring to reduce or abandon Uruguay's welfare programs, as suggested by the International Monetary Fund and other economists, although inflation had made many of the programs worthless, by holding the line as best he could, Pacheco did end the year 1969 with only a 20 percent inflation. Tightened credit and restrictions on wages brought further labor unrest.

During 1969–70, amid charges that the police were customarily torturing political prisoners, the Tupamaros significantly intensified their antigovernment activities. Because of the administration's determination to crush them, police methods had become more severe. Interspersed with robberies, bombings, gun battles with security forces, and other hostilities, the Tupamaros stepped up their kidnappings of some and murder of other carefully chosen victims. In September 1969 they seized a prominent banker and publisher, who had been involved in the bitter dispute with bank employees, held him seventy-three days, and released him after a large ransom had been paid to a welfare organization. After killing several other policemen over a period of months, in April 1970 they shot to death the head of the police intelligence branch, who had been trying to crush the guerrillas. In July they abducted a criminal judge who had handled most of the recent cases involving Tupamaros, but he was released unharmed a week later after promising to try no more guerrilla cases. Three days after this kidnapping they seized a U.S. citizen and a Brazilian but failed in attempts on three other men.

One of those taken was Dan A. Mitrione, chief U.S. adviser to the Uruguayan police force, stationed in Montevideo to train officers in combating guerrillas. He was killed a few days later, after President Pacheco refused the kidnappers' demands to release all political prisoners (estimated at about 150). The other victim was the Brazilian consul in Montevideo, freed in February 1971 after his family paid a ransom reportedly over $250,000. On August 7, 1970, the Tupamaros kidnapped Claude L. Fly, a U.S. adviser to the Uruguayan agriculture ministry. After being held in a four by six-foot wire cage in a hideout never located by police, he was released March 2, 1971, following a heart attack, as his captors feared he might die.

The same day Fly was seized, Raúl Sendic and twelve other Tupamaro leaders were caught. But although more than 12,000 policemen and soldiers, operating under a suspension of civil rights approved by the General Assembly for twenty days, made a house-to-house search through Montevideo and arrested approximately 200 more suspected Tupamaros and sympathizers, their captives were not found. Even with most of the guerrilla leaders in prison, the Tupamaros undertook a successful campaign to frighten away many of the tourists who normally would arrive with the summer season. Since the prisons were operated by the Ministry of Education as rehabilitation centers, the inmates were permitted frequent visitors and it was easy for the imprisoned Tupamaro leaders to send instructions to members outside. On January 8, 1971, they kidnapped the British ambassador. A spokesman for the Tupamaros stated that Ambassador Geoffrey Jackson was kidnapped to counteract the impression that Uruguay was returning to normality. The U.S. ambassador would have been a more desirable hostage, he commented, but he was too well guarded by U.S. marines. Three days later Tupamaros shot down the eleventh policeman known to have been killed by them.

President Pacheco steadfastly adhered to his policy of not negotiating with the Tupamaros, claiming they were common criminals; but he did request another suspension of civil rights, which the congress approved for forty days. This suspension facilitated another intensive but fruitless search for the British, Brazilian, and U.S. captives. Seeking to end rule by decree, the legislators refused to extend this suspension of rights as Pacheco requested.

By early March only the British ambassador remained in captivity, but in less than a month the Tupamaros seized two more Uruguayan officials—Attorney General Guido Berro Oribe and Ulises Pereira Reverbel, kidnapped once before. Berro Oribe was questioned for thirteen days and then released. In a "people's court" Pereira, allegedly a leader of the antiguerrilla campaign, was sentenced to life imprisonment. Subsequently Pacheco, being unable to rescue him, appointed a new head of the telephone and electric service corporation. Finally, in late April 1972, Pereira was rescued when security forces found the "people's jail" where he was hidden.

In late July and early September 1971, more than 150 Tupamaros, including Sendic and other leaders, gained their freedom in two spectacular escapes from a maximum-security penitentiary. Shortly thereafter, having spent 245 days in their "people's jail," the British ambassador was released by the Tupamaros with the announcement that all the prisoners whose freedom they had demanded had freed themselves. The Tupamaros still held four hostages who had been seized in recent months—three Uruguayans and an Argentine.

Three hours after the ambassador's release, President Pacheco turned over to the military control of anti-Tupamaro operations, which until then had been the sole responsibility of the police. The mass escape of the Tupamaros and their subsequent release of the ambassador, which dramatized police weakness in dealing with them, enabled him to convince the military chiefs they should assume this role.

Undeterred by the mockery the Tupamaros had made of his efforts to suppress them and hopeful of winning another term as president, two days later Pacheco, in a radio and television address to the nation, promised a tougher fight to exterminate them. He accused prison guards of having been corrupted or frightened into letting the guerrillas escape and said those guilty would be punished. "I will take all, hear me well, all the steps needed to defeat this subversion of your security," he affirmed.[5]

Tupamaro success was due largely to their skill in profiting by the widespread discontent with, as well as the weaknesses and divisions within, the government. The 1969 clashes between President Pacheco and striking bank employees resulted in many disgruntled clerks who readily supplied the Tupamaros with inside information that enabled them to carry out spectacular bank robberies. In one such raid on the Bank of the Republic in November 1970, they reportedly got away with about $8 million in jewelry and other valuables on deposit as security against loans. They took advantage of disorganization and inexperience in Uruguay's security forces—a situation the U.S. government belatedly helped remedy by providing special training in counterinsurgency. Assassinations of policemen had a demoralizing effect on the entire force and led to a police strike in June 1970 for higher pay and the right to work in civilian clothes. Many officers were so intimidated by the Tupamaros that they hesitated to move against them for fear of reprisals. Pacheco was also handicapped by political divisions within the government and particularly by the Tupamaros' skillful exposure of corruption and incompetence among several high administration officials, including members of his cabinet.

While at times cooperative, on other occasions the General Assembly proved a stumbling block by refusing to extend the president's emergency powers when they were needed. Pacheco became so despondent over the situation that on August 7, 1970, right after the kidnapping of Claude Fly, he was reported to have written his resignation, but he destroyed it later in the day after the capture of Raúl Sendic. Uruguay's tradition of democracy and the determination of many politicians to protect civil rights, as they saw them, made it difficult to apply extreme measures when these were really necessary to combat terrorists who sought to destroy those rights and the entire fabric of democracy.

With the November 1971 elections approaching, the Tupamaros temporarily curtailed their violence and appeared willing to take their chance at the polls. Previously they had condemned the electoral process and insisted that the people could win power only through armed struggle. But in early 1971 Uruguay's leftist parties joined in a coalition known as the Broad Front (Frente Amplio). After a time, the Tupamaros offered their grudging support in the forthcoming elections. The Broad Front included the far left Socialists and other extreme Marxists, the well-disciplined Communist Party, the Christian Democrats, and dissidents from the Colorado and Blanco Parties. As in

Chile, Uruguay's Socialists were more radical than the Communists, while the Uruguayan Christian Democrats, unlike those in Chile, were a very small and militantly socialist group. The Broad Front was viewed by many as similar to the Popular Unity coalition in Chile, which had elected Allende the previous year, but actually this Uruguayan alliance covered a broader political spectrum and lacked the experience and cohesiveness of its Chilean counterpart. As in Chile's Popular Unity, the Communists were the strongest party and, should the coalition remain intact, could be expected to emerge eventually as the real power.

The Broad Front chose as its candidate for president a recently retired army general, Liber Seregni Mosquera, who claimed he was not a Marxist and described himself as a "popular nationalist" and a "lifelong member" of the Colorado Party. Although Seregni and other leaders denied that the front was Marxist or socialist, its announced platform appeared very leftist. It advocated nationalization of all private banks and other industries not already under government control, nationalization of foreign trade, renegotiation of the foreign debt, reform of the electoral laws, agrarian reforms with conversion of the large cattle and sheep ranches into "cooperatives," and an "anti-imperialist" (meaning anti-United States) foreign policy, including diplomatic relations with Cuba.

In the months preceding the November 28 elections, public opinion polls indicated the Broad Front had a large following. This fact created a fear that, in a three-way split with the two traditional parties, it might have a chance of winning, as had happened in Chile the previous year. During this time also President Pacheco became convinced that, despite a constitutional provision to the contrary, he should serve a second term. Prior to the elections, other Colorado and Blanco candidates joined him in warning voters of dangers in supporting the Broad Front.

In the meantime, cracks had appeared in Pacheco's austerity policy under which Uruguay had made impressive economic strides. From the world's highest annual inflation rate, which the country was experiencing when he inherited the presidency in 1967, he had managed to bring it down to around 20 percent for 1969 and 1970. Although unemployment remained excessive, the gross national product, which had declined about 15 percent from 1956 to 1968, climbed approximately 5 percent in 1970. But in October 1970, with elections a little more than a year away, General Assembly members began appealing to the voters. Over the president's veto, they approved an inflationary budget that suddenly increased the deficit from $18 million to $52 million. Almost immediately the peso, which for two and a half years had remained rather steady at around 250 per dollar, dropped to 300 on the free market. The $8 million robbery of the Bank of the Republic a few weeks later was followed by Tupamaro sabotage of the 1970–71 tourist season, on which the government had relied to balance the budget. Reportedly the number of tourists declined about 50 percent. Then, as Uruguay approached the

1971 elections, Pacheco, anxious for a second term, abandoned part of his stabilization program. With a budget deficit now at about 30 percent of expenditures and the government issuing increasing amounts of new currency to pay the bills, the peso experienced a precipitous fall in value. According to government statistics, the cost of living rose 36 percent in 1971—almost double the annual rate of the two preceding years. Other estimates placed it as high as 60 percent.

On election day, November 28, 1971, voters had a choice of ten candidates for president. Besides Seregni, there were seven Colorados, including Pacheco, and two Blancos. But even if he should win the most votes, in order for Pacheco to continue in office, he would also have to win a plebiscite amending the constitution to permit him a second term.

The heaviest voter turnout in Uruguay's history resulted in defeat of this amendment but a close victory for his designated alternate candidate, Juan M. Bordaberry, prominent rancher and minister of agriculture. The Broad Front won slightly over 18 percent of the total vote—about twice as much as the parties comprising it had received in previous elections but far short of a victory. Since the Tupamaros had identified themselves with this coalition, its defeat was considered a defeat for them. Early on the morning after the elections, crowds, celebrating what they termed "a victory over Communists," marched through Montevideo streets carrying portraits of Pacheco and chanting, "¡Policías, sí! ¡Tupamaros, no!"[6]

Bordaberry pledged to follow Pacheco's hard-line policy dedicated to eliminating Tupamaro terrorism and the disturbing agitation by students and labor unions. To accomplish these ends, he foresaw the need for extraordinary presidential and police powers, as well as organizational reforms in the national university and secondary schools to end Marxist influence there. But the results of congressional elections raised serious doubts as to what cooperation he could expect from the legislative body. In the new congress the Colorados had only 14 senators and 41 deputies, the Blancos 12 and 40 respectively, and the Broad Front 5 and 18. Thus no party had a majority. With the traditional rivalry between Colorados and Blancos heightened by the close outcome of the presidential race, Broad Front members appeared to be in a very strategic position.

Senator Wilson Ferreira Aldunate, head of the liberal wing of the Blanco Party and himself more liberal than Bordaberry, had opposed Pacheco's economic policies and the use of drastic measures against the Tupamaros. Bordaberry barely nosed out Ferreira for president in a bitterly contested election that was so close the results were not determined until mid-February. After his defeat, Ferreira showed no desire to cooperate with Bordaberry and rejected his offer to form a national unity government.

Initially Broad Front support enabled the Blancos to elect the president of the Chamber of Deputies, but fear of popular repercussions made many Blancos reluctant to join these leftists in opposing administrative policies. In

June, after appointing three more Blancos to his cabinet, President Bordaberry gained a working majority in both chambers of the General Assembly
when the three smaller of five Blanco factions decided to support his administration.

Following the failure of Seregni's presidential candidacy, there were indications that the Tupamaros would renew their terrorist campaign. In early
January 1972 they seized a Montevideo radio station and broadcast an announcement that attacks on the government would be resumed. But despite
this warning, within a few days after taking office on March 1, the new
congress, at the instigation of Broad Front members, repealed most of the
curbs on individual rights that had been imposed by President Pacheco in
his fight against the Tupamaros.

In mid-April fifteen Tupamaros and ten other prisoners dug their way out
of the Punta Carretas maximum security penitentiary, from which more than
100 guerrillas had escaped the previous September. Two days later Tupamaro assassinations of four prominent security officers provoked street battles with military and police in which eight of the guerrillas lost their lives.
Thereupon President Bordaberry asked the General Assembly to declare a
state of internal war and suspend all constitutional rights. So shaken were
the legislators by the bloody clashes that almost immediately such a measure,
which placed the country under martial law, was approved for a period of
thirty days. This action enabled accused guerrillas to be incarcerated in military prisons and tried in military courts rather than in civil prisons and courts
whose officials were believed to be intimidated by Tupamaros. Subsequently
martial law was extended until it was replaced in July by a tough security
law that granted broad authority to the combined military and police.

With these emergency powers, the security forces began an effective drive
against the terrorists. A significant break came in late April when they found
a "people's jail" containing two prominent victims of kidnapping. This was
followed by discoveries of many other Tupamaro hideouts and large quantities of weapons and ammunition. The key that unlocked important guerrilla
secrets was provided by a disgruntled Tupamaro leader who, after his arrest,
betrayed his comrades by revealing the locations of at least thirty of their
hideouts. When it became clear that the military meant business, many people, who had distrusted the police, supplied information regarding the
whereabouts of Tupamaro members.

The internal war, which resulted in the arrest of more than 1,000 Tupamaros and the death of 20 others and 23 soldiers, policemen, and noncom-
batant civilians, culminated on September 1, 1972, with the capture of Raúl
Sendic in a shootout in which he was seriously wounded. Mopping up operations continued another three years, but with him and his top lieutenants
in military custody, the steam had gone out of the Tupamaro movement.

Under the firm leadership of Pacheco and Bordaberry, the Uruguayan government, whose dedication to democracy and individual freedoms had fa-

cilitated the rise of urban terrorism, had managed to bring the Tupamaros under control. But this antiguerrilla campaign had succeeded only after the army assumed direction of security forces and the congress declared a state of internal war and placed the country under martial law. Now a new question appeared. Would the customarily nonpolitical military leaders, who had been drawn into a political turmoil, be willing to return to their traditional status? Or would they feel obliged to play a more active role in the affairs of their country which, while now relatively free of terrorists, still was plagued with other very serious problems?

During the political campaign of 1971 and the Tupamaro roundup of 1972 the economy continued to deteriorate. When Bordaberry assumed the presidency in March 1972, he found the treasury bare, the currency's value debatable, and much of the approximately $500 million foreign debt due within a few months. Because it had been deemed politically unwise to acknowledge its decline in the election year, the peso remained officially at 250 per dollar, but actually it was worth far less. Several devaluations over succeeding months brought it, by mid-July 1972, down to an official exchange rate of 572 per dollar; but on the black market it was close to 1,000. Between April and December the government secretly sold about 20 percent of its gold reserves to satisfy the most pressing foreign debts. For this measure Bordaberry was severely criticized by leading opponents, but Uruguay's international standing improved. The one bright spot in the economic picture was the return of tourists to Uruguayan beaches in the summer of 1971–72. This was during the recess in terrorist activities before the elections and afterward while they awaited the outcome to determine which of the two major parties should be the object of their renewed attacks.

Mindful of a trade deficit of almost $19 million for 1971 despite a considerable decline in imports, in March 1972 Bordaberry announced a four-month ban on domestic beef consumption, beginning July 15, to provide more beef for export. Uruguay had arrived at a predicament similar to Argentina's under Perón two decades earlier. Over the years cattle and sheep production had stagnated. Now, with approximately the same number of beef cattle as in 1908, there were not enough to export and also satisfy domestic demand—normally among the highest per capita in the world. But although the politically inspired high export duties, which resulted in so much smuggling, had been lifted after the elections, by the end of 1972 it was found that beef exports had continued to decline while domestic prices had increased 83 percent.

With the cost of living rising about 50 percent during the first half of this year, the president succumbed to labor demands and paralyzing strikes and granted modest wage increases in the private sector. He also agreed to price hikes for foods and services. In return for a standby credit to alleviate its balance-of-payments problem, the International Monetary Fund demanded that Uruguay balance its budget; but the administration did not live up to this commitment. According to government statistics, the inflation rate for 1972 was 94.6 percent; while during the decade since 1962 living costs had increased 6,457 percent. Based on the annual rates previously cited, the ten-year figure was actually more than 10,000 percent. Nevertheless, a five-year budget, approved for the period beginning January 1, 1973, forecast a large deficit and was based on the assumption that a high rate of inflation would continue.

In mid-1972, as the drive to subdue terrorism was reaching a climax, military leaders began investigating some of the irregularities that the Tupamaros had exposed. Reportedly the anti-Tupamaro campaign had uncovered numerous documents linking certain prominent political figures with financial scandals. After capturing the top Tupamaros and crushing their worst subversive activities, the armed forces, eager to retain their broad powers, undertook a crusade to eliminate corruption. This effort together with their crackdown on the terrorists led to clashes with politicians, who retaliated with accusations that the military was trying to seize power.

In August, as a result of military pressure, the Chamber of Deputies voted to strip a Broad Front member of his parliamentary immunity so he could be brought to trial on charges of belonging to the Tupamaros. In October there was a confrontation over military charges of corruption by Jorge Batlle, leader of a major faction of the Colorado Party, and his subsequent criticism of the armed forces. In this instance, President Bordaberry bowed to military pressure, reversed his initial position, and ordered Batlle's arrest. This action precipitated one of the most serious crises in decades. In what appeared to be a clear confrontation between civilians and the military, the entire cabinet resigned; and in the congress various parties and factions united in opposing this action. A few days later Bordaberry, under strong military pressure, ordered the arrest of a former foreign minister, Jorge Peirana Facio, charged with misusing state funds.

What appeared to be a military bid for power led to an even more severe crisis in February 1973. The immediate cause was the president's appointment of a defense minister whom the army and air force chiefs considered unacceptable. The new minister, retired Gen. Antonio Francese, was instructed by Bordaberry to persuade the armed forces to return to their nonpolitical role. This order brought a confrontation between the 20,000-man army and air force on the one hand and the president supported by the 2,000-man navy on the other. Subsequently, as a column of tanks and trucks loaded with troops approached the capital and air force jets buzzed overhead, Bordaberry backed down and accepted the minister's resignation. This episode boosted the power of the military and severely weakened civilian government.

The next day army and air force officers broadcast a nineteen-point "national reconstruction" program aimed at eliminating corruption, eradicating "the influence of Marxism-Leninism," reviving the economy, controlling inflation, promoting agrarian reform, and abolishing political influence in government. Amid pressures on Bordaberry from leaders of all three major political groups to resign because of his humiliating surrender, the military chiefs made clear their desire that he remain and constitutional rule continue. But they also expressed determination to carry on their crusade against what they believed to be the evils that had bred Uruguay's urban terrorism.

MILITARY IN GOVERNMENT

As a result of an agreement reached between Bordaberry and the military commanders, the latter achieved virtual control of the government. But, respecting their nation's democratic traditions and mindful of the problems Argentina's armed forces had encountered in trying to govern that country, Uruguay's officers chose for the time being a supervisory role rather than an overt assumption of power. Thus they agreed to remain in the background and preserve the semblance of a constitutional system. They would direct the administration through a National Security Council, composed of the commanders of the three armed services and the ministers of defense, interior, foreign affairs, and economy. Granted control over the nominations of the defense and interior ministers, the military would dominate the council.

Army and air force commanders insisted they were engaged in a nationalist movement with no specific political philosophy except "an ideal conception of Uruguay." They defined their aims as "recovery of national moral values, patriotism, austerity, idealism, generosity, honor, abnegation, and strength of character." As one officer put it, "What we want is clean, effective government."[7]

Bordaberry promised to work toward these objectives, while the armed forces pledged to support the constitution and democratic institutions and guaranteed elections in 1976 as scheduled. As a condition for the continuation of civilian rule, the military chiefs also demanded a crackdown on "economic crimes" and reform of the government utility corporations.

Military leaders praised the agreement as one that would permit the armed forces to pursue their mission of safeguarding national security and promoting development within the constitutional framework. "We never wanted to overthrow the government," an air force officer stated. "We are very respectful of constitutional laws. We did not use one shot, but we attained our objective—to exert direct influence over national affairs."[8]

As the crisis tentatively subsided, President Bordaberry announced the military's new role as one "to safeguard national developments" and stated that "all the republican institutions remain intact."[9] Technically his capitulation had preserved constitutional government, but now the military was actually in command. The Tupamaros, by creating a situation through which the armed forces acquired extraordinary powers, had achieved their goal of destroying democracy in Uruguay.

Over the next few months Bordaberry, with a working majority in the General Assembly, was able to persuade this body to approve extensions of the suspension of civil liberties, which enabled the armed forces to continue rounding up Tupamaro suspects and also intensify their anticorruption campaign. But this policy led to other clashes with the congress, and relations between the military and civilian branches of the government continued to deteriorate. In May 1973 a controversy arose over alleged connections with the Tupamaros of a left-wing senator, Enrique Erro, who was head of the far left Popular Union, part of the Broad Front. Bordaberry supported a military demand that the Senate revoke Erro's parliamentary immunity so he could be prosecuted. Anxious to resist military pressure, the Senate refused.

President Bordaberry's alignment with the military on this issue led to the resignation of a Blanco cabinet member, Luis Balpardia Blengio, whose appointment had helped create the fragile coalition with the three factions that provided him a working majority in the congress. The resignation of this commerce minister was a particularly serious blow because he had played a key role in the February crisis and was one of those credited with preventing an outright military takeover at that time. With his departure, the coalition began to disintegrate, and Bordaberry's congressional majority soon disappeared. On June 1, with the suspension of civil liberties expiring and little chance of a renewal, the president bypassed the General Assembly and decreed an extension.

In mid-May, as a compromise solution to the Erro affair, it was agreed that the Chamber of Deputies would conduct an impeachment hearing; but in late June this body rejected the administration's impeachment resolution. Thus both congressional chambers had defied the armed forces. Although many members believed him guilty, they were now determined to save Senator Erro in order to preserve congressional authority and prevent a complete military takeover of the government.

In view of this impasse, on June 27, 1973, President Bordaberry dissolved the General Assembly and announced that it would be replaced by a twenty-member Council of State, composed of prominent nonpolitical elder statesmen chosen by himself, which would oversee presidential acts and perform legislative functions, including the drafting of constitutional reforms. After Vice President Jorge Sapelli refused to preside over the Council of State unless the nation's political parties were granted freedom of action, Bordaberry appointed as its president Martín Echegoyen, former senator and leader of the Blanco Party's conservative wing. He died in May 1974 and was succeeded by Alberto Demicheli, a seventy-eight-year-old lawyer.

The elected municipal councils were supplanted by "neighborhood councils" to be selected by the president from names submitted by mayors and police chiefs. As a justification for this move, Bordaberry declared there had been a serious deterioration of constitutional rule and attributed the crisis to "the criminal actions of the conspiracy against the country, aligned with the complacency of political groups without national spirit."[10]

Referring to the rejection of impeachment proceedings against Erro by both the Senate and Chamber of Deputies, Bordaberry said it "signified the collapse of the spirit to fight subversion, and that I could not permit."[11] Subsequently Senator Erro, Senator Wilson Ferreira, and a few other leading congressional opponents set up a resistance committee in exile in Buenos Aires.

It was announced that Bordaberry would rule by decree until constitutional reforms should be approved in a national plebiscite. But it was obvious that his claim to absolute power was a hollow one and that he was really a front for the military, who would be calling the plays.

The Communist-dominated National Convention of Workers protested the dissolution of the General Assembly and military occupation of the congressional palace by immediately calling a nationwide strike that soon paralyzed major industries. President Bordaberry retaliated three days later by outlawing the CNT and ordering the arrest of its leaders and confiscation of its property. On the same day troops were ordered to break up the strike by clearing factories, banks, public offices, and other affected sites. But protesting workers persisted and repeatedly reoccupied factories and offices that had been cleared. During this period, as in previous crises, strict press censorship was imposed.

On July 4, 1973, police dispersed an antigovernment demonstration by more than 1,000 women in the streets of Montevideo. (It is interesting to note that 1973 also witnessed significant demonstrations by women in Santiago, Chile.) Five days later security forces broke up a protest march by several thousand workers and students, during which at least two were killed and many wounded. Finally, after secret negotiations between government representatives and those of the CNT, which had continued to operate underground, on July 11 the strike was called off—fifteen days after it had begun. By then most of the nation's industrial establishments had been closed for two weeks, transportation had been seriously curtailed, and many parts of the country were suffering food shortages.

With the aim of making the CNT nonpolitical and free of foreign influences, in late July the government announced that it would be replaced by a new organization whose officers would be forbidden to participate in political activities. Union funds would be audited by the state; and strikes, which must be approved by a two-thirds vote of the affected union members, could be called only for economic purposes.

Consistent with their open support of Bordaberry during the crisis and in an apparent attempt to bolster his prestige, the military commanders issued a communique stating the armed forces were "completely subordinated" to the president. They insisted that Uruguay remained under civilian control. With the strike now ended, on the surface the president appeared to have emerged victorious. But in mid-August an "Uruguayan revolutionary army," formed by some young army officers, sent to the top command an ultimatum calling for implementation of the agreements reached in February by the president and the military. They also demanded Bordaberry's resignation and the establishment of a full-fledged military government.

In October 1973 President Bordaberry, backed by the National Security Council, ordered the closing of the national university (University of the Republic), where a few weeks earlier elections of directors had resulted in victory for the leftists and defeat of progovernment candidates. At least 150 members of the directing staff and faculty were arrested, including the rector and nine of the ten deans. (The other dean was out of the country.) The directors were held ultimately responsible for the death of a student, who was killed when a bomb he was making in one of the university laboratories accidentally exploded. In his decree Bordaberry alleged that subversive literature found there proved the university guilty of "indoctrination of youths in the Marxist ideology," and the discovery of materials for the manufacture of explosives indicated this academic institution was being used for "incitement to armed struggle." He accused the rector and deans of permitting the university to become a "refuge for conspiracy against the fatherland, its institutions, and the security of its inhabitants."[12]

The university, whose independence was guaranteed by the constitution, was the last center of strong opposition to the government. Several months later, after it had been reopened under new directors, Bordaberry issued a decree authorizing university authorities to dismiss any professor or employee who lacked a "well-known affiliation with democracy." Following continuing leadership difficulties and alleged Marxist infiltration in educational institutions, especially the university, in early 1975 military officers were appointed to key posts in the school system.

In December 1973 the government outlawed the Communist and Socialist Parties along with eleven other leftist organizations and closed the Communist newspapers. Only three legal political parties remained—Colorado, Blanco, and Christian Democrat.

The roundup of stray Tupamaros extended well past this year. In November Raúl Sendic and eight other leaders were reported to have been tried in secret by a military tribunal and sentenced to death, with the understanding that they would be executed if their confederates continued to operate. The following April three women Tupamaros were killed in a gun battle with troops and police who surrounded the house in which they were staying. By this time the number of political prisoners, who included even such prominent figures as Liber Seregni and some of Uruguay's best-known writers, was estimated at between 2,000 and 3,000. In November 1974, after sixteen months in prison, Seregni was granted "provisional liberty," but later he was taken into custody again and not released until March 1984.

In July 1975 the military reported that twenty-two Tupamaros had been arrested and three killed in raids since late May. The Tupamaro movement was believed to be directed now from a secret base in Buenos Aires with the objective of sending fugitives back to Uruguay and reviving activities there. A few days later security forces reported the arrests of more than fifty members of a Maoist group accused of attacks jointly with Tupamaros on Uruguayan military units.

After suffering an inflation of about 90 percent in 1973, Uruguay began 1974 with government announcements of a 33 percent increase in salaries and from 10 to 60 percent rise in the prices of approximately 1,000 consumer items. As all of its petroleum had to be imported, the country was hit especially hard by the 1973 oil crisis. Gasoline quintupled in price and by May 1974 was selling for the equivalent of over $2.50 per gallon. The peso, which had gone through numerous "mini devaluations" since the beginning of Bordaberry's administration, was officially down to over 1,000 per dollar. During the next six months it dropped to 1,500. With a foreign debt estimated at $600 million and a trade surplus of the past year turning into a deficit of over $100 million for 1974, the economic picture was far from bright. By October 1973 government officials had become so alarmed over the number of young people leaving the country (estimated at about 240,000 since 1968) that a decree was issued requiring university graduates to remain in Uruguay a specified number of years before being eligible to emigrate.

Fearing that their efforts were being discredited and facing a potential loss of prestige, army leaders were especially disturbed by the government's apparent inability to stem the inflation. One officer voiced an opinion frequently heard in both military and civilian circles when he said, "If we are going to be blamed for all the failures, then we should assume complete power and responsibility."[13] Bowing to military pressure, President Bordaberry agreed to overhaul his cabinet and announced that in the future the armed forces would play a key role in managing the nation's economy. In late July military officers were placed in charge of the major government economic enterprises.

As Uruguayans looked for scapegoats on whom to lay the blame for their plight, one of the most frequently mentioned was José Batlle y Ordóñez. "It is difficult to admit it," said one former Colorado senator, "but many of our problems can be traced to *batllismo*. Batlle was one of the greatest political leaders this continent has produced, but his programs had nothing to do with the reality of this country."[14]

Members of the military tended to view the situation differently. To them the real villains were politicians of the day and especially the many leftists who had infiltrated various classes of society. A document published by the armed forces in February 1974 concluded with a warning that every Uruguayan "must be conscious of the deterioration in the republic caused by Marxist erosion."[15]

The army continued to push vigorously an anti-Marxist campaign. In June

1974 several hundred tons of Marxist publications in two bookstores were confiscated, and the publishing house, Pueblos Unidos, that owned the stores was closed temporarily. This company was closed permanently in November 1975 and its properties seized because it was allegedly the main South American distribution point of Communist propaganda. In July of that year approximately 20,000 books were destroyed as part of a drive to purge schools of pro-Marxist texts. A few days later the government abolished the Uruguayan-Soviet Cultural Institute in Montevideo, charging that it was a mouthpiece of outlawed Marxist groups. Late December brought a series of raids on the now illegal Communist Party headquarters that netted about 1,000 weapons and valuable party records and led to the arrest of at least 300 members.

The military campaign to eradicate leftist influences was especially vigorous in the educational system. A purge of allegedly left-wing professors and teachers resulted, by the end of 1975, in many dismissals from the university faculties as well as all levels of public education, including some 1,300 grade-school and 800 secondary-school teachers. The colonel who was director of the National Education Council summed up the philosophy behind these moves when he said, "We must develop a nationalist doctrine in our schools with which to confront and eradicate the doctrines of international Marxism that penetrated our classrooms."[16]

By 1976 Bordaberry's policy of economic austerity was beginning to show a few favorable results, although there were still serious problems. An emphasis on private enterprise had attracted some foreign capital. This capital in turn helped stimulate growth and the economy expanded by about 4 percent in 1975. But the drastic increase in the cost of oil imports together with a sharp decrease by several European countries in their purchases of Uruguayan beef disastrously affected the balance of trade, and this loss was only partly offset by a variety of new exports that had resulted from new industries and more realistic exchange rates. The balance-of-payments deficit for 1975 rose to approximately $170 million, but the first half of 1976 showed a trade surplus. With the foreign debt at over $700 million, a World Bank study near the end of 1975 indicated that Uruguay was paying over 30 percent of its export earnings in debt service charges. Despite the removal of price controls from virtually all articles by mid-1976, the inflation rate dropped from 107 percent for 1974 to 58 percent in 1977. Some articles actually declined in price, with gasoline down to the equivalent of $1.80 per gallon by early 1976. Increased construction and the opening or expansion of many small industries, together with the exodus of thousands of professionals and skilled workers, had alleviated for the time being the serious unemployment problem.

During 1972–76 the government succeeded in curbing some of its operating expenses—except the military budget. In these years the armed forces increased in number to an estimated 25,000 men. The enlarged military, with its additional duties and power, was to a considerable degree responsible for the continuing annual deficits in public spending of at least 25 percent. The deficits in turn were the primary factor in the shrinking value of the currency. By July 1975, with the exchange rate at 2,780 pesos per U.S. dollar, the Uruguayan government adopted a "new peso," worth 1,000 of the old. It began with an exchange of approximately 2.90 per dollar but subsequently steadily declined in value and by December 1978 was down to 6.73 per dollar on the free market.

Part of the agreement between President Bordaberry and the armed forces, following the power crisis of February 1973, was a guarantee by the military that elections would be held in November 1976 as scheduled. But as that time approached, Bordaberry had some second thoughts about the desirability of holding elections at all. He decided he should remain in office beyond his legal term, which was due to expire March 1, 1977. In a letter to the military commanders on December 9, 1975, he suggested that, by military mandate, he be given an additional three years. He blamed the old political party system for corrupting Uruguay's government and for the influence of Marxism there; and he proposed that the constitution be amended, either by plebiscite or military order, so as to ban the traditional parties and establish the armed forces in a permanent political role. In an Independence Day address the previous August 25, Bordaberry had ruled out a return to "formal democracy" and said, "Our main responsibility is to prevent, ever, either directly or indirectly, a return to the conditions that pushed the country to the verge of chaos and dissolution."[17]

With the press strictly censored and overt political party activity prohibited, negotiations over this issue went on quietly for several months. It did become known that a serious split had developed between Bordaberry and some cabinet members and military commanders, who preferred a gradual return to democratic government. The latter particularly objected to his attempt to remain in office and reshape the governmental system to conform with his own concept.

On June 12, 1976, the armed forces issued a communique stating they had "withdrawn their confidence in and support of" Bordaberry.[18] Shortly after this was broadcast on national radio and television, Alberto Demicheli, president of the Council of State, was sworn in as temporary president of Uruguay. The removal process was handled very smoothly and calmly. Bordaberry was told he could remain in the official residence a few days and that, if he wished, he and his family would be provided air transportation to their ranch about 100 miles away. There was little public impact and scheduled events went on as though nothing had happened.

MILITARY DICTATORSHIP

Instead of abolishing political parties and setting up a corporate state with participation of the armed forces, as Bordaberry had proposed, military leaders decided to preserve the status quo and retain the civilian front while appearing to support a return to Uruguay's traditional system. For three years they had been the real power in the government. Bordaberry had been permitted to continue in office because he agreed generally with their policies and his presence preserved a semblance of democracy. During this period he was not exactly a puppet and frequently differed with military commanders on important matters; but, as he well realized, he was not free to formulate policies alone.

Following this coup, it was understood that Demicheli would be replaced within seventy days by another chief executive chosen by military leaders and members of the Council of State. He would remain in office about three years, at the end of which the Colorado and Blanco Parties, purged by the military of their most prominent members, would be reactivated and select another president to serve for five years. At the end of that period, the armed forces would permit the two parties to run their own candidates in a nationwide election. No other parties would be allowed. Subsequently, after considerable outside pressure, the military-controlled government announced in August 1977 that it would permit the return of civilian administration in 1981, when elections for a president and congress would be held.

Another elder statesman, seventy-two-year-old Aparicio Méndez, a conservative lawyer, was installed for a five-year-term as Demicheli's successor on September 1, 1976. One of his first acts was to issue a decree, demanded by the military in return for his appointment. (Demicheli had refused to do this.) It suspended for fifteen years the right of some 3,000 public figures, including Bordaberry, Pacheco, and leaders of all political parties and factions, to hold public office. The ban, which pertained to members of party structures before the General Assembly was dissolved in 1973, was considered punishment for "the subversion and inertia of the political parties that led to shedding of innocent blood, limitation of liberties, collapse of security and administrative chaos." Disqualification of the old politicians was termed essential to "prepare for the incorporation of new generations to political life through the traditional parties."[19] All parties were declared in recess, and there was no indication as to when any of them would be allowed to resume activities.

HUMAN RIGHTS ABUSES

In June 1974 Amnesty International and the International Commission of Jurists released a report to the United Nations accusing the Uruguayan government of torturing political prisoners as a means of securing confessions. The charges were made after representatives of these two private organizations had visited Uruguay the previous month. It was estimated that approximately 3,500 persons had been arrested for security reasons since the far-reaching security law was enacted in July 1972, and that about 1,150 were still awaiting trial. The majority of these were Tupamaros, but many were not. Uruguay's antisubversion campaign had been extended to include all groups in the Broad Front coalition and eventually came to embrace members of any faction that disagreed with the national administration. It was alleged that various—and often extreme—forms of torture were practiced regularly.

In February 1976 Amnesty International, from its headquarters in London, charged that torture of political prisoners in Uruguay was routine and that twenty-four had died there from torture in the past three and a half years. At this time it estimated that, with at least 6,000 people in jail, Uruguay had more political prisoners per capita than any other country. A member of the Amnesty International staff termed Uruguay's system of government "a rule of terror . . . as brutal and as far-reaching as any in the world."[20] Although some of these charges were obviously excessive, there appeared to be justifiable grounds for complaint.

Among the many Uruguayans who had left the country for political reasons was Wilson Ferreira Aldunate, whom Bordaberry had defeated for the presidency in 1971. After dissolution of the General Assembly in 1973, he and a number of other legislators had fled to asylum in Argentina; but when the Argentine military seized absolute control again there in March 1976, he and his family went to Europe and then to the United States. In testimony before a House of Representatives subcommittee in Washington, and also in statements to the press, he appealed to the U.S. government to withdraw support from Uruguay's military regime. In September the U.S. Congress did approve a ban on further military aid to Uruguay because of alleged violations of human rights. This action did not affect economic aid; but in March 1977 the Uruguayan government termed U.S. foreign aid linked to respect for human rights unacceptable intervention in its internal affairs, and it notified the U.S. ambassador in Montevideo that it was withdrawing all requests for economic assistance.

In a lengthy report by the Inter-American Commission on Human Rights to the eighth General Assembly of the Organization of American States, meeting in Washington in June 1978, Uruguay was charged again with wholesale violations of human rights, including arbitrary arrest, torture, and murder of political prisoners. The Uruguayan government replied with a detailed denial of these allegations and claimed that such repressive actions as it had taken were necessary to combat left-wing terrorism; but before the Washington meeting adjourned on July 1, the assembly adopted resolutions urging Uruguay, along with other allegedly guilty states, to eliminate the human rights abuses that were believed to exist.

About this time a few signs were beginning to appear that indicated the Uruguayan armed forces were relaxing a bit in their treatment of prisoners. A number of military leaders had become disturbed by international criticism of alleged human rights violations in their country and especially by the OAS rejection of Uruguay's offer to serve as host of its 1978 General Assembly.

Moreover, the political ambition and rivalry that had appeared among some of these officers were bringing them to a greater awareness of human rights and of the need for moderate policies that would be more appealing to the Uruguayan public.

Particularly was this attitude true of Gen. Gregorio Alvarez, commander in chief of the army, who was anxious to cap his military career with a term as president of the republic. In the late 1970s he was engaged in maneuvers designed to bring the presidency within his grasp. He reaffirmed the previous military commitment to elections in 1981 and a return to civilian administration, but became involved in a power struggle with other ambitious commanders. He believed the military would play a primary role in the forthcoming elections. As a consequence, after his retirement as commander in chief in early 1979, Alvarez tried to maintain his position as front runner in the renewed political struggle.

Meanwhile government practices showed some improvement, with gradually increasing respect for human rights. According to official figures in mid-1979, the number of political prisoners had declined from between 6,000 and 7,000 to 1,600. This reduction led the United States in 1979 to restore some of the military aid that it had withdrawn in 1976. But an improved human rights position did not carry with it greater political freedom, and determined repression of political dissent continued. In mid-1981 Amnesty International was still dissatisfied with the human rights situation in Uruguay.

Desiring to improve its image, gain greater popular support, and perpetuate its power, the military-controlled government formulated a new constitution in 1979, to be ratified by the Council of State and submitted for public approval in a late 1980 plebiscite. This document conferred upon the military a permanent role in government, with final authority over most policies. It also provided for a tribunal of nine members, initially appointed by the armed forces, empowered to impeach any government official, including the president. Assuming approval of this constitution, elections in 1981 would be limited to one military-approved candidate for each administrative office. Choices for a contemplated weak congress would be confined to candidates of the purged Blanco and Colorado Parties with no left-wing entrants permitted.

Confident that it would be approved, about a month before the plebiscite the government relaxed its long-standing restrictions and permitted public debate on the proposed constitution. At the same time it launched a vociferous radio and television campaign urging people to vote for it. But the results were surprising. Although handicapped by limited time and lack of open support by most former political leaders, who were prohibited from participating in political affairs, the opposition mounted an effective campaign which succeeded in defeating the constitution. Peaceful balloting on November 30, 1980, resulted in the new charter being rejected by a vote of approximately 58 to 42 percent. Contrary to custom in many Latin American countries, the military had permitted a fair election—and lost. But Uruguay is not a typical Latin American country; and the plebiscite clearly demonstrated that seven years of military dictatorship had not destroyed the tradition of democracy for which this republic had been justly famous.

Following their defeat at the polls, government leaders reimposed restrictions on political activities while they considered their next move. Although reiterating his firm belief in democracy, Lt. Gen. Luis V. Queirolo, commander in chief of the army, stated a few days after the plebiscite that the armed forces would not hasten to withdraw from power. He claimed the people had rejected only the proposed constitution—not the government—and that Uruguay was not yet ready for restoration of democracy. He envisioned the military retaining an effective administrative role because of the very difficult years the country had experienced. For the time being government would continue under control of the Council of State, headed by Aparicio Méndez, with a junta of twenty-eight top army, navy, and air force officers really calling the shots.

Defeat of this constitution brought infighting among the armed forces as members argued over who was to blame. It also resulted in increased rivalry between former political leaders, with Blancos and Colorados splitting into factions and seeking advantageous positions in anticipation of eventual return of political freedom.

After further maneuvering among military officers and increasing efforts by General Alvarez to satisfy his presidential aspiration, in July 1981 the military decided on an earlier return to democratic rule than previously intended. With the term of Méndez due to expire September 1, the Council of State chose Alvarez to succeed him for a period of three and one-half years. He was directed to prepare for national elections before the end of his term March 1, 1985. The armed forces also relaxed their ban on political activities by opposition politicians. After the installation of Alvarez as president, negotiations were begun between his government and the Colorado and Blanco Parties with the aim of restoring all political freedoms.

More than a year later—November 28, 1982—an important step toward democracy was taken in the holding of elections to choose approximately 500 delegates to conventions of the three approved parties—Blanco, Colorado, and Civic Union. (The Christian Democrats, Communists, and Socialists were not recognized.) These parties would designate representatives to a constitutional convention in 1983 and also select party leaders and candidates for president and the congress in elections to be held in November 1984. Of the 1.2 million votes cast, 84.8 percent of the Blanco and 68.4 percent of Colorado ballots went to candidates opposed to the military government. Among prominent presidential potentials, opposition leader Julio María Sanguinetti received 39 percent of the Colorado total and progovernment Jorge Pacheco Areco, former president, 29 percent. With their antimilitary leader, Ferreira, still in exile, the Blancos polled slightly more votes than the Colorados. Thus twice in two years the military-controlled government had been defeated in free nationwide elections.

Popular dissatisfaction with the government was due not only to latent democratic tradition but also to current economic problems for which present leaders appeared to have no solution. Boosted by new export industries, the economy grew more than 8 percent in 1980, but it declined thereafter, leading to approximately 17 percent unemployment by mid-1983. Inflation, which reached 83 percent for 1979, still hovered around 46 percent in 1983, contributing to a decrease of approximately 50 percent in purchasing power of the average wage earner during the decade of military rule.

With at least 85 percent of the summer beach population of Punta del Este and other resorts normally composed of Argentines, much of the building construction by Argentine capitalists, and an estimated $1 billion in Uruguayan bank deposits owned by Argentines, these neighbors played an impressive role in the Uruguayan economy. By 1983 serious recession in Argentina was making itself felt in Uruguay.

Hope for an early return to democracy faded in 1983. Formal negotiations on provisions of a new constitution broke down in July as civilian and military negotiators clashed over proposed changes. After ten years in power, military leaders were divided. Some favored reestablishing fully a traditional democratic system, with legalization of all political parties. But others, arguing that only they could protect the country from international Communism, advocated reasserting military control and canceling the promised 1984 elections. Especially vocal in this group was General Alvarez, who, after gaining the presidency in 1981, had sought to increase his power and discourage movements toward democracy. After the July 1983 breakdown in negotiations, he was reported seeking to extend his term as president until 1987 or later.

Another problem in civilian-military negotiations was the position of the Blanco Party regarding its leader, Ferreira. Not only was he considered by many armed forces officers to be their worst enemy but he also was believed to be the likely victor in a free presidential election. He had been permanently barred from political activity, and Blanco leaders now refused to join in further negotiations until he was allowed to participate.

In early August 1983 the military government issued a decree banning all unauthorized public political activity. This ruling led to expressed fears by politicians that the promised 1984 elections would be canceled, although military rulers indicated they would not. The following months witnessed increasing antimilitary demonstrations. Encouraged by neighboring Argentina's repudiation of military government and return to democracy, many thousands of Uruguayans voiced their protests by marching, carrying banners, beating on pots and pans, and in other ways expressing their opposition to military rule and desire for restoration of their democracy. One protest rally in November, officially permitted by the government, drew a crowd of participants conservatively estimated at over 200,000. These antigovernment demonstrations culminated on January 18 in a twenty-four-hour general strike—the first in eleven years—which was called by organized labor demanding higher wages, amnesty for political prisoners, and restitution of democracy. It brought Montevideo to a virtual standstill and was effective throughout the country. On June 27, the eleventh anniversary of the dissolution of the General Assembly that had led to military dictatorship, a general strike called by opposition political groups paralyzed the capital as well as other cities and towns.

On June 16, 1984, Ferreira, who had been nominated by the Blanco Party as its candidate for president in the November 1984 elections, returned to Uruguay after eleven years in exile. Now the only Blanco or Colorado leader still banned from public office, he expected to be jailed by the Alvarez government. Upon his arrival by chartered ferry from Buenos Aires, accompanied by approximately 400 friends, relatives, and journalists, he was arrested and booked on several charges, including inviting foreign intervention by his criticism of Uruguay's government. His son, Juan Raúl, who was with him, was also arrested on accusations of insulting the military and attempting to undermine the government. During their years in exile, both had loudly criticized the military regime. This carefully staged return home after his long absence was designed to boost Ferreira's prestige and promote the antimilitary campaign and his own chance for election as president. It did succeed in bringing out more than 50,000 greeters and well-wishers to utter antimilitary protests. His arrest and detention sharpened the friction between political and military leaders and served as an impediment in Uruguay's return to democracy.

Members of the Blanco Party refused to continue transition negotiations with the government until Ferreira and his son were released, and in this they were supported temporarily by Colorado and Broad Front leaders. By now most generals and admirals, weary of their unsuccessful attempts to solve the disastrous economic problems, appeared anxious to shift the burden of government to civilians. But mindful of prosecutions of military officers for human rights abuses taking place in Argentina under the new civilian government there, they hesitated to give up power until assured they would not be in danger of a similar fate. Also, while many military leaders desired to remove the ambitious and unpopular Alvarez from the presidency, they did not want to appear to be bowing to their political enemy, Ferreira. They had been holding out for a major role in future civilian governments and amnesty from any prosecutions for their past deeds. Now, however, they appeared willing to relinquish their control with merely some face-saving assurance that a future civilian government would not initiate prosecutions for past civil rights abuses by military officers. Well aware of Ferreira's enhanced popularity, they showed no inclination to restore his political freedom.

While the Blancos still refused to participate because Ferreira had not been released, leaders of the Colorado and Civic Union Parties and the Broad Front coalition entered into negotiations with military commanders that led to an agreement in early August 1984 providing for national elections November 25 with the winners taking office March 1, 1985. The armed forces were granted an advisory council but not a major role in future civilian governments as they had wanted. They also obtained a guarantee that only military courts would investigate alleged past human rights abuses. The Blancos rejected this agreement, and Ferreira charged that it confirmed the military system of government; but Colorado leader Julio M. Sanguinetti claimed it was the best possible arrangement and would phase the military completely out of political decision making. Although factions opposed it, all parties except the Blancos officially approved. Some 45,000 people participated in a demonstration of support and celebration of what they believed was a return to democracy.

Prior to this agreement the government, by way of clearing the air for serious negotiations, had begun backing away from some of the restrictions it had imposed, including arbitrary dismissal of public employees and extension of its curbs on citizens' political rights. Under pressure to free all the remaining approximately 700 political prisoners, it agreed to hasten the release of many. On August 20 Juan Ferreira was set free. By November an estimated 500 remained in prison.

With the military still firmly maintaining its prohibition of his running in the November 1984 elections, in mid-August Wilson Ferreira renounced his candidacy and urged his party to pick a new candidate who would be acceptable. At a party convention, however, the delegates asked him to reconsider, realizing that without him at the head of the ticket their chance of winning was considerably reduced. But on August 23, with time running out, they chose Alberto Sáenz de Zumarán, a human rights activist, as a stand-in for Ferreira. He promised that if elected he would conduct a short, transitional administration, with all political rights restored, and then hold a second election in which Ferreira and other politicians could participate. The feasibility of this proposal was questioned as calling new elections would require approval by two-thirds of the congress.

Although the Alvarez government had permitted the Broad Front to participate in the November elections and had freed its longtime leader, Liber Seregni, it had not restored his political rights. Under these circumstances the Broad Front nominated as its presidential candidate Seregni's 1971 running mate, Juan José Crottogini, an elderly physician. With its leader, Sanguinetti, a forty-eight-year-old lawyer and political moderate, heading the Colorado ticket, opinion polls gave him a slight edge in the presidential race. But at this time Uruguayans generally appeared more interested in getting rid of the dictatorship than in which political candidate would win the presidency. Desirous of assuring the permanent demise of military rule, Colorados, Blancos, and members of the Broad Front, containing Communists, Socialists, and Christian Democrats, agreed to work together to strengthen the new democratic government, whatever its political orientation.

DEMOCRACY RESTORED

Amid great popular enthusiasm Uruguayans went to the polls on November 25, 1984. With no troops on the streets and only one unarmed soldier guarding each voting place, the military allowed civilians to cast their ballots freely in the first general elections since 1971. Political exiles returning to Uruguay for this event were estimated at over 60,000. Although pessimistic regarding the ability of civilian politicians to run the country, in bowing out of political control the armed forces were following the general trend at this time toward democracy in Latin America.

The nation not only restored free elections but also the old system of permitting political parties to present several lists of candidates. As a result, both Sanguinetti and Pacheco appeared on the ballot as Colorado candidates for president, while the Blancos ran two others in addition to Sáenz de Zumarán. Of these Sanguinetti, principal author and skillful negotiator of the plan whereby the military agreed to free elections, emerged as the winner of a five-year presidential term with 38.8 percent of the votes. A few days later the military government dropped its charges against Wilson Ferreira and released him.

Sanguinetti called upon his defeated opponents to join with him in forming a "government of national understanding." He well understood that, while the armed forces were relinquishing control, they were still well organized and for the time being only fading into the background from which they might reemerge should the new democracy show signs of weakness. Moreover, with above 50 percent annual inflation, over 15 percent unemployment, and a foreign debt of $5.3 billion, the country was experiencing an extreme economic crisis. The new civilian administration was coming to power saddled with economic problems for which earlier civilian politicians were largely to blame and which military administrators had been unable to solve.

As the generals and admirals eased their way out of power, President Alvarez hastened the process by resigning on February 11—some eighteen days before Sanguinetti was scheduled to take office. This action was seen as a move to prevent any embarrassment at the inauguration of the new president. According to custom, Alvarez should present to his successor the presidential sash and baton, traditional symbols of power; but Sanguinetti had indicated he would not permit Alvarez to participate in the inaugural ceremonies. The Council of State therefore asked Rafael Addiego Bruno president of the Supreme Court, to serve as provisional president of the republic until March 1.

On February 15, 1985, thousands of people cheered as the thirty senators and ninety-nine deputies who had been elected to the General Assembly in November entered the congressional palace and revived this legislative body, which had been closed in 1973. In an inaugural ceremony on March 1, attended by members of the new congress, heads of six Latin American republics, and prominent representatives of many other countries, Julio Sanguinetti took the oath of office as Uruguay's first freely elected civilian president in thirteen years. Enrique Tarigo was sworn in as vice president.

President Sanguinetti began his administration by announcing that his government would seek diplomatic relations with all countries. This policy meant reestablishing ties with Cuba, although Sanguinetti was known to be strongly pro-United States. He also restored the rights of more than a dozen groups formerly banned, including the Tupamaros and the Communist Party. He proposed to the congress amnesty for the approximately 325 political prisoners still held, and he launched investigations of some 80 known deaths in prison and between 150 and 200 people who had disappeared during military rule. But Sanguinetti recognized Uruguay's greatest problem to be economic: inflation had drastically lowered the standard of living, and a scarcity of jobs had caused more than 300,000 people—over one-tenth of the population—to leave the country in search of employment. He well understood the difficulties in performing the miracle that was needed to turn the situation around and provide the prosperity Uruguayans now expected from their democratic government.

As the military regime relaxed its grip, increasing numbers of political prisoners were freed. This process was stepped up in the days following inauguration of the Sanguinetti administration. Nearly 2,000 of those who had been arrested were Tupamaros, but numerous others had been seized merely because they held leftist views or had criticized the government. Upon their release they spread stories of horrible mental and physical torture suffered while in prison. Many found it extremely difficult to shake off the effects of their long incarceration. There were several suicides, and a large number of people with serious mental problems wound up in hospitals.

The military had tried to obliterate leftist influences in Uruguay, but by now it was clear that their efforts had met with little success. Once they were free to operate again, left-wing political groups flourished, especially in the capital, where the Broad Front came close to winning control of the Montevideo government in the November 1984 elections.

After regaining their political rights, the Tupamaros sought respectability by abandoning armed struggle and seeking to achieve their goals democratically. They organized as a legal political party, established headquarters in Montevideo, and applied for membership in the Broad Front, which initially was denied because of opposition by the Christian Democrats. Subsequently they expanded their activities, gained additional followers, acquired a radio station, published a very popular magazine, were admitted into the

Broad Front, and continued working toward their objective of establishing socialism in Uruguay. The Tupamaro founder, Raúl Sendic, played a leading role in the party until his death in 1989.

President Sanguinetti skillfully maneuvered the Uruguayan ship of state between extremists on the left and right. As investigations revealed more shocking details regarding individual disappearances and harsh treatment of political prisoners, there was increasing pressure to punish military officers for their alleged misdeeds. Although in the agreements leading to restoration of democratic government the armed forces had been assured by civilian negotiators that they would be subject only to military tribunals in human rights cases, many people did not approve of this provision. As time passed there were increasing demands that perpetrators of these crimes be brought to justice in civil courts. But while there were many demands for "justice," there also was the awareness that the armed forces, still well organized, were standing by and might again seize control if pushed too far. No one realized this danger more than Sanguinetti. Arguing that the military should be dealt with as leniently as the Tupamaros had been, he recommended burying the past by granting total amnesty. He pushed for adoption of such a measure by the General Assembly, but in September 1986 it was defeated. A few weeks later the congress rejected a proposal by Ferreira and his fellow Blancos to limit trials to thirty-eight specific cases then under way. Nevertheless, in December, with the army threatening to defy the courts, after very heated debates, amnesty for military officers won congressional approval.

Staunch opponents of amnesty for the military refused to accept this decision. Led by the Tupamaros and the Broad Front, in the hope of overturning the congressional act, they began campaigning for a referendum whereby the public could vote on this issue. They managed to gain the required signatures of a fourth of the voting population, and on April 16, 1989, the referendum was held. It resulted in victory for the pro-amnesty side, although in Montevideo more than half the ballots were against amnesty.

Uruguayans had restored democracy, but restoring economic prosperity was quite another matter. After more than a year of democratic government, the country was still experiencing serious depression, over 60 percent annual inflation, and a continuing exodus of young people in search of jobs abroad. Many older persons who remembered the prosperity of the 1940s and early 1950s longed for a return to those days and appeared unable to accept the fact that they now were living in another era. From all sides the Sanguinetti administration felt pressure for economic improvements. It was especially strong from organized labor, which, after relegalization, had emerged with renewed strength largely under left-wing leadership. Militant unions continually agitated and staged strikes. These brought demands from the business community and middle classes in general for more effective government control, but in his desire to preserve freedom of expression, Sanguinetti refused to crack down.

With regard to the national debt, Sanguinetti would not accede to leftist demands that the nation default on its payments. Instead he sought to protect Uruguay's credit rating by entering into an arrangement with the International Monetary Fund that made possible renegotiating the debt and obtaining additional capital. With an eye to expanding Uruguayan trade, he made two visits to the United States, one in September 1985 and another in June 1986. On both occasions in numerous meetings with business and government leaders he sought to obtain greater access to foreign markets.

Two powerful forces strangling economic development were organized labor and the government industrial corporations. The inefficient and expensive operations of the latter were a severe drain on the treasury. A frequently proposed solution to Uruguay's economic problems was the sale of some or all of these corporations and their return to private enterprise. Another proposal was exchange of equity in state companies for part of the foreign debt. But labor organizations fought such ideas and also opposed other schemes to attract foreign capital. Instead, leftist leaders preferred to reduce or eliminate interest payments on the foreign debt and bring about cancellation of at least part of the debt itself. They would use money so acquired for larger salaries to government workers and various welfare needs. By the late 1980s a split was appearing in the Uruguayan Communist Party resulting from division in the Soviet Union, and this split was bringing diversion in the philosophy and policies of Uruguayan labor.

A principal factor discouraging foreign investments in Uruguay was the freedom of labor organizations to operate with little or no restrictions and the numerous demands and strikes that resulted. With national elections scheduled for November 26, 1989, leading presidential candidates of the Blanco and Colorado Parties were advocating much stricter regulation. They also favored eliminating or greatly reducing the state's role in industry and promised significantly increased efforts to attract foreign capital. Such policies were opposed by the left-leaning Broad Front.

Well before the November elections, polls indicated the probable winner for president to be Luis Alberto Lacalle of the Blanco Party, grandson of the earlier Blanco leader, Luis Alberto de Herrera. Lacalle, a forty-eight-year-old senator, had moved up to Blanco leadership after the death of Wilson Ferreira two years earlier. The top Colorado contender in the 1989 presidential race was Jorge Batlle Ibáñez, great nephew of José Batlle y Ordóñez and close friend of President Sanguinetti, who was ineligible for a second term. Batlle had been prohibited by the military from participating in the 1984 elections. The Broad Front candidate was Liber Seregni.

In the balloting on November 26 Lacalle and his running mate, Gonzalo Aguirre, were elected as predicted, receiving about 38 percent of the votes. Batlle, who polled approximately 31 percent, was adversely affected by public displeasure with the Sanguinetti administration's lack of economic improvement. Inflation was now over 80 percent annually. By this time pensioners constituted more than a fourth of the electorate. Batlle lost much of their support by opposing constitutional revision whereby pensions would be increased every few months instead of yearly to offset inflation.

Not surprising also was the showing by the Broad Front. Winning 34 percent of the local votes, it captured the Montevideo city government, electing Tabaré Vásquez, a Socialist, as mayor and gaining a majority of city council seats. This impressive attainment emboldened Broad Front members to speak out more forcefully against free enterprise, labor union regulations, and other reforms advocated by Lacalle and fellow Blanco and Colorado leaders. Thus the way was prepared for growing conflict between leftists, represented by the Broad Front, and more moderate elements led by the Blancos and Colorados. To strengthen the moderate position, Lacalle proposed that these two parties form a governing coalition that would provide a clear majority in the General Assembly. But with both Blancos and Colorados split into factions, he found such a coalition very difficult to achieve.

When Lacalle was inaugurated president on March 1, 1990, the economy was still depressed, annual inflation was running at about 100 percent, and the Uruguayan peso, which had been sliding for many years, was down to an official exchange rate of over 800 per U.S. dollar. He quickly set about the formidable task of moving Uruguay away from its state corporations toward free enterprise, as he had promised in his campaign. But bills designed to permit disposal of all or parts of some of these companies met stiff opposition in the congress. And in Montevideo the leftist local administration was moving in an opposite direction with such inflationary steps as increased salaries and property taxes.

One of the cardinal points of President Lacalle's efforts to improve the Uruguayan economy was greater international trade. When in June 1990 U.S. President George Bush, in a good will gesture toward closer United States-Latin American relations, announced his offer of free trade with all Latin American republics, Lacalle enthusiastically accepted, the first head of state to do so. He saw this offer as the answer to his dream of turning Uruguay away from stifling protectionist policies and toward trade and investments that were needed. In December President Bush included Montevideo in a six-day-tour around South America. In a speech to the Uruguayan congress he praised Lacalle for being the first president to call him after announcement of his inter-American trade plan. But it is interesting to note that about a dozen left-wing members boycotted Bush's speech and several others departed without joining in the applause.

At the beginning of 1991 Uruguay was still beset by inflation. During the past year the currency had declined even more rapidly, and the peso was officially over 1,600 per dollar. It continued a rapid slide until by the end of April 1993 it was down to almost 3,900 per dollar. On April 30 the government issued a new peso worth 1,000 of the old ones. At this time the exchange rate was 3.89 per dollar. Since then the new peso has slowly declined until by the beginning of November 1994 it was approximately 5.50 per dollar. It should be remembered that this is actually a "new new peso" worth 1 million of the pesos that in 1935 were on a par with the U.S. dollar.

During these years the Lacalle administration worked diligently to improve the economic picture, but the problem was difficult and the opposition to change was strong. A key part of Lacalle's privatization program was sale of the state-owned telephone company, Antel; but in a December 1992 referendum on this issue, voters rejected it 72 to 28 percent. By November 1994 Lacalle had succeeded in disposing of only Montevideo port facilities and several smaller companies. Inflation had been reduced to 52.9 percent for 1993 and approximately 40 percent in 1994. The government had virtually stopped printing additional currency but had imposed large tax increases to cover its budgets. A boost in the economy was provided by the arrival in 1993 of some 2 million tourists, an increase of 11 percent over the previous year. About 80 percent of them were from Argentina.

As one of Latin America's top financial centers, Uruguay still lives up to its reputation as the "Switzerland of South America." With strict security laws, Uruguayan banks continue to attract foreign depositors. As of June 1994, they held $5.7 billion in deposits, an increase of 4.8 percent in a year. Approximately 60 percent of all deposits were from outside the country, about 90 percent of them from Argentina.

Of special interest in Uruguay has been the new South American Common Market (Mercosur), including Argentina, Brazil, Paraguay, and Uruguay, scheduled to go into effect in January 1995. It has been promoted vigorously by President Lacalle as a means of greatly expanding Uruguayan trade and in the hope that Montevideo would become the official capital of Mercosur.

In elections held November 27, 1994, Julio Sanguinetti won another presidential term, permitting him to return to office for five more years, until 2000. In the Senate, Colorados won in addition to the vice presidency, 10 seats, Blancos 10, Broad Front members 9 and a new party, Nuevo Espacio, gained 1 seat. In the Chamber of Deputies, Colorados captured 34 seats, Blancos 31, the Broad Front 30 and Nuevo Espacio 4.

These elections—the third in a decade—confirm that Uruguayans again have their democracy and freedom, enabling the various political groups to express themselves openly. The General Assembly is back to business as usual, with a wide range of views represented. Many Uruguayans long for the "good old days" before the mid-1950s; but in a population of about 3 million composed of well over half as many retirees as workers, there is hardly enough of the "good life" to go around. Yet as long as the armed forces remain in their barracks, there is plenty of room to debate and experiment in the hope of recreating something of the old Uruguayan utopia.

NOTES

1. *The New York Times*, March 2, 1967.
2. *The New York Times*, August 9, 1967.
3. *The New York Times*, August 11, 1970.
4. *The Evening Star* (Washington), August 8, 1968.
5. *The New York Times*, September 12, 1971.
6. *The New York Times*, November 30, 1971.
7. *The New York Times*, February 14, 1973; March 2, 1973.
8. *The New York Times*, February 15, 1973.
9. *The New York Times*, February 18, 1973.
10. *The New York Times*, June 28, 1973.
11. *The Evening Star* (Washington), June 28, 1973.
12. *The New York Times*, October 30, 1973.
13. *The New York Times*, March 13, 1974.
14. Ibid.
15. Ibid.
16. *The New York Times*, February 12, 1976.
17. *The New York Times*, August 25, 1975.
18. *The New York Times*, June 13, 1976.
19. *The New York Times*, September 2, 1976.
20. *The New York Times*, March 10, 1976.

Chapter 3

Argentina: A Divided Land

On September 6, 1930, crowds of Argentines stood in the streets of Buenos Aires and cheered the army as it moved toward the Casa Rosada (the Pink House, the presidential palace). President Hipólito Yrigoyen, Argentina's first "man of the people," had just been forced to resign, and the remnants of his party were about to be ousted. But in their desire to get rid of a once popular and now despised ruler, most of those who cheered failed to ask, "What are we getting in his place?" The result was more than a year of military dictatorship before the country returned to constitutional normality.

Then followed nearly a dozen years of conservative, stable government, similar in many respects to that under which Argentina had prospered in the late nineteenth and early twentieth centuries. By the end of that period the people were ready for something different. At dawn on June 4, 1943, troops of the Campo de Mayo garrison on the outskirts of Buenos Aires moved against the administration. As they marched through the capital and seized strategic points, they were cheered with cries of "¡Viva libertad!" and "¡Viva democracia!" from thousands of *porteños* (residents of Buenos Aires) engaged in frenzied demonstrations against the doomed regime. Within a few hours the president had fled and a new government was in power. Again a brief display of armed might had determined the nation's future. Once more, however, the Argentine man in the street, in the spirit of "anything for a change," failed to ask, "What are we getting instead?" This time it was military rule, the rise of Juan Domingo Perón, and the disappearance of "liberty" and "democracy" in Argentina.

The 1930 revolution had been a triumph for the army and the conservative politicians. The one of 1943 was a victory only for the army. For over two years thereafter, several high army officers contended for supreme power. Out of this struggle emerged Perón as the strongman of Argentina.

What happened in 1930 and 1943 was not typical of Argentina during the previous seven decades. Politically stable and economically progressive, by 1930 the country had reached an enviable position in Latin America, and it certainly would not be classed with the "underdeveloped" or "developing" states of more backward regions. In the late nineteenth and early twentieth centuries it had grown rapidly into one of the world's greatest meat and grain producers and had become unquestionably a leading Latin American republic. By the early twentieth century it had surpassed Chile in economic and social development. Economically similar to Canada and Australia, for many years it has been culturally on a par with the most advanced nations.

Argentina's spectacular rise was due largely to its several advantages over most other Latin American states—particularly in regard to location, topography, people, and history. With an area of more than 1 million square miles, extending about 2,300 miles from just above the Tropic of Capricorn to the southern tip of South America, the nation embraces a climatic range from subtropical in the extreme north to cold, windswept Patagonia and Tierra del Fuego in the south. On the west the high Andes, which so effectively divide it from Chile, tower over a vast expanse of lowlands. To the east, stretching across a radius of approximately 400 miles south, west, and north of Buenos Aires and enjoying a fine, temperate climate, lies one of the world's flattest and most fertile regions, a really important breadbasket—the pampas, the heart of Argentina.

Across these broad plains and beyond, many railroads were constructed in the late nineteenth and early twentieth centuries, giving Argentina the most extensive rail network of any Latin American country and the seventh largest in the world. They were financed principally by British and French capital. About two-thirds was British, which by 1910 controlled approximately 65 percent of these railways. About one-fourth of the system was state owned. In a pattern designed to develop and serve the important overseas trade, these lines fan out from the principal ports of Buenos Aires, Rosario, and Bahía Blanca. They tie the interior to the coast, as well as provide access to Chile, Bolivia, and Paraguay. The level pampas facilitated the building of this system, which in turn provided necessary transportation for the many settlers attracted to the fertile land and made possible its fantastic economic development. Because of mismanagement and financial difficulties, especially after the first Perón government purchased them, these railways deteriorated in quality and efficiency; but they still form a significant part of the overland transportation.

One of Argentina's greatest advantages has been its people. At the time of the Spanish conquest, this part of South America was similar in aboriginal composition to the North American region that became the United States, with a small, mostly hostile Indian population. There, as in the United States, the Indians were gradually pushed toward the far frontiers or exterminated. This left a large, virtually empty land, which attracted numerous foreign immigrants. Net immigration during 1880–1910 was more than 2 million, resulting by the end of this period in a population approximately 30 percent foreign born. In these three decades the total number of inhabitants increased from about 2.6 million to over 7 million. In modern Argentina almost all of the settlers have come from Europe, principally Italy and Spain. Only by a stretch of imagination can Argentina be termed a Spanish American country. At least one-third of the people are of Italian extraction, and in several parts of the republic Italians are in the majority. There are also many Argentines from northern Europe, especially Germany and the United Kingdom. The latter have wielded an influence far out of proportion to their numbers. Indeed, Argentina has been termed a land populated by Italians who speak bad Spanish and think they are British!

With a population almost entirely of European origin, there are no racial problems of consequence. Today there are virtually no blacks; and the few Indians, except recent immigrants from Bolivia, have been mainly in remote areas. Such ethnic friction as has appeared has resulted primarily from differences in European background. But many Argentines believe they do have a population problem—too few people. With only 35 million and a growth rate of about 1.3 percent annually, they fear Brazil, their big rival, which with a population of approximately 155 million and a more rapid rate of increase, appears to them a potential danger.

In the colonial period the Río de la Plata area profited, as did Chile, by its remoteness and lack of precious metals. Until the latter half of the eighteenth century, because of Spain's stereotyped navigation routes and trade policies, which kept ports in this part of South America officially closed, Argentina was one of the most distant and backward parts of the Spanish American empire and an open market for smugglers. Considered of minor importance by the crown, this region experienced considerably less control by the mother country than the economically more desirable colonies, and its inhabitants frequently ignored Spanish authority altogether. With this relative political freedom, they gained valuable experience in government.

Rivalry with the Portuguese over part of the Río de la Plata basin led to Spain's establishing in 1776 the Viceroyalty of the Río de la Plata, embracing present-day Argentina, Uruguay, Paraguay, and Bolivia, with Buenos Aires as the capital. This action gave the region a new prominence in the empire and set off rapid economic and cultural development. Two British attempts to seize Buenos Aires in 1806–07, the lack of Spanish support in defending it, and the success of local residents in driving off the British had a profound effect. The Argentines found they could not depend on Spain for protection. Their political training together with their successful confrontation of the British gave them needed confidence to achieve independence and self-government. These experiences helped mold their concepts of freedom as well as their belief in the necessity of protecting themselves without relying on outside assistance.

Although Argentina has enjoyed these and other advantages, it has suffered from one serious handicap. It has been and still is a divided land. In the nineteenth century the division was geographic. In the twentieth century, although geographic problems have been partially solved, there has been an even more severe division between classes of people.

Buenos Aires is not only the nation's capital, largest metropolis, and chief port, but also one of the world's most sophisticated cities—quite a contrast to what it was in the colonial and early independence years. Today more than one-third of all Argentines live there. The province of Buenos Aires, which surrounds it, has long been the most populous and advanced in the country. In the late colonial era, after becoming a viceregal capital, the city progressed rapidly. Not only was it the focus of political power, but, together with the surrounding province, it attained economic and cultural levels considerably above those of the interior regions.

Independence from Spain was achieved rather easily, with an initial break in 1810 and a formal declaration in 1816; but establishing a united republic was a far greater problem. *Porteños*, believing they alone had sufficient political capability to govern, generally insisted on a centralized state ruled by Buenos Aires; but leaders in the interior, determined to maintain their provincial and individual freedoms, bitterly opposed any such arrangement. For half a century Argentina was plagued by internal conflict over this issue before anything resembling a united nation appeared. In the meantime, the nearest approach to a government for the entire country was the dictatorship of Juan Manuel Rosas from 1835 to 1852. Officially he was only governor of the province of Buenos Aires, but he managed to extend his control over much of the country and speak for most of Argentina in international affairs.

ARISTOCRATIC REPUBLIC

In 1853 Argentines formulated a new constitution modeled closely after that of the United States. (Argentine envy and dislike of this country appeared later. Such intellectual leaders as Juan B. Alberdi, whose ideas profoundly influenced the constitution, and Domingo F. Sarmiento, later Argentine president, were ardent admirers of the United States.) With the exception of a few years during the Perón era, the Constitution of 1853 has remained the official framework of government until the present, although in recent years it has been ignored rather consistently. It now is the oldest extant constitution in Latin America.

In theory the constitution provided for a federal form of government with considerable autonomy reserved to the individual provinces—a necessary concession for any prospect of national unity. But because of the many problems of government Argentines had experienced before 1853, together with the tradition of *caudillismo* that had long existed, the framers of this constitution were impressed with the need for a strong executive and created one who would be more influential in the political system than the congress or courts. They provided for a president elected indirectly for a six-year term and ineligible for immediate reelection. (The term limitation was inspired by the difficulties experienced in disposing of the dictator Rosas, who had been overthrown the previous year.) He must be a native-born Argentine, at least thirty years of age, and a Roman Catholic. There was also provision for a vice president with duties similar to those of his U.S. counterpart. The constitution established a bicameral National Congress composed of a Senate, representing the provinces, and a Chamber of Deputies representing the people. The Roman Catholic Church was declared the official, state-supported church, but freedom of worship was guaranteed.

With the president possessing, among his various powers, the right of intervention in the provinces, Argentine federalism proved considerably more theoretical than real. Over succeeding years the chief executive acquired important additional powers. Of special significance has been his right to bypass Congress and the courts by executive decrees. Argentina provides a prime example of the extremes to which government by decree has been carried in Latin America.

In 1860, some seven years after the promulgation of this constitution, a semblance of unity was finally attained. This unification marks the beginning of Argentina's great age of development, which transformed it from a poor, backward land into the advanced nation it became within the next half century. Under the leadership of such outstanding statesmen as Bartolomé Mitre, Domingo F. Sarmiento, Nicolás Avellaneda, and Julio Roca, government in the 1860s, 1870s, and 1880s was stable, sound, conservative, and progressive. With suffrage normally limited to the propertied and educated classes, Argentina was a republic of the aristocracy—similar to that of the United States during its early decades of independence. Contrary to most Latin American states of that era, it was civilian government in which the military, controlled by the civilian commander in chief, the national president, remained nonpolitical. Although a ruling oligarchy appeared, whose members often perpetuated themselves in office by fraudulent elections and other unethical methods, it was a government that provided stability and encouraged economic progress. This farsighted leadership deserves much credit for Argentina's very rapid economic and cultural growth in the late nineteenth century.

One of the unsolved problems still remaining after 1860 was the relationship between Buenos Aires (city and province) and the interior. For nearly two decades the city served as the temporary residence of the federal government, but no permanent capital was agreed upon. In 1880 a compromise solution was reached by separating the city of Buenos Aires from the province and making it a federal district and the permanent capital. Since this arrangement theoretically decreased the power and influence of the city and placed it under the national government, which interior provincials controlled, it was a political compromise they could live with; and *porteños* liked it because they retained the seat of government. But today there are still two

Argentinas—the great city and province of Buenos Aires, with their economic and cultural advantages, overshadowing the rest of the country.

For half a century government by the few maintained a climate that encouraged economic development and attracted the numerous European immigrants who were needed. In the three decades preceding World War I, per capita wealth increased five times as fast as the rapidly growing population. By the early 1880s significant improvements in Argentine cattle and sheep, together with the appearance of refrigerator steamships and increasing demands in Europe for beef and mutton, set Argentina on the road to prosperity as one of the world's greatest meat producers. The 1890s brought an additional source of wealth—production of grain, principally wheat, for which the pampas soil and climate were very suitable. Again it was European demand that stimulated this industry, which proved to be even more profitable than beef. By 1910 Argentina led the world in grain exports. Grain crops were ideal for large-scale farming in what was already a land of big estates (*estancias*). Argentina was then and has been since a country of a few great landholders living in sharp contrast to the many farm laborers, who have had little opportunity to acquire property. In this respect it has been like most other Latin American states.

Not only was the country a boom land economically, but also during the late nineteenth century a great interest in education appeared, due largely to the rapidly increasing middle class and the presence of men such as Sarmiento, who provided the leadership. A result was nationwide building of public schools that enabled Argentina to emerge in the twentieth century with a level of literacy among the highest in the world. From only 18 percent, as shown in the 1869 census, the literacy rate has risen to reportedly over 90 percent today.

Unfortunately, economic prosperity together with the carefully manipulated political system bred corruption, which reached a peak in the late 1880s, when it prevailed in numerous forms through all levels of the administration. Virtually every government employee seemed to have his price. Among unethical schemes engaged in by the president and other top officials were huge and very questionable sales of public lands to speculators or outright grants to friends, as well as secret, unauthorized issues of large quantities of paper money that devalued the currency and caused serious inflation. A peso freely convertible to gold, established early in Julio Roca's first administration (1880–86), was soon abandoned. Prior to this Argentina had no national currency. Subsequent emissions of paper money resulted in the peso's corresponding decline in value, and the currency issues of 1886–89 worsened an already unstable monetary situation. Financial stability was achieved only with a return to the gold standard during Roca's second term (1898–1904).

When a worldwide depression in 1889 burst Argentina's prosperity bubble, it brought loud cries for political reform and resulted in the resignation the next year of President Miguel Juárez Celman, elected in 1886. By the 1890s the nation was experiencing considerable political unrest and increasing agitation to clean up the government and make it more democratic.

Unlike their Chilean and Uruguayan neighbors, Argentines had not developed strong, long-lived political parties. For more than half a century after 1860 the country was ruled by a conservative oligarchy, but it was not one highly organized political unit. The first serious challenge to this regime was the appearance in 1889 of the Civic Union (Unión Cívica), a loose organization of dissenters from several walks of life, including some from the old oligarchy and the army. Part of them were rebelling against recent political scandals. Others, representing the increasingly influential middle class, looked with jealousy on the conservative political monopoly and longed to seize this power and the accompanying spoils of office. Still others were genuine believers in a more liberal political philosophy. An armed revolt led by the Civic Union in July 1890, while helping to bring about the resignation of the president, failed to terminate the conservatives' hold on the country. The Civic Union soon split; but the stronger faction, which took the name Radical Civic Union (UCR), often called Radicals, eventually played a significant role in Argentine politics. It was at least two decades, though, before this party overcame its internal differences and gained sufficient organization and strength to lead an effective opposition to the entrenched aristocracy.

The conservatives, now operating through their National Autonomous Party, remained in control of the government until 1916. But although it was a time of great prosperity and the spotlight was on economics rather than politics, a step was taken that transformed the nation's political life. This was the passage in 1912 of a series of electoral reform bills, which were forced through a reluctant, conservative Congress by President Roque Sáenz Peña who, during his campaign for this office in 1910, had loudly denounced fraudulent elections and promised reforms that would confer control of the government upon the general public.

MASS ENFRANCHISEMENT

These measures were designed to satisfy demands by labor and the middle classes, led by the UCR, for universal manhood suffrage. The Sáenz Peña laws required, for the first time in Argentina, secret ballots in all elections and, with the exception of certain specified groups, enfranchised all males over eighteen years of age. (Women did not vote in national elections until 1951.) For those qualified, voting was made compulsory, but this rule was not consistently enforced. Another provision stipulated that one-third of the seats in the Chamber of Deputies and the provincial legislatures would go to the highest ranking minority party regardless of the number of votes received.

During a time of economic prosperity and rising expectations by the disenfranchised majority, the conservative rulers had been pressured into political suicide. As Argentines proved in the next elections, if these laws were honestly administered, it now was possible to elect to public office candidates not endorsed by the aristocracy.

The victorious presidential candidate in 1916 has often been referred to as Argentina's first "man of the people" and also the first in this country to gain the presidency in a free election. Sáenz Peña had died in 1914 and some doubts were voiced as to whether his successor, Victoriano de la Plaza, would honor the 1912 electoral reforms or permit them to be violated by fraud. Apparently they were adhered to and the 1916 elections were relatively free. The winner, by one electoral vote, was Hipólito Yrigoyen who, for more than a quarter century, had been the recognized leader of the Radicals. A poor speaker, an incoherent writer, and a man who shunned large gatherings, he had, mainly by individual contacts, gathered numerous, devoted adherents and developed the UCR into a powerful political organization. His popular appeal was based in part on vague pronouncements that were unclear as to meaning and open to varying interpretations. He attracted primarily the middle and laboring classes, although his followers also included some former members of the conservative oligarchy. The methods upon which Yrigoyen relied to win power were the secret ballot or revolution. Attempts in 1890, 1893, and 1905 to gain control by military insurrection failed, but he continued to build up the Radical Party and insist on free elections. Trends of the times, which witnessed the growing importance of the middle and laboring classes, favored the Radical movement.

The fourteen-year Radical administration of 1916–30 began with Yrigoyen and ended with Yrigoyen, with the six-year term of Marcelo T. de Alvear (1922–28) in between. But although this period witnessed a continuing increase of Radical power, it did not really bring radical changes. The Radical Party actually was not very radical. It was a moderate party that represented primarily the middle classes—white-collar workers, including merchants and professional men. Although there were some modifications, these years did not see sweeping revisions in the nation's social and economic structure. Economically Argentina remained primarily a meat and grain producer controlled by the landholding aristocracy and relying on foreign markets.

Yrigoyen assumed power in the midst of World War I and remained steadfast in his determination to keep Argentina out of this conflict. The nation benefited as a result. Greater demand for meat and grain brought quick recovery from economic difficulties experienced at the war's beginning, while the curtailment of available consumer imports improved the balance of payments and stimulated new Argentine industries. World prosperity of the mid- and late 1920s was also reflected in Argentina, which, until the crash of October 1929, continued its spectacular economic and cultural growth. As in previous decades, it prospered from more foreign investments and the arrival of additional European immigrants.

Although little was done to change the overall economic orientation, Yrigoyen did take one major step toward what was considered economic independence. That was the creation in 1922 of a national petroleum agency, known as Yacimientos Petrolíferos Fiscales (YPF). It was especially significant in establishing the principle that public utilities should be owned by the state rather than private enterprise, especially foreign enterprise.

The labor vote had contributed in no small measure to Yrigoyen's election, but labor leaders soon found that they could expect few favors from his government. Reforms for the benefit of labor were considerably less than had been anticipated and meager as compared with the example set by neighboring Uruguay. Collective bargaining was approved and many restrictions on labor unions were removed, thus stimulating labor organization. There were also several public housing projects. But the Radicals did not enact meaningful social security legislation, and the few minimum-wage laws adopted were quite limited in scope. Wartime scarcities stimulated small industries, but the Radicals did not really promote large-scale industrial development. When postwar depression and unemployment led to serious labor agitation culminating in outbreaks of violence in Buenos Aires, Yrigoyen called out troops to quell the riots, which resulted in many casualties.

The failure of Radical administrations—both Yrigoyen's and Alvear's—to do more for labor was the result of conservative opposition as well as of Radical inertia and disorganization. Even with extensive presidential intervention in the provinces, Radical influence was slow to penetrate the interior, where the middle classes were considerably weaker and conservatives remained in control of many local governments. The national Senate, composed of members elected by provincial legislatures, remained a conservative stronghold until 1930. But the Radicals themselves were seriously divided. Many appeared content to have gained national power and the spoils of office. Very few middle-class politicians, who really controlled the party, were genuinely concerned about the problems of the laboring masses. Thus internal division and lukewarm interest among the Radicals together with conservative obstruction spelled doom to many reforms the administration claimed to support. Nevertheless, most Argentines appeared more impressed with what Yrigoyen said than with what he and his party did or failed to do, and by the end of his first term he had achieved tremendous popularity. Such reforms as were provided, although not as impressive as contemporary ones in some other countries, did set the stage for much greater labor demands, achievements—and problems—in future decades.

MILITARY IN POLITICS

Of special significance during this time was the rising military influence. Unfortunately, the Radical Party's advocacy of revolution as a means of gaining control had brought the traditionally nonpolitical military into the power struggle. This was followed by growing intervention by the armed forces in political affairs, particularly aimed at securing a greater voice in economic and foreign policies as well as obtaining various benefits for themselves. An army colonel was appointed director of the new YPF; and as the government became increasingly involved in economic matters, it relied more heavily on the military for technical expertise. Subsequently the military participated extensively in industrial development and management, including YPF, petrochemicals, steel and light metals, shipbuilding, armaments, and other products, as well as operation of a large airline and much of the railway system. Well before 1930 it was obvious that henceforth civilian administrations would be dependent on military support for their tenure of office; and, alarmingly, the army had become divided regarding political power, with only one faction really dedicated to constitutional government.

Alvear, Yrigoyen's handpicked successor who became president in 1922, was fortunate. His term of office coincided with a period of extreme prosperity. He followed a middle-of-the-road policy, similar to Yrigoyen's, which made some concessions to labor but really was attuned to the middle classes. Yrigoyen had been popular with the people but was dictatorial in ruling the Radical Party. His attempts to extend his party discipline to policies of the Alvear government led to clashes between the two men, which resulted in a party split. The Alvear group allied themselves with the conservatives— now known as the National Democrat Party (PDN)—in opposition to a majority of the Radicals.

In 1928 Yrigoyen, aware of his personal popularity and desirous of regaining control over the government, announced his candidacy for a second presidential term. Although he declined to campaign, he was reelected by an overwhelming majority. But his return to the presidency at this time was unfortunate. Now seventy-eight years old and more feeble physically and mentally than many men his age, he was really incapable of directing governmental affairs. Moreover, while he began his second term in an era of prosperity, the Great Depression was just a year away.

Yrigoyen himself lived frugally and apparently was scrupulously honest, but his first administration had been quite corrupt. His second term was even worse. It soon became apparent that he was president in name only and the government was being run by subordinates whom he could not or would not control. Nevertheless, Argentina was so prosperous at this time that administrative deficiencies and political scandals were easily ignored. But then came October 1929.

National administration may be relatively easy when times are good economically; but when the economic picture turns sour, as it did in Argentina following the 1929 crash, it is a different story. Whether justifiably or not, the government in power is blamed. Unless it is able to perform miracles and quickly solve the most pressing economic problems, the people become restless and begin seeking a change. In many countries in the early 1930s there were sudden—frequently violent—shifts of administration. Argentina was no exception. After a few months of depression, it became obvious that the Yrigoyen government was drifting and apparently incapable of improving the economic situation. Opposition then appeared, not only from conservative politicians, who longed to resume the control they had held before 1916, but also from many of Yrigoyen's formerly devoted supporters. Moreover, there now was another element—the armed forces, who had become very concerned with political affairs.

By mid-1930 voices of opposition were being heard from various quarters. Repudiation of the Radicals in local elections was followed by labor and student demonstrations against the Yrigoyen regime, leading to bloody riots in the streets of Buenos Aires. By early September the situation had grown so serious that the president was persuaded to resign, whereupon the vice president, Enrique V. Martínez, assumed the presidency—but only for a few hours.

In the meantime, the army became involved in a plot to overthrow the government. This was a personal affair, led by Gen. José F. Uriburu, a distinguished officer and member of a family long prominent in Argentine politics. A conservative who had looked with disfavor on Yrigoyen's policies, Uriburu now saw an opportunity to restore conservative government and gain power himself. Apparently for several months prior to September he had been quietly engaged in promoting anti-Yrigoyen street demonstrations and spreading exaggerated rumors about the president's alleged senility. A coup was planned for September 6 and proceeded on schedule, although Yrigoyen had already resigned the previous day. The coup was carried out by General Uriburu, supported by a relatively small army contingent, including many cadets. These forces met only nominal opposition from a few loyalist troops in their march through Buenos Aires and soon succeeded in capturing the Casa Rosada. Within a few hours Martínez agreed to resign, and Uriburu and his staff took complete control of the presidential palace.

By 1930 a vibrant spirit of nationalism had developed in Argentina. Also many people had been led to believe that democracy had failed, largely because of corruption, and that it was now the duty of the armed forces to save the country from the politicians. Ironically, it was Yrigoyen and his Radical followers who initially had involved the military in struggles for political power. Now Yrigoyen's Radical administration was the first Argentine government since 1860 to be ousted by an army coup. Among the participants in that day's action was a little-known captain named Juan D. Perón.

This September 1930 revolution is of special significance in Argentine political history. For seventy years the republic had enjoyed civilian, constitutional government and political stability. In spite of the corruption that had crept in and other faults that appeared from time to time, these administrations had provided the climate in which Argentina had grown from a rude, divided land into an economically and culturally advanced nation. While both conservative and Radical governments had catered primarily to the aristocracy and the middle classes, individual rights of all people, including freedom of speech and freedom of the press, were scrupulously respected. Within this environment, well before 1930 Buenos Aires had attained respectability as one of the Western Hemisphere's leading cultural centers, with outstanding accomplishments in music, art, architecture, and literature. It also had become a publishing capital of top rank; and its press freedom had encouraged the establishment of many newspapers, including *La Prensa* and *La Nación*, classed among the world's greatest. But the revolution of 1930 marks a turning point in these developments. With the restoration of constitutional government the following year, the country experienced another decade somewhat similar to the previous seven. Nevertheless, the spirit had changed. The specter of military intervention and military government had cast its shadow over the land.

It quickly became clear that the palace revolt of September 6 had not been merely for the purpose of ousting Yrigoyen. Uriburu had seen an opportunity to seize power and had taken advantage of it. He proclaimed himself provisional president. While claiming to establish a new constitutional government that would respect all individual rights, he dissolved Congress and made himself a dictator. Radical officeholders were replaced by conservatives. At the same time, he promised new elections at an appropriate date, a promise typical of many a Latin American strongman under similar circumstances.

Until early 1932 Yrigoyen was held prisoner on the island of Martín García in the Río de la Plata, one of Argentina's favorite detainment centers for unwanted politicians. He died in July 1933. By that time popular sentiment had shifted once more, and the estimated half million mourners who turned out for his funeral indicated that Yrigoyen again had a large following.

A few weeks after his coup, Uriburu revealed a plan to abolish political parties and set up a corporate state. This proposal met with widespread disapproval, not only among civilians but also within the military. One of those who most strongly objected was Gen. Augustín P. Justo, leader of a rival army faction and himself ambitious for power. Actually he was planning a revolt of his own. Subsequently, with an armed power struggle in the making and seeing that he had been outmaneuvered, Uriburu gracefully bowed to conservative pressures, scheduled presidential and vice presidential elections for November 1931, and declined to be a candidate. It was understood that sufficient fraud would be practiced to insure a conservative victory at the polls despite a resurgence of Radical popularity. Realizing this fact, the Radicals, reverting to their pre-1912 practice, boycotted the elections. Under these circumstances, Justo, backed by a coalition of conservatives (National Democrats), Antipersonalist (anti-Yrigoyen) Radicals (Justo's party), and Independent Socialists, faced with only token opposition (Lisandro de la Torre, leader of the Progressive Democrats, a minor party), and aided by various forms of fraud, was declared the winner by a comfortable majority. Thereupon Argentina returned for a time to constitutional government. Once more the aristocracy was in control, but it was a government in which the military played an influential role.

Justo provided a firm and effective administration without dictatorship. To be sure, it was rule by the few, with corruption at all levels; but although they were not free to elect Radicals to public office, Argentines again enjoyed their long-cherished civil liberties. Recognizing that the government could not be run exclusively for the benefit of one class, the president promoted some far-reaching labor legislation, most of which was passed. These measures included vacations with pay, protection from arbitrary dismissal, and compensation for job-related injuries; but they applied primarily to workers in industry and trade, not to agricultural laborers on the *estancias*. Even though they did improve working conditions, they were rather modest as compared with advanced social and labor legislation in Chile, Uruguay, and a few other countries in the 1930s.

On the other hand, by sound fiscal reforms, including reduction of government expenditures, Justo strengthened the nation's financial position. With realistic economic policies, he made rapid progress in bringing the country out of the very serious depression, and by 1936 prosperity had been restored. Unlike other Latin American republics, during the depression years Argentina regularly met its foreign debt-service payments. While usually favoring British investors, Justo ignored opposition from the British-owned railroad companies and launched the building of an extensive system of competing highways. Argentines at all levels profited by these improvements. One of Justo's unsuccessful efforts was to get the military out of politics.

The Justo government not only restored political authority to the old oligarchy and their allies but also continued and improved close economic relations with Europe, especially Great Britain, on which the fortunes of the cattle and grain producers were based. Nevertheless, during the 1930s significant economic changes were occurring. An economy founded on beef and grain was beginning to be eclipsed by urban industry. The number of European immigrants declined, while the migration of farm workers to the cities was rising. And in both business and politics the landholding oligarchy was being seriously challenged by the increasingly influential industrialists.

Election day in November 1937 appeared to many Argentines like the Resurrection—so many dead people came out to vote. Justo's choice for president was Roberto M. Ortiz, a well-known corporation lawyer and Antipersonalist Radical, who the aristocrats believed was conservative enough to be acceptable. They insisted, however, that the vice presidency go to a National Democrat; and the nominee was Ramón S. Castillo, distinguished University of Buenos Aires law dean of very conservative views. Various methods were used to discourage opposition voters, including the seizure of thousands of enrollment booklets, which were required identity at polling places. With conservatives controlling the tally, the outcome was certain.

To the surprise of many, shortly after his inauguration on February 20, 1938, President Ortiz began to look like another Roque Sáenz Peña. He worked diligently to assure free and honest elections, often intervening in the provinces to set aside those believed to be dishonest. It was a time of political freedom such as Argentines had rarely experienced. Under these circumstances, the Radicals once more began to win. By 1940 they gained control of the national Chamber of Deputies; and it was obvious that, if honest elections continued, within another few years they would have a majority in the Senate. But this situation did not endure. Ortiz became very ill and, in July 1940, turned over the presidency to Castillo, who served as acting president until June 1942, when Ortiz resigned. Ortiz died the following month. Unfortunately, the political liberties Argentines had enjoyed from 1938 to 1940 quickly disappeared after Castillo became chief executive. He began intervening in the provinces as Ortiz had done—but for the purpose of ousting Radicals rather than guaranteeing free elections. Ortiz cabinet and other appointees were replaced by ultraconservative friends of Castillo. Ortiz's illness had turned the tables, and the conservatives were in the saddle again.

By this time Argentine domestic politics had become affected by events in Europe. During World War I Argentina had maintained strict neutrality. The outbreak of World War II set off political struggles between Argentine factions that were both ideologically and economically oriented. Britain had long been Argentina's best commercial market and one of its chief sources of development capital. There were also economic ties with France, and many Argentines looked to Paris as the cultural center of the world. With so many inhabitants of Italian extraction, there was naturally much interest in Italy, although little enthusiasm for Mussolini's government.

There was also considerable German influence in Argentina. Beginning in the mid-nineteenth century, many German immigrants had arrived. Most of them, who had left their homeland to escape Europe's troubles and seek a better life in the New World, settled in colonies in the hinterlands. There was, however, a second, and politically more significant, wave of German immigration, which began about 1890. This penetration had been planned by the German government in order to establish in key centers around the world representatives who might be valuable to Germany in future developments. A number of these immigrants had settled in Buenos Aires and other strategic urban areas, where some achieved political, economic, and social prominence and a few even married into leading Argentine families. Before and during World War II, Hitler tried to make use of such individuals to further Nazi interests in South America. These efforts were ignored by most provincial German-Argentines; but among the more recent Buenos Aires arrivals and their descendants, there were activists promoting the Nazi cause. Then there was the Argentine army, which included many officers with pro-German sentiments, based partly on their admiration for German military techniques.

While maintaining a show of neutrality, President Ortiz had been definitely opposed to the Axis powers; but his replacement by Castillo immediately reversed the picture. Neutrality was still the official policy; but in this administration, characterized by censorship and repression, pro-Axis agents and propaganda found a friend.

Argentina was now undergoing far-reaching changes. The political parties were experiencing serious disintegration. The middle class had grown to comprise at least 40 percent of the population, but it was badly divided— actually it was a group of several classes with widely diverse interests. Rapid industrialization, stimulated by a sharp drop in foreign imports due to the war, created new capitalists and an expanded labor force. Soaring prices of food and other essentials brought loud complaints from wage earners, who saw the cost of living outrunning income. The preceding decade had witnessed a greatly magnified spirit of nationalism, but that discouraged needed foreign investments and soon proved to be more of a restrictive than a constructive phenomenon. Now there was a growing concern with world affairs and the nation's ability to protect itself from possible foreign aggression. Although Argentina was not directly involved, World War II inspired fear and confusion in the country. Castillo appeared out of tune with the times and the factors promoting domestic changes, and he showed no more skill in dealing with them than to impose a state of siege in December 1941, which he maintained throughout the remainder of his administration in a futile attempt to stifle the rising opposition to his foreign and domestic policies.

In the meantime, there were growing ideological divisions within the armed forces. A wide gulf existed between those officers who believed they should stick strictly to military duties and those who believed they also had a political mission. Within the latter group there was considerable diversity as to what their political mission should be, and these differences became intertwined with varying points of view regarding the war in Europe. As the political fabric deteriorated and Castillo's extreme conservatism and dictatorial methods made him increasingly unpopular, revolutionary plotting among members of the armed forces significantly intensified.

Argentina's deteriorating political situation together with the growing interest of military officers in political affairs made another coup almost inevitable. The events that immediately set it off revolved around the approaching 1943 elections. Castillo's choice for president was an ultraconservative politician named Robustiano Patrón Costas, a pro-British member of the landholding aristocracy who was very unpopular among a large majority of people, including the military. While himself pro-Axis, Castillo apparently had come to believe the Allies eventually would win; and although unwilling to change his own position, he could save face by naming as his successor a pro-Allies candidate. It was obvious that no matter how strong the opposition, in an election controlled by the Castillo government, his chosen candidate would win. Many pro-Axis members of the armed forces were disturbed by the prospect of an anti-Axis president; and by now there were several military officers, ambitious for political power, seeking an excuse to seize control. One of these was Gen. Pedro P. Ramírez, minister of war in Castillo's cabinet, who had been forced upon Castillo by the military. Rumors that the UCR was about to choose him as its presidential nominee set off a cabinet crisis, which precipitated the June 4 coup. The Radicals, who had tried the revolutionary road to power on previous occasions and entered into military conspiracies as recently as 1932 and 1935, saw the armed forces as their only hope in 1943 in face of what promised to be rigged elections. Ramírez, himself ambitious for power, was not averse to using the Radicals as a means of achieving his goal.

Castillo, disturbed by what appeared to be disloyalty on the part of his war minister and unable to force his resignation, ordered his arrest. Ramírez reacted swiftly, and within a few hours troops were moving into Buenos Aires. But in the race to the Casa Rosada, Ramírez was beaten by another general, Arturo Rawson, commander of the Campo de Mayo cavalry and leading army moderate, who captured the palace and declared himself provisional president. Castillo and members of his cabinet escaped from Buenos Aires on board a naval vessel. A struggle for power was on. Within two days Rawson was pushed out and Ramírez took over. Congress was dissolved, martial law declared, and the forthcoming elections suspended. Argentina's traditional democracy, which long had seemed firmly established, was dead—destroyed really by politicians who abused it and were too divided to preserve it.

Rawson, who appeared to favor an early return to democracy, was overthrown by Axis sympathizers in the army, who feared his pro-Allies leanings, together with extreme nationalists, whose objective was a dictatorship. Although the Supreme Court had recognized the new government, following a promise to uphold the constitution, and Ramírez now held the title of "president," he was only part of a junta and not in complete control. The real direction of the coup and its aftermath came from a secret organization of generals and colonels known as the GOU. The initials stood for the name of the organization—Group of United Officers (Grupo de Oficiales Unidos) as well as their motto—"Government, order, union" (*Gobierno, orden, unión*). Within this group were several top- and middle-rank officers clawing their way toward the same goal—the presidency. One of them was Col. Juan Domingo Perón.

It quickly became obvious that Ramírez was the chief of a military dictatorship. In key positions at all levels—from the cabinet to provincial and municipal governments—civilians were replaced by military officers. With Congress abolished, decrees supplanted legislative enactments. But the administration did take steps to solve some of the more pressing economic problems. Inflation was attacked by a policy of fiscal economy. Rents and other basic living costs were rolled back by decree, while minimum wages were imposed for agricultural workers and middle- and lower-echelon government employees. In regard to World War II, Ramírez continued for a while a policy of neutrality despite evidence of eventual Allied victory and increasing pressure for a break with the Axis.

Within a few months after seizing power, Ramírez and his government had become notorious for violations of long-established civil liberties. Hundreds of people who criticized the administration or were even suspected of being anti-Ramírez were arrested, and many of them ended up in concentration camps, where conditions allegedly were horrible. With freedom of speech and freedom of the press destroyed and spies lurking in private homes as well as public places, many Argentines came to term the Ramírez regime a reign of terror and wish for the "good old days" of the once-hated Castillo. But Ramírez remained popular among many of the working classes who appreciated the reduction in living costs. Another strong element of support was the Roman Catholic Church, which the government courted by a pro-church policy that included restoration of obligatory Catholic religious instruction in the public schools, abolished more than half a century earlier.

In January 1944 Ramírez, succumbing to British and United States pressure, broke diplomatic relations with Germany and Japan. Momentarily the GOU was caught off guard; but following widespread condemnation of the administration for yielding to outside influences, it took action. In late February some of its younger officers, known as the "colonels' clique," led a bloodless palace coup in which the president was replaced by his minister of war, Gen. Edelmiro Farrell. For many army leaders it was an expression of determination to retain control of the government as well as an effort to protect Axis interests in Argentina. Among the principal instigators of this move was Perón, now surfacing as head of the colonels' clique, which supplanted the GOU. Viewing Ramírez as a probable stumbling block in his projected rise to power, Perón took advantage of the tide of anti-Ramírez criticism to get him out of the way.

Farrell remained president more than two years, but it soon was evident that he was merely a front man—considered safe in this office since apparently he was not ambitious to rule. Under Ramírez, Perón had been head of the secretariat in the War Ministry, which enabled him to influence army promotions and thus increase his power in the GOU. He also was head of the Department of Labor and Social Welfare, a position he soon managed to raise to cabinet status. When Farrell became president, Perón acquired the posts of vice president and minister of war, in addition to minister of labor, which he already held, and emerged as the most powerful figure and leading spokesman of the regime. He played upon the strings of nationalism with loud criticism of the United States and its alleged attempts to pressure Argentina into declaring war on the Axis powers, and thus rallied support from the many Argentines who objected to what they considered U.S. interference in their national affairs. His kind words for the laboring classes created a power base on which he rode to the presidency.

A man of impressive physique, keen mind, abundant craftiness, and amazing personal magnetism, Perón, now in his late forties, was emerging as the real ruler of Argentina. From a rural, middle-class family and lacking the advantageous background of a landed aristocrat, he had risen slowly through the army ranks. But his career had included a tour as military attaché in Italy (1939–40), where he became acquainted with Mussolini's army. Prior to this stint he had served as military attaché in Chile, but his stay there had been abruptly terminated by charges that he had attempted to buy Chilean defense secrets. He had long been an admirer of German military discipline; and while in Europe he had visited Germany and also Spain. Europe's dictators, especially Mussolini and Franco, made lasting impressions on him. He became convinced the Axis powers would win the war and that Argentina could profit by a close association with them. About this time he began to have illusions of grandeur and imagine himself a man of destiny, born to lead his country to greatness. Boasting that he was going to imitate Mussolini but avoid his mistakes, he returned to Argentina in early 1941 determined to gain control, transform the country into a totalitarian state, and establish it in its rightful place as the dominant power in Latin America. What he envisioned was a self-sufficient nation in which democracy and individual freedoms would be replaced by prosperity based on a new social and economic order—a projection of what he later tried to explain as *justicialismo* (justicialism), a "third position" between capitalism and communism.

PERÓN ERA

Perón's rise to power and his subsequent dictatorship were founded on three principal pillars—labor, the army, and the church. Of the three, labor was the most influential. Perón was one of several recent political leaders around the world who recognized and capitalized on the increasing ability of the masses to make their demands heard. The lure of urban industry together with low wages and unfavorable working conditions in rural areas had resulted in an impressive migration of Argentine laborers to the cities, especially Buenos Aires; but there most of them encountered only low wages, unfavorable working conditions, and slums, while all about them were examples of the wealth and privileges of the middle and upper classes. Regardless of where they came from, there, herded together in crowded, unattractive surroundings, were members of a newly powerful element, desirous of a better life and looking for someone to lead them to it. These people were ripe for deception. Perón recognized the potential of such support—and he was a proficient opportunist. He stood out from his military colleagues by pretending a genuine interest in the welfare of the laboring classes; and he used his position as minister of labor to court them and gather them into unions under his control through a broad-range labor organization, the General Confederation of Labor (Confederación General de Trabajo), familiarly known as the CGT. By decreeing higher wages, shorter working hours, and paid vacations and providing numerous other benefits, including more schools, hospitals, public housing, and recreational facilities, Perón skillfully appealed to laborers and molded them into an extremely effective political organization for his own benefit. At the height of his power, CGT membership was estimated at from 4 million to 6 million.

In capturing labor, as well as in other respects, Perón was greatly aided by his attractive mistress, Eva Duarte, whom he married in late 1945. His first wife, Aurelia Tizón, had died in 1938. In addition to their control through the CGT, the Peróns made good use of their personal magnetism and their skill as masters of mob psychology. The ability of both to gather thousands of their followers into the Plaza de Mayo and harangue them to action was well recognized. Evita (Little Eva), as she was commonly called, was especially adept at handling the *descamisados*, as Perón often termed his labor adherents. (Literally "shirtless ones," they were not really shirtless but were poorly dressed. The Peróns apparently adopted this term from a derogatory newspaper caption that appeared with a picture of some labor demonstrators.) When, in October 1945, he was arrested by order of military colleagues who disliked his proposed social reforms, and shipped off to Martín García, Evita played a leading part in gathering the *descamisados* for an impressive rally in the Plaza de Mayo that resulted in his triumphal return and assured his rise to the presidency.

Perón realized that he must have military backing to attain and remain in power. His sojourn in Spain had impressed upon him the importance of cooperation between the military and labor and the disaster that could result from a clash of these two. His retention of military support for a decade was due not only to his army background and skillful maneuvers among members of the armed forces but especially to his great following among the masses.

In a country in which the Roman Catholic Church claims to embrace more than 90 percent of the people, its support can be quite significant. Perón gained power with the blessing of the church, and for some eight years after his election to the presidency in 1946 he got along well with the clergy. Church and state used each other to mutual advantage, as they had done on some previous occasions, and until late in his regime the church received numerous favors in return for its support of Perón's government.

As a means of boosting national prestige as well as increasing his own influence in the army, Perón, as minister of war, began a drive to build up the armed forces. With this goal Farrell agreed. The resulting program, which quickly tripled the size of the army and included development of heavy industry to supply the nation's military needs, was very expensive. By 1945 over half the greatly expanded national budget was allocated to the military, and total government expenditures were twice as large as income.

In March 1945 Perón, having reversed his position, prevailed upon Farrell to declare war on Germany and Japan. This was done in part to permit Argentina to secure a seat at the forthcoming San Francisco conference. It was also for the purpose of obtaining U.S.-made consumer goods and war materials, which thus far during World War II had been denied Argentina, and thereby offsetting the advantages its rival, Brazil, had enjoyed as a U.S. ally.

By the middle of 1945, partly as a result of the end of the European war and the fall of dictatorships in Germany and Italy, there was a loudly voiced reaction against Perón. Leading merchants and industrialists as well as cattle and grain producers were alarmed by his economic policies, especially the unbalanced budgets and rapidly mounting public debt. By this time not only the military buildup but the loss of democracy, muzzling of the press, and curtailment of other freedoms were of serious concern and led to numerous demonstrations against Perón in many parts of the country. There was also growing fear that in time he would maneuver the people into electing him president. By a skillful propaganda campaign he tried to counteract such opposition. One of his most successful weapons was an army of several thousand laborers who were paid to go about Buenos Aires and other cities agitating for Perón. They often participated in violent demonstrations. As *gritones* (criers), at opportune times in public gatherings they would shout for Perón and come out with such cries as "Perón for president!" They played a significant role in bringing him back from Martín García.

It was the vocal, widespread opposition that inspired the military attempt to oust Perón in October 1945. But the leaders bungled the job; and after his temporary exile and triumphal return to the Plaza de Mayo eight days later, he felt strong enough to face the electorate. He appeased his opponents by relinquishing all his government positions, including his army commission. Thereupon he announced his candidacy for president on a platform of far-reaching social and economic reforms. (Perón had been stripped of his offices after his arrest. Renouncing them after his return was a popular formality. Once in the presidency, he resumed his army commission and promoted himself to general.)

Elections were scheduled for April 1946 but were suddenly moved up to February, which gave the opposition less time to campaign. Most political parties united under what was known as the Democratic Union to oppose Perón and the newly formed organization of his followers he called the Labor Party. After he became president, this group was developed into the tightly organized Peronist Party. With José Tamborini, a good, honest, but colorless former senator and cabinet member, as an opponent, and a campaign characterized by violence, in which his rowdies harassed the opposition in almost every conceivable way, the charismatic Perón had many advantages. Presenting himself as a defender of Argentine independence against Yankee intervention, he also capitalized on a brazen attempt by the U.S. State Department to defeat him. This effort included issuance of the well-known Blue Book, *Consultation Among the American Republics with Respect to the Argentine Situation*, which purported to prove that Perón had collaborated with Nazi Germany. Under these circumstances, even if the elections were fair, as claimed, Perón's announced victory with almost 56 percent of the votes should have been no surprise. His party also won an impressive control of Congress, with two-thirds of the Chamber of Deputies and all but two members of the Senate. When this Congress convened the two non-Peronist senators were denied their seats.

On June 4, 1946, exactly three years after the coup that overturned civilian government, Perón was inaugurated president. He then set out to strengthen his grip on the nation. With a subservient Congress, he used congressional impeachment procedures to gain dominance over the judiciary. Mindful that the six national universities were normally political hotbeds, he brought them under control by replacing with his trusted followers all rectors, deans, and professors whose loyalty was questionable. Censorship of the press and radio became more rigid; and among the numerous newspapers, only the two most powerful dailies, *La Prensa* and *La Nación*, retained for a time any significant independence.

On July 9, five weeks after his inauguration, President Perón observed Argentine Independence Day by staging what he termed the greatest military parade ever held in South America. It was three hours in length, very colorful, and presented the military as quite impressive by comparison with those of other South American republics. This parade was another attempt by Perón to convey to neighboring countries, as well as to the Argentine people, a hint of his power.

But on the Avenida de Mayo, within sight of the Casa Rosada, *La Prensa* was celebrating Argentine independence in quite a different way. After Perón's parade was over and darkness had brought an early end to this gray, winter afternoon, the paper's building was ablaze with lights from top to bottom; and the torch held by its famous statue, representing freedom of the press, shone brightly from the roof. This light was a symbol not only of *La Prensa*, long recognized as one of the world's greatest newspapers, but also of the free press throughout Argentina. *La Prensa* was actually more than a newspaper—it was an institution that, since its founding in 1869, had stood for freedom and democracy in Argentina and had built an enviable record of victories in the causes it espoused. As I viewed this spectacle on that Independence Day evening, mindful of the newspapers that already had fallen before Perón and the attempts that had been made to crush *La Prensa*, I asked myself, "Will this light be shining this time next year—and the following year?" So strong was *La Prensa* that it was nearly five years before

Perón was able to seize it and extinguish its torch. He ordered the statue destroyed. When *La Prensa* was returned to its rightful owners after his downfall, its publisher, Alberto Gainza Paz, searched for his statue and found it. It had not been destroyed—only broken into pieces and thrown in a warehouse. It was restored to its former position atop *La Prensa*'s building; and on July 9, 1956, exactly ten years after the aforementioned Independence Day celebration, the torch was relighted.

Perón came to power at a time of great economic prosperity, a result of postwar demands for Argentine meat and grain and also of the large foreign exchange balances accumulated in Europe during the war. But he spent nearly half of the nation's cash reserves—estimated at approximately $1.25 billion—in carrying out one of his principal objectives: acquisition of the foreign-owned railways, about three-fourths of the entire rail system. Carefully avoiding giving any offense to Argentina's major trading partners, especially the British, the government did not confiscate these properties but purchased them at high prices and for cash. The rail lines were in a bad state of disrepair, and most were nearly bankrupt. Indeed, their owners were glad to get rid of them. Under government management they continued to decline and were heavily overstaffed. With the rising costs of operation and political pressures on the government to keep rates low, railroad operation became one of its most serious financial burdens. But initially acquisition of the railways and other public utilities was very popular.

After the railway deal, Perón purchased most of the remaining foreign-owned utilities. By 1949 the government had spent over 60 percent of its exchange reserves on such projects. Argentines could boast that they had rid themselves of the foreign capitalists who had controlled the country and were now completely independent. Nationalism had won! During this acquisition process Perón played it up to gain votes for his candidates in the March 1948 congressional elections.

In tampering with the economy Perón made some of his greatest blunders. Before his appearance, Argentina had enjoyed economic growth and prosperity based on its position as one of the world's greatest cattle- and grain-producing countries, and in recent decades it had also experienced rapid development of light industries. In 1946, however, Perón introduced a "five-year plan" that aimed at creating "economic independence" by quickly transforming Argentina into an advanced industrial state, including heavy industry. This change would be accomplished without foreign capital. To pay for it, cattle and grain producers were forced to sell their products to the government's Instituto Argentino de Promoción del Intercambio at ruinously low prices, while the institute in turn sold these in the world market for as much as the traffic would bear.

The inevitable happened. With profit gone, farmers and ranchers sharply curtailed their output. On top of this drop came two years of drought. As a result, by 1952 Argentina reached the point where it no longer was able to supply both its foreign and domestic customers. But exports were necessary. Thereupon, the health minister warned the country of dangers in eating meat; and a leading Perón mouthpiece proclaimed that beef would provoke serious digestive disorders. Meatless days were decreed—in one of the world's highest per capita meat-consuming lands. Initially it was one meatless day per week, but soon one day was increased to two. Subsequently there were meatless weeks. In Argentina "meatless" really means "beefless." Other meats, fish, and poultry normally have been available. White bread was replaced by substitutes as wheat became scarce. Both wheat and corn production dropped from nearly 6 million metric tons each in 1946 to 2 million each in 1951.

Not only was Perón's method of financing fallacious, but his program to create heavy industries was undertaken without due consideration of Argentina's deficiencies in many of the raw materials essential for such development. Moreover, a large part of the money that was supposed to go for industrialization apparently ended up in grafters' pockets. Much of it also was invested in unprofitable enterprises or in wild schemes such as the highly publicized atomic energy project, which even Peronist members of Congress finally termed a fiasco.

In his relations with labor, Perón also eventually found himself in trouble. Continued deficit financing and printing-press money set off rampant inflation, and frequently decreed wage raises hardly kept pace with the rapidly rising cost of living. The Argentine currency, which for a number of years before 1946 had been quite stable with a free exchange rate of approximately 4 pesos per U.S. dollar, began to decline under the Perón government until by 1955 it was down to 30 per dollar. Living costs in Buenos Aires more than quintupled during the same period. In his attempts to keep prices down and, at the same time, grant labor's numerous demands, Perón almost squeezed industry out of existence. When he finally reached the point of having to refuse substantial wage boosts, the result was serious labor unrest with riots and other disorders. The labor problem had been further complicated by increased migration of workers from the rural areas into the cities in search of industrial jobs. This influx created unemployment in Buenos Aires and other centers while leaving a shortage of farm labor.

Finally the Perón government was forced to reverse itself on several matters of economic policy. For the purpose of alleviating the grain and meat shortages, it began lending a hand to agriculture. In an effort to relieve a dangerous situation in the capital, it started a back-to-the-farm movement. During his last two years in office, Perón also toned down his nationalistic insistence on "economic independence" and invited foreign capital back into Argentina. But all these efforts were too little and too late.

In 1949 Perón had a new constitution formulated and adopted to replace the one under which Argentina had lived since 1853. Although the 1949 document contained a number of changes, the real reason for it was to eliminate the provision in the old constitution denying the president a second, successive term in office. With this handicap out of the way, Perón declared his candidacy for reelection in November 1951. But by this time the evils and errors of his regime were becoming obvious. Military objections stifled his attempt to name Evita as his running mate; and in late September some army officers led an unsuccessful revolt to unseat him before elections. Perón was saved by loyalist troops and an effective labor demonstration in front of the Casa Rosada. With sufficient propaganda and intimidation during the campaign and the election machinery strictly controlled, he had no difficulty winning a second term.

From this point Perón's downhill slide gradually gained velocity. Labor unrest, economic crises, and the death of Evita in 1952 all contributed toward weakening his hold on the country. Evita's demise was considered a special blow by the poor. Many had looked upon her as their fairy godmother, who, through her Social Aid Foundation, provided numerous benefits. But this organization, which received contributions from government, business, and labor estimated at more than $100 million annually, also provided fabulous welfare to Evita, who disbursed its funds without restrictions—to herself as well as others.

As he felt his popularity slipping, Perón drastically increased his civil police force and stepped up terroristic practices. By mid-1953 the number of police in Buenos Aires alone was estimated at 80,000—four times as many as in New York City. Under the "state of internal war" decreed after the 1951 revolt, they could arrest anyone and hold him indefinitely without bringing charges. But these police were not only to keep the people in line. Perón apparently relied on their support should the military turn against him. Freedom of the press and freedom of speech had long been dead; and during the last years of his dictatorship, a casual anti-Perón remark to a relative or friend sent many an Argentine to jail. Perón's spies did not even have to "hear" such comments. He had lip readers in public places to "see" what people were saying.

Late in 1954 came the almost inevitable clash between the church, ever seeking to extend its power and uphold its rights, and the dictator, who demanded complete submission to his personal rule. An increasing boldness on the part of the clergy brought retaliation by the totalitarian political ruler, which included suspension of Catholic religious instruction in public schools, a large reduction in government financial aid to Catholic schools, laws legalizing divorce and prostitution, and threats to disestablish the church. These steps led to a church-state split that culminated with expulsion from Argentina, in June 1955, of two Argentine-born prelates and the pope's excommunication of Perón in return. (The excommunication remained in effect until early 1963.) His break with the church, which apparently could have been avoided, hastened Perón's downfall and was one of the most serious blunders of an administration loaded with errors.

Clerical influence in the September 1955 revolution was somewhat over-played, with the clergy claiming more credit than they actually deserved. But certainly the loss of church support contributed significantly to the decline of Perón's power. The church provided a rallying ground for some of the divided opposition and apparently encouraged disaffection among members of the armed forces. Even more decisive, though, were the general economic plight of the country, growing dissatisfaction in the ranks of labor, and the failure of Perón's *descamisados* to rally sufficiently to his support when the crisis came.

Perón managed to weather a bloody, poorly organized revolt in June 1955, led by the navy and its air wing, that included air raids on the Casa Rosada. But three months later, in mid-September, another one, in which the navy and air force, normally cool toward him, teamed up with disgruntled members of the army, broke out simultaneously in several parts of the country. After four days of fighting, during which Perón remained hidden and the *descamisados*, who formerly had shouted, "Our lives for Perón," were conspicuously absent from the heavily attacked Plaza de Mayo, he took refuge on board a Paraguayan gunboat in Buenos Aires harbor on September 20. Subsequently Maj. Gen. Pedro E. Aramburu, termed him a coward and said if he had led an armed resistance, the revolt would have been crushed. Nearly two weeks later, following delays in getting a safe-conduct pass out of the country, Perón was flown to exile in Paraguay.

To millions of Argentines longing for their former freedoms, the overthrow of Perón came as a great relief. But as in 1930 and 1943, they were not sure what they were getting in place of the fallen dictator. Nevertheless, faced by mounting evidence of the corruption practiced by him and his cronies and the staggering economic blows inflicted on the nation, many appeared to believe any government would be an improvement.

PERONISM VERSUS MILITARISM

While Perón's departure in September 1955 officially brought an end to what is commonly referred to as "the Perón era," the dictator's influence remained. After a month in Paraguay, where he was an unwelcome guest, he moved farther away, with stays in Panama, Venezuela, and the Dominican Republic before settling down in exile in Spain. He would have liked to remain in Paraguay, as it was an ideal spot from which to try to regain his power. But he was already unpopular there, and President Alfredo Stroessner feared domestic political repercussions if he allowed him to stay very long. Argentina's new government also exerted pressure to get him out. At Argentine request, most of the time Perón was there he was kept outside Asunción and away from the border. In Panama he met a future president of Argentina—an Argentine-born cabaret dancer named Isabel Martínez, who became his third wife.

Although host governments tried to prevent Perón from engaging in political activities, from Spain as well as stops on the way he conducted an
effective propaganda campaign aimed at an eventual return to power in
Argentina. Alleged subversive actions directed by Perón from Caracas led to
a diplomatic break between Argentina's government and that of Venezuelan
dictator Marcos Pérez Jiménez. Perón's move to the Dominican Republic,
after the ouster of Pérez Jiménez in early 1958, brought interruption of diplomatic relations between Argentina and that country. Perón's Argentine enemies were disturbed by his political meddling from abroad and especially
by the knowledge that he had gotten away with so much money that he had
no difficulty financing such interference.

Argentina was left saddled with several serious problems. One was an
extreme degree of nationalism. Nationalism was already rampant before Perón appeared on the scene, but he played upon this theme and helped build
it up to a much higher intensity. He also left a legacy of militarism. He had
climbed to power through the 1943 coup, of which he was a principal pro-
moter; he had remained in the presidency with military support and had
departed only because the armed forces turned against him. Having thrown
him out, they inherited the responsibility of governing the country. Perón
also left a formidable economic imbalance. He had seriously upset Argentina's agricultural economy and actually contributed little toward industrialization, which was already developing rapidly before he gained control. One
of his most damaging legacies was the soaring inflation. It was inflation that
proved decisive in toppling him in 1955, and it became much more serious
later.

Another problem growing out of the Perón era was the dominant, and
often irresponsible, role of the laboring classes. It is true that they had been
victims of discrimination before Perón and he gave them dignity, which they
had not hitherto enjoyed. But during his regime they were pampered out of
all proportion to their just needs—not because he was really interested in
their welfare but because he wanted their support. Wage increases did not
have to be earned but were decreed nationwide by the government, and
labor laws made it almost impossible to dismiss lazy or incompetent employees. A result was constant demands for higher wages and other benefits
while efficiency declined. Since 1955 organized labor has been very uncooperative and many difficulties have resulted from labor agitation and influence.

Argentina had long been a land divided between port and interior provinces. But division proliferated, and it evolved into a land also seriously
divided between classes of society. By his overtures to labor and discrimination against the middle and upper classes, Perón dramatically accentuated
this division but did not effect any meaningful realignment. Actually he created a class war. When he departed in 1955, he left the country not only

economically devastated but considerably more divided than before his regime.

Probably the most disturbing legacy left by Perón was *peronismo*. From his places of refuge, he succeeded in keeping Peronism very much alive; and his followers continued to look and work for the time he might return to power. For two decades Peronism contributed effectively to Argentina's political demoralization. During the balance of the 1950s, through the 1960s, and into the 1970s, there were various attempts to restore sound, orderly government, stop inflation, and put the country back on its feet economically. In the numerous failures Peronism played a significant part.

It was a political vacuum surrounded by these and other problems that the military inherited in September 1955. Inexperienced in governmental administration and beset by so many difficulties, military leaders seemed confused. A short-lived regime, headed by Maj. Gen. Eduardo Lonardi, chief of the revolutionary forces, assumed control immediately following Perón's departure. With foreign obligations of $1.2 billion, an internal debt of $4 billion, and the economy a shambles, Lonardi termed this "the most disastrous situation" in the nation's economic history. Claiming there were at least 150,000 unnecessary government employees, he called for "austerity, work and sacrifice" and promised no "pie in the sky."[1] But as he seemed too conciliatory toward the Peronists and hesitant in righting the wrongs Perón had imposed on the country, he was set aside by a palace coup in November, and Maj. Gen. Pedro E. Aramburu, army chief of staff, took over as provisional president and head of a ruling military junta.

The 1853 Constitution was reinstated; but there was no Congress and, with disturbances in many places, a state of siege continued until 1957. Civil liberties were restored—to all except Peronists. Newspapers regained their former freedom. *La Prensa* was returned to its rightful owners, as were most other confiscated properties. The universities, again free and autonomous, welcomed back professors who had been ousted by Perón. One of the really dramatic changes was in foreign relations. The anti-United States policy was immediately reversed and a new ambassador arrived in Washington with friendly overtures to the Yankees Perón had despised. Argentina now desperately needed U.S. assistance. Recognizing the necessity for development capital even more than Perón had reluctantly done in his last two years, the Aramburu government opened wide the doors to foreign investments. Most economic controls were lifted and other steps were taken to encourage development under a free economy.

But efforts to impose austerity and balance the budget encountered determined resistance. Inflation persisted, the laboring classes grumbled, and under instructions from their exiled leader, the Peronists continued to harass the nation. From exile Perón promised a bloody return to power. In June 1956 a violent uprising, financially backed by Perón and aimed at restoring Peronist control, was put down by the alert Aramburu government.

During his two and a half years as head of state, Aramburu tried very hard to get the military out of politics and restore civilian, constitutional government. In an effort to prevent another dictatorship, he attempted to reform the Constitution. He realistically recognized that the 1853 document, again in force, conferred so much power on the president that Perón did not have to depart very far from it to assume his dictatorial position. It was Aramburu's desire to curb presidential powers by a revised constitution. A constituent assembly was elected for this purpose, but it did not adopt the amendments he thought were needed. Nevertheless, he succeeded in restoring constitutional government to the extent of holding elections in February 1958, barring military officers as candidates and making sure that the duly chosen president, whom he did not really favor, was inaugurated on May 1.

Aramburu had done exceedingly well in leading the country back to a semblance of order and democracy; but merely holding elections and installing a civilian president had not really removed the military from politics. Although temporarily they faded into the background, there were still within the armed forces many officers who, having experienced power, wanted to retain it. Actually the military was now divided between those who wanted to rule the nation themselves and those who preferred a civilian government. But, fearful for both their careers and their lives, one thing on which most of the army, navy, and air force were united was that Perón should not return. Until the early 1970s, virtually all military officers were obsessed with making sure that he never regained control. For this reason, the Peronists were restricted and denied their political rights. The armed forces kept a watchful eye on every president—be he civilian or military—and unseated him if he appeared to be succumbing to Perón's influence.

The victorious presidential candidate in 1958 was Arturo Frondizi, nominee of the UCR left wing, known as the Intransigent Radicals (UCRI). He was opposed by Ricardo Balbín, candidate of the People's Radical Civic Union (UCRP). Balbín and Frondizi had run for president and vice president respectively on the UCR ticket in 1951. Before the 1958 elections, this party had split over choice of a presidential candidate and also the Peronist issue.

Mindful of Perón's lingering popularity, Frondizi had courted some of his principal backers, including such diverse groups as the Peronists, extreme nationalists, and the church. Reportedly, under instructions from Perón, about 1.5 million of his followers voted for Frondizi, while many others cast blank ballots. This Peronist support was a significant contribution to his victory, but it also proved to be a primary factor in the difficulties he encountered after his inauguration. On the one hand, the armed forces were suspicious of him because of his Peronist association. On the other hand, the Peronists were impatient for a return of their political rights, which Frondizi had promised before his election but which the military consistently opposed.

With inflation already very high and growing worse, Frondizi made conscientious attempts to solve the nation's economic difficulties. He recognized the need for reduced government spending to cut budget deficits; but with a third of the population government employees and their dependents and with other workers spoiled by frequent wage increases, austerity was extremely unpopular, especially among the liberals who had elected him. Many Argentines also objected to Frondizi's visits to the United States in 1959 and 1961 in search of financial and technical assistance. Even more controversial was a stabilization agreement with the International Monetary Fund, which his government entered into at the urging of the United States and with a promise of financial aid. To his credit, however, foreign capital again flowed into Argentina in large quantities; and heavy industries, including a steel mill and manufacturing plants turning out automobiles, railway cars and engines, aluminum products, petrochemicals, and numerous other items, augmented the economy.

One of the serious financial drains on the country was the importation of oil, which cost about $300 million annually. YPF, the government oil monopoly, had been unsuccessful in developing much of the nation's large petroleum resources, and the extreme nationalists had consistently opposed bringing in foreign oil companies to do the job. Perón belatedly had admitted this need, and shortly before his overthrow he had been in the process of making a deal with the Standard Oil Company of California. Opposition to this negotiation had hastened his fall and the arrangements were incomplete at the time of his departure. Although during his campaign he had courted nationalist support, early in his administration Frondizi entered into agreements with several oil companies in the United States and Europe for development of Argentine resources in connection with YPF. This arrangement paid off handsomely. In about three years Argentina became self-sufficient in oil and even began to export a little. But the extreme nationalists voiced loud objections; and this issue turned into a political football that has been kicked around various times since.

Approximately $300 million more per year was being drained out of the national treasury by deficits in railway operations. Frondizi managed to return some costly nationalized industries to private ownership, but the government remained saddled with the railroads as well as other likewise unprofitable public utilities. Frondizi was able to entice more than 25,000 employees of the heavily overstaffed railway system to retire, thus relieving some of the unnecessary overhead. For a time he also stabilized the currency at 83 pesos per U.S. dollar; but after his ejection from office, it resumed its rapid slide and by July 1962 was down to approximately 135 per dollar.

The military problem was especially difficult for Frondizi. Before he was unseated in 1962, he survived some thirty-five major crises caused by military attempts to interfere in or take over his administration. They stemmed from different factions in the armed forces trying to gain advantages in the government, as well as from efforts to prevent the Peronists from strengthening their position. Although he was committed to restoring Peronists' political rights, for nearly four years Frondizi avoided such a showdown. He was removed from office in late March 1962 because he permitted free elections in which the Peronists participated and, with Communist and other allies, won 10 of the 14 governorship contests, including the important province of Buenos Aires, 47 seats in the 192-member Chamber of Deputies, and many representatives in provincial legislatures. (Only 86 of the deputies were up for election at this time and there were no senatorial contests.)

Opposition to Frondizi's austerity program was a primary reason for the Peronist victories. If these results were allowed to stand, it was feared that at the next elections the Peronists would gain control of the country. This possibility the military refused to accept. The result was a palace coup a few days later in which Frondizi was arrested. Rejecting demands that he resign, he was imprisoned on the island of Martín García. He was kept there until March 1963 and then taken to Bariloche, where he was held another five months, insisting he was still president. He was freed after the July 1963 elections. With the office of president declared vacant since Frondizi had violated the law by leaving the capital without permission of Congress, the president of the Senate, José M. Guido, next in line of succession, as the vice presidency was vacant, was sworn in as chief executive in March 1962.

Guido, controlled by the army, annulled the elections and established federal control in all twenty-two provinces. At military insistence, Frondizi had annulled them in five provinces. Not satisfied with this act, the military forced Guido to make a clean sweep. New elections were announced for October 1963, at which time a president would be chosen to take office May 1, 1964, the date on which Frondizi's term would legally expire. A few months later, amid another crisis, elections were advanced to July 1963, with Peronist and Communist parties outlawed.

During the year and a half of Guido's presidency, crises continued. The instability of this period was due principally to a struggle between military factions regarding the best way to control the Peronists. In September 1962 a new political leader emerged from the army and quickly rose to prominence as chief of a rebellion against the army high command. He was Lt. Gen. Juan Carlos Onganía, commander of the Campo de Mayo garrison, who said he became involved in politics because of Argentina's slow drift toward dictatorial government. Asserting that Guido must face up to the issue of "democracy or dictatorship," Onganía called for early elections and a quick return to real civilian control. While both major military factions were anti-Peronist, the Onganía group advocated a softer line, declaring that one-fourth of the nation's population could not be outlawed by executive decree and that Peronists should be given some kind of electoral outlet. After battles between rival military forces in densely populated sections of Buenos Aires, Rosario, and La Plata, the Onganía "legalists" won. In the meantime, Guido had switched sides and emerged with the winners. Claiming victory for the insurgent forces, he appointed Onganía interim commander in chief of the army.

Nevertheless, the victory of the pro-democratic military faction did not cure Argentina's real troubles, which ran far deeper. Although both seriously tried, neither Frondizi nor Guido made much progress in solving the nation's economic problems, especially inflation. With an annual budget deficit of $400 million, a foreign trade deficit of $500 million, and a bankrupt government pension fund that had been depleted to meet other expenses, Guido inherited a very unenviable position. As the cost of living soared and austerity measures brought unemployment and other hardships, many Argentines, refusing to admit that this predicament was largely a result of Perón's mismanagement, looked to him as the great father who could solve their problems—if only he could get back. Although the Communists tried to take advantage of the growing dissatisfaction, they could make little headway as long as the Peronists were active and Perón's image still cast its spell over the country. But after being subdued for some seven years, the Peronists were seriously divided over how to proceed in their efforts to regain control.

In the elections of July 7, 1963, a country physician from the province of Córdoba, Arturo Illia, candidate of the UCRP, won the presidency with only about one-fourth of the popular vote. In the congressional races this party won 24 of the 46 Senate seats and elected 71 of the 192 members of the Chamber of Deputies. Illia's election was a victory for the moderates and a defeat for Perón. As the Peronists were prevented from presenting candidates, Perón had ordered them to cast blank ballots, but only about half did so. With Illia's inauguration on October 12, the nation again settled down for a while with an elected, civilian government.

These elections revealed quite dramatically the multiplicity of parties that had appeared. Out of about 200 political parties of various sorts around the country, some 60 actually participated in the balloting. And of the approximately 10 million voters, an estimated 20 to 30 percent were Peronists.

A key issue at this time was the contracts with foreign oil companies. Just before Illia's inauguration, a national board investigating these contracts termed them illegal since they were signed without congressional approval. A month later Illia, prodded by the nationalistic vice president, Carlos Perette, followed up this decision with decrees annulling the contracts. Gradually over the next year the rights and properties that had been leased to foreign oil companies were turned over to the YPF; and compensation settlements were arranged with several of them. The subsequent Onganía government renegotiated oil contracts with foreign companies. Without sufficient funds, equipment, and technical capabilities, YPF again proved incapable of supplying the nation's petroleum requirements and Argentina soon reverted to large and costly imports. Thus did nationalism prevail over economic realism.

In 1964 the annual budget deficit reached $1 billion, the cost of living continued to rise more than 25 percent, and there were still two "meatless" days per week. By August, in order to continue its vital exports and not cut domestic consumption too drastically, Argentina reached the humiliating predicament of importing beef from Uruguay and Paraguay. This measure was a real morale booster as well as an economic windfall for Uruguay, which the latter did not fail to publicize. But for Argentina it was further evidence of the sad decline of one of its leading industries for which nature had so richly endowed it. Two years later high consumer prices had cut domestic consumption, and European restrictions had decreased foreign markets so much that Argentine beef producers were desperately seeking customers and beefless days were no longer desirable. Nevertheless, by the early 1970s the need for rationing reappeared, resulting in beefless days—and even weeks—during this decade.

Meanwhile, Perón, from his headquarters in Spain, kept the Peronist political pot boiling in Argentina. Then, after many promises to return, in December 1964 he left Madrid on a trip that ostensibly would take him home. But when he arrived in Rio de Janeiro, Brazilian authorities, at Argentine request, detained him at the airport, refused to permit him to continue, ordered him back to Spain, and made sure he was aboard when his plane left the same evening on its return flight. Armed with a Paraguayan diplomatic passport, which he had acquired as a result of having once been made an honorary Paraguayan general, he was headed for Montevideo and thence to Asunción, where he apparently hoped to remain until he could make his way back into Argentina; but both Uruguayan and Paraguayan governments announced that he would not be permitted to land. It is doubtful that he really expected to reach Argentina; but the attempt, feigned or real, served to reassure his followers that he had not forgotten them. After this episode, the Spanish government demanded that Perón either state in writing that he would give up all political activity or leave Spain within a month. Originally he had been granted asylum in Spain upon his promise not to engage publicly in politics. As he wished to remain in Spain, he promised to refrain.

In October 1965 Perón sent his wife, Isabel, to Buenos Aires to participate in demonstrations planned for October 17—the twentieth anniversary of his return from captivity that had carried him to power. Her arrival set off violent clashes between Peronists and anti-Peronists, which were followed by a twenty-four-hour general strike, called by the Peronist-controlled CGT, that paralyzed factories and transportation facilities throughout the country. In January Isabel announced in Buenos Aires the names of a forty-two-member "high command" dedicated to returning Perón to power. This message precipitated a split of the fifty-two Peronist congressional deputies into two factions, with seventeen of them supporting absolute obedience to Perón and the other thirty-five preferring to promote Peronism as an integral part of the national political and economic life. Isabel came as a "messenger of peace" to reunite the quarreling Peronist factions and reassert Perón's personal leadership at a time when his image was fading and many Peronists were advocating "Peronism without Perón." But during her eight months in Argentina she succeeded only in intensifying the factionalism and thus weakening Peronism.

Since 1961 Argentina had enjoyed a favorable balance of trade. In 1965 the gross national product (GNP) had increased 7 percent in real terms, unemployment had dropped from 6.3 to 4.6 percent, and financial reserves had reached about $300 million; but the cost of living had risen approximately 40 percent. During the decade since the fall of Perón, the United States had poured about $1.5 billion in grants and loans into Argentina, but in the same period Argentines had shipped an estimated billion dollars to safer investments outside the country. By mid-1966 growing political turmoil, spiraling inflation, a foreign debt of more than $2 billion, and a mounting fiscal deficit had led to a feeling that the country needed stronger leadership than President Illia was providing. Even more significant, from a military viewpoint, was fear that he was allowing the Peronists and Communists to get out of hand and a dangerous political situation was developing. In November 1964 Illia had signed a bill passed by Congress permitting resumption of Peronist and Communist political activities providing they promised to abide by the legal restrictions for other parties. In the March 1965 congressional elections the Peronist Popular Union had slightly outdistanced the UCRP in total votes. In early 1966 elections in the northwest province of Jujuy, Peronists had gained 71 percent of the votes, winning the governorship and 23 of the 30 legislative seats. The result was a bloodless coup d'état on June 28 whereby the Illia government was overthrown.

By this time the military coup had become a customary method of changing presidents, and this one was accepted with indifference by many Argentines and greeted with considerable enthusiasm by others. Financially poor and unwelcome in his hometown, Dr. Illia went to his brother's suburban home. As he was being led out of the Casa Rosada to a car waiting to carry him there, shouts of "Long live democracy and liberty!" were heard from the small crowd of about seventy people who had gathered to see him off.[2]

The military leaders who seized control in 1966 were not men hungry for power. They thought they saw a job to be done and became involved. In their opinion, the country could not be freely turned over to the people because the Peronists would gain control, Perón would return, and the miserable cycle of corruption and economic blundering would start again. Those who headed this coup conscientiously set out to curb inflation, set the country back on the path of sensible economic development, and try to find some way to bring the Peronists back into the political framework without allowing them to acquire too much power.

After Illia's hastened departure from the Casa Rosada, a three-man military junta assumed control and General Onganía, who had been an outspoken advocate of civilian, constitutional government, was named provisional president. The previous December Onganía had resigned as army commander in chief because he objected to Illia's weak administration and especially the freedom permitted Peronists and Communists. Subsequently he had indicated his possible candidacy for president in 1969.

The junta dissolved Congress and the Supreme Court and ousted all provincial governors and legislative bodies. A "Statute of the Argentine Revolution" provided that the president would exercise both executive and legislative functions, while in the provinces executive and legislative duties would be performed by governors appointed by him.

More than 200 political parties had presented candidates in the 1965 congressional elections. Now all parties were abolished; but following an apparent promise by the CGT to refrain from political activity, the trade unions were left intact. Nevertheless, three months later the CGT denounced the Onganía administration and called on all loyal Peronist members to resume their propaganda and protests. There followed a lengthy conflict between Onganía and the CGT that seriously weakened it and caused the big labor federation to abandon its antigovernment demonstrations and strikes. This action was hailed as a defeat for the trade unions and a major achievement for Onganía. By 1968 he, like Perón before him, appeared hopeful of using "unified" labor and the military as twin bases on which to build a "new Argentina"; but these plans were shattered by a serious split in the CGT and the revival of a strong Peronist faction that renewed the fight with the government.

Because the eight national universities provided to subversive groups places of refuge free from police interference, a decree in late July 1966 abolished their autonomy and ordered all rectors and deans of faculties to pledge loyalty to the minister of education within forty-eight hours or resign. This order resulted in wholesale resignations of administrators and professors and led to student demonstrations and serious clashes with authorities. Nine months later the government restored autonomy but imposed stricter regulations by means of a new law that withdrew student and graduate voting representation from university governing bodies, forbade academic officials to engage in political propaganda or agitation, attempted to remove the numerous "professional" students from universities, and gave the government the right to intervene in a university when it was deemed in the national interest. These and other restrictions stimulated further student reaction. Violent academic protests, including the bloody Córdoba riots of 1969, appeared periodically throughout Onganía's four years in office and hastened his departure from the presidency.

By 1966 the cost of living was approximately fifty times as high as in 1946. The peso, which had been very stable at 4 per U.S. dollar when Perón became president in 1946 and had fallen to 30 per dollar by the time he was ousted, was down to an official rate of 205 per dollar when Onganía took over in 1966. In an effort to improve the economy and especially the government's fiscal position, he issued a decree reorganizing the railway system.

With losses reaching approximately $1 million per day, the railroads accounted for about half the national deficit and were a major source of inflation. Although Frondizi had managed to get rid of many superfluous employees, this haven of political patronage still had about 173,000—at least 50,000 more than necessary.

The Onganía administration was rather successful in straightening out the economic mess it inherited. Following a decline in oil production, in December 1966 the government began renegotiating contracts with foreign oil companies. A decree of June 1967 offered private companies exploitation concessions on equal terms with YPF. In less than four years the oil policy pendulum had swung from one extreme to the other. In early 1968 a $70 million contract was awarded a West German company to build in Argentina the first nuclear power plant in South America.

In other respects the economy was showing improvement by late 1967. Credit and trade agreements with several European countries, the sale of Argentine bonds abroad, and a new flow of private capital into the country indicated a restored international confidence in Argentina's economy and government. By 1969 monetary reserves had risen to $1 billion; inflation, which ran between 30 and 40 percent annually before the 1966 coup, was slowed to 6.7 percent; and this year witnessed a GNP growth of 6.6 percent. But the increasing foreign debt had reached an estimated $3 billion.

On January 1, 1970, the peso, which since March 1967 had been maintained at 350 per dollar and had temporarily regained its pre-Perón status as a fully convertible hard currency, was replaced by a new peso worth 100 of the old. By June, under Onganía's successor, it was devalued to 4 per dollar—one-hundredth of the Argentine currency's value in 1946. The new peso soon lost its rating as a hard currency and began an accelerating decline that carried it to unbelievable lows before the end of the decade.

The economic minister, Adalberto Krieger Vasena, credited these achievements of his "Great Transformation" to the effectiveness of government by decree. But unfortunately, the Onganía administration was not able to balance its budget and move away from heavy annual deficits. The slowing of inflation was mainly by artificial wage and price controls and thus was only temporary. As long as the government continued deficit financing with large issues of printing-press money, inflation would continue. Moreover, the "invasion" of foreign capital soon aroused much opposition because, under liberalized investment policies, foreign companies, principally from the United States, were buying up Argentine firms. Also the austerity measures imposed to retard inflation created restlessness, especially among the laboring classes to whom the "good old days" of Perón looked ever more inviting.

During the Onganía regime drastic measures were taken to curb the Communists, who were now considered a real menace. After an early beginning in 1918, the Argentine Communist Party had operated with some success in the 1920s but had been suppressed by the Uriburu government following the 1930 revolution. It enjoyed a semi-legal status in the late 1930s and early 1940s but was driven far underground as a result of the 1943 revolution. During his bid for the presidency, Perón had tried to make a deal with the Communists in 1945 to secure their support. As a result, the party had regained legality, but it had opposed him in the 1946 elections. During his years in power, he and the Communists had frequently criticized each other, but they had occasionally cooperated when there seemed an advantage in doing so. In the last years of the Perón era the official Communist Party line was one of opposition, but a branch had secretly cooperated with Perón.

The Communists had been suppressed during the Aramburu administration but were permitted to participate in the 1958 elections, in which they supported Frondizi. After he became president, the war ministry warned of a Communist plan, inspired by the Soviet Union, to provoke disorder in Argentina. Alleged Communist involvement in strikes and riots led to a decree in April 1959 banning all Communist activity throughout the country, although the party was not outlawed. Just before this, six diplomats from Communist countries, including the Soviet ambassador, were forced to leave. As has been noted, after the fall of Perón, Communist subversive activities were overshadowed by those of the Peronists. Nevertheless, by August 1967 President Onganía considered the Communist threat serious enough to issue a controversial "Defense Against Communism" law, which prohibited the entrance of foreign Communists and permitted the government's National Intelligence Center to investigate suspected Argentine Communists, bring charges against them, and blacklist them if convicted in a court of activities "proved to be undoubtedly motivated by Communist ideology."[3]

Austerity measures imposed by the Onganía government together with Peronist and Communist meddling inspired increasing resistance and turmoil. This disturbance reached a climax in May 1969 with a week of student-police clashes around the country. The violence was especially heavy in Córdoba, where workers and students fought the police and military forces in street battles that resulted in several fatalities. A general strike led to more violence there as well as in Buenos Aires and other cities and virtually paralyzed the country. It was the most serious outbreak since the September 1955 revolution that toppled Perón and the most precarious situation yet faced by Onganía. Because of repressive measures to control hostile demonstrators and government efforts to prevent large wage increases, the ministers of interior and economy were special targets; but even their resignations did not materially lessen the tension. Further labor troubles led to the proclamation of a state of siege at the end of June and government seizure of the CGT.

TERRORISM

October 1969 brought the beginning of terrorist attacks against foreign business firms, universities, and the homes of politicians throughout Argentina. For the purpose of calming troubled waters, in late November President Onganía announced a general amnesty for all persons jailed under the state of siege or during the earlier wave of labor unrest. As several reform-minded bishops were increasingly critical of his administration, he drew closer to the powerful conservative elements in the church. But violence continued. The kidnapping of a Paraguayan consul in Buenos Aires in March 1970 was only the beginning of a long series of such acts. Although the government refused to free two prisoners, as the kidnappers demanded, the consul was released unharmed after four days. Far more serious was the abduction from his home on May 29 of former President Aramburu. Four days later a note from the kidnappers, a left-wing Peronist group called Montoneros, stated that he had been executed. Subsequently his body was found.

The kidnapping and murder of Aramburu stirred to action army, navy, and air force leaders, who were already jealous of Onganía's power, disturbed by his apparent intent to perpetuate his authoritarian regime, and alarmed over the deteriorating economic situation. In a bloodless coup on June 8, 1970, led by Lt. Gen. Alejandro A. Lanusse, army commander in chief, Onganía was set aside. Subsequently a brigadier general, Roberto M. Levingston, was called home from his post as military attaché in Washington and sworn in as president. Reasons for his selection included a wide acquaintance with Argentine labor and press leaders as well as his experience in Washington.

Although Levingston was made chief executive, the most powerful political figure was General Lanusse. All three of these military leaders—Onganía, Levingston, and Lanusse—were dedicated to returning Argentina to constitutional government, but they differed as to how and when this might be accomplished. Onganía, while long an advocate of civilian administration, had become disillusioned about the ability of the Argentine people to govern themselves and thought it might take ten years or more to restore anything like a meaningful democracy. Levingston held a similar view. Lanusse, in contrast, desired to return the country to civilian control much more quickly.

Levingston retained the presidency nine and a half months. During this time acts of violence escalated alarmingly. By this time kidnappings, assassinations, bank robberies, and raids on military posts for uniforms and weapons had become commonplace; and on July 1 Montonero terrorists, who had abducted and killed Aramburu, seized La Calera, a town of over 5,000 people ten miles from Córdoba and close to a major military base. These and other such acts bore a striking resemblance to Tupamaro activities in neighboring Uruguay, except that in Argentina there were many unrelated guerrilla groups representing a wide range of political philosophies, including Nazi, Communist, and especially Peronist views.

During his relatively short term in office, Levingston sought to make friends with labor, but compliance with union demands for relaxation of wage controls contributed to inflation of 20 percent in 1970. He also appealed to the widespread nationalist sentiment by abandoning Onganía's free enterprise policy and returning to state ownership of basic industries, which discouraged foreign investments. Nationalization of all private communication companies was an immediate result. But, reflecting intensified Peronist militancy, the CGT issued a manifesto calling for more rapid national development, redistribution of wealth, regional integration, popular elections, and economic independence for Argentina. It warned that the alternative would be increased violence. This threat was followed by a series of three nationwide strikes in support of these demands, partly inspired by accelerated inflation and also by unemployment, which reached 5 percent for the first time since 1965. Concurrently there was a call for early elections from the leaders of five of the most important (but still outlawed) political parties.

In the meantime, Perón, from his Spanish exile, was calling for violent revolution. "Violence already reigns and only more violence can destroy it," he told a representative of the Cuban news agency, Prensa Latina. "To free the country like Fidel, that is the solution," he added. Blaming his fall from power on the "Yankees" rather than the Argentine people, he stated, "I am ready—the day when I decide to go there, no one will be able to stop me."[4]

An outbreak of strikes and riots in Córdoba in March 1971, termed the worst student and labor disorders since the "Cordobazo" of May 1969, involved an estimated 10,000 rioters and resulted in partial or total destruction of more than 100 business establishments. An attempt by President Levingston to dismiss army commander Lanusse for not preventing the rioting led to Levingston himself being deposed on March 23, 1971. Thereupon the military junta resumed political power to complete the "Argentine revolution" begun in 1966, and General Lanusse was sworn in as president. This change of presidents, as was the case the previous June, aroused little reaction in Buenos Aires. Levingston, like Onganía, was given several days to move out of the presidential offices and residence.

The previous year Lanusse had said, "The military have the sacred Christian duty to deliver Argentina to its legitimate place among nations. Toward that end the continuing revolution must place national goals above all. Elections can be held only when basic problems are solved."[5]

Nevertheless, upon assuming the presidency, he, in effect, admitted that the military was unable to solve the "basic problems." One of his first acts was to remove the ban on political activities and restore confiscated property to the political parties. By September, sixty-six parties had filed petitions for recognition. Lanusse announced that his government welcomed suggestions from any Argentine desirous of contributing to the solution of national problems, and he solicited advice from the CGT—and even Perón.

As a friendly gesture intended to facilitate negotiations between Lanusse's government and the Peronists, in September 1971 the Argentine ambassador to Spain delivered to Perón in Madrid a coffin containing the remarkably preserved body of Evita (embalmed by a special process for which Perón had reportedly paid $100,000). In December 1955 it had been removed, by military order, from a mausoleum in the CGT headquarters in Buenos Aires and, after being hidden in several places, had been secretly buried in Italy. Many times since then the Peronists had demanded its return. In November 1974 it finally was brought back to Buenos Aires and interred beside the body of Juan Perón.

Within a few months preparations were under way for general elections in March 1973 to select officials of a civilian government. Prior to this date, constitutional revisions, decreed by the chief executive, included direct election of the president and vice president and reduction of the term of office from six to four years, with a two-term limit.

President Lanusse's efforts to hold elections and restore constitutional government aroused strong opposition among many military officers and led to abortive coups in May and October 1971. But although his military support was questionable, by this time Lanusse enjoyed almost solid backing from the various political parties, including the Communists, as well as the Peronist-dominated CGT.

Meanwhile kidnappings, murders, bank robberies, and other terrorist activities continued. By August 1971 guerrilla strength was officially estimated at 6,000, and the antisubversive campaign was placed under direct command of the armed forces. On February 2, 1972, an army spokesman reported that during the previous five months the People's Revolutionary Army (ERP) had participated in 90, the Armed Forces of Liberation (FAL) in 8, the Armed Revolutionary Forces (FAR) in 3, and unidentified groups in 196 guerrilla actions throughout the country. One objective was to prevent the proposed elections and bring about a great social upheaval through violence. Government attempts to curb violence were met with loud charges of military and police brutality and unjustified detention of political prisoners.

Terrorism was not the only difficulty that beset Argentina. Economic problems that contributed to an early end of Levingston's term subsequently grew much worse. With accelerated printing of currency, inflation, which had been slowed to 6.7 percent for the year 1969 and returned to 20 percent in 1970, was 40 percent in 1971 and spiraled to 70 percent in 1972. During the latter year, wages rose only 35 percent. The new peso, which stood at 3.5 per dollar for nearly six months after its creation on January 1, 1970, was down to approximately 12 per dollar before the end of 1972. By this time the public debt to foreign banks and governments had risen to more than $4 billion, while an estimated $8 billion in domestic capital had left the country during the previous three years. Argentines themselves had been departing on an average of about 4,000 per month. Highly unfavorable trade balances together with the flight of local capital and increasing inflation brought foreign exchange reserves, which stood at about $800 million in October 1970, down to less than $100 million by early 1972 and created one of the most serious government economic crises of the century. The Lanusse administration was reaping the consequences of its reluctance to impose restrictions that might irritate any group.

Of even greater concern to many people was the beef shortage, resulting in part from discriminatory tax and price policies. In a country where beef consumption had averaged four pounds a week per person—a third more than in the United States—soaring prices and now alternate beefless weeks were considered intolerable. And previous governments had found that hunger for beef made Argentines dangerously restless.

In January 1972 the federal electoral court recognized Perón's Justicialist Party as legal, since it had produced the required number of signatures. In April Perón announced his presidential candidacy, and on June 25 the Justicialist Party officially chose him its nominee. In the meantime, his civil rights had been restored and charges against him of treason and misappropriation of public funds had been dropped. He was no longer a political exile and was free to return to Argentina when he wished. But other military leaders made it clear to General Lanusse that they would not accept Perón's candidacy. They also made known their objections to Lanusse's apparent attempt to promote his own candidacy. He subsequently announced that he would not run.

Hoping to eliminate Perón, on July 7 Lanusse decreed that all potential presidential candidates must reside in the country by August 25 and that members of the military government who wished to run for office must resign from their positions by that date. Two weeks later Perón advised from Madrid that "for security reasons" he would not comply with Lanusse's order but would remain the Justicialist presidential candidate. In November he did return to Argentina on what he claimed was a "peace and tranquillity" mission, but he seemed tired and ventured out only on rare occasions. Except for attending a few political conferences, during most of his four-week stay he remained secluded in a heavily guarded suburban mansion, appearing sporadically at a second-floor window to greet the thousands of admirers who gathered outside. There were rumors that extreme leftists might try to kill him to prevent a possible political settlement between Peronists and the military.

Upon leaving Buenos Aires, Perón issued a statement that he would not accept the presidential nomination of the newly formed Justicialist Liberation Front (Frejuli), composed of the Justicialist and fourteen minor parties. Despite Peronist pressure, Lanusse and other junta members had stood firm on their residency requirement that disqualified him. After he left, Perón was prohibited from returning until after the inauguration. He proposed instead his personal representative in Argentina, Héctor J. Cámpora, a sixty-four-year-old former dentist, veteran politician, and secretary general of the party. The following day Cámpora was named the Justicialist coalition's candidate for president.

In the national elections, held on March 11, 1973, after a dull campaign,

Cámpora gained 49.58 percent of the total vote and was declared the winner, although he did not quite have a now required majority. The UCR nominee, Ricardo Balbín, was far behind with only 21.2 percent, and the remaining ballots were split between several other candidates. Frejuli won 145 of the 243 seats in the Chamber of Deputies, 43 of the 69 Senate seats, and 20 of the 22 provincial governorships. Many of the Senate and governor races were decided in runoffs on April 15. By this time Peronism had expanded considerably beyond its original labor base and included right-wing nationalists, young leftists, and people who were just dissatisfied with military rule. These elements helped swell the Peronist vote.

After nearly seven years of complete control, many military leaders had grown weary of trying to solve Argentina's political and economic mess and were willing to turn the problem back to civilians, hoping to participate in an advisory capacity in the conduct of national affairs. But the armed forces chiefs openly disapproved of a Peronist victory. Nevertheless, in free elections the people chose Cámpora, who had called himself "an obsequious servant" of Perón; had campaigned on the slogan, "Cámpora in government, Perón in power"; and after his election promised to represent Perón "with all fidelity, as I have in the past."[6] On top of this choice, they elected a Peronist-controlled Congress. Thus the Argentines brought back to "solve" their problems the same politicians who had created them. Ironically, the man who scheduled the elections that permitted the Peronists to regain power was Gen. Alejandro Lanusse, who had spent four years and undergone torture as a political prisoner of Perón for his part in the 1951 attempt to unseat him.

Cámpora spent much of the time between his election and the May 25 inauguration in Rome and Madrid conferring with Perón on the composition of his government and policies to be followed. The two agreed on a five-point program of "national reconstruction," which called for an economy independent of foreign influences. In the meantime, increased violence gripped the nation, and Cámpora was persuaded by Lanusse to return and discuss internal security problems. Despite considerable pressure, the president-elect refused to condemn guerrilla activities. Along with other Peronist leaders, he maintained that terrorism had resulted from the years of military rule and was a temporary phenomenon that would disappear after installation of his civilian government. This attitude encouraged the terrorists, and criminal acts increased dramatically, especially kidnappings. Reportedly the Marxist ERP was responsible for most of these, but common criminals recognized a profitable venture and joined in. According to reliable sources, some 200 of the approximately 500 hard-core ERP members had been trained in Cuba. Victims included not only the wealthy but also members of less affluent families; and ransom demands ranged from $2 million to as little as $50.

In his inaugural address Cámpora called for a "political and social truce";

and he promised additional economic benefits for workers and broadened public health, educational, and welfare programs. The same day he announced a major shakeup in the military leadership to force into retirement high-ranking anti-Peronist officers. Frightened by rioting, looting, and threats unintentionally set off by some of his inaugural remarks, he pardoned more than 500 prisoners—despite efforts of the outgoing junta to deter him. Then, two days after his inauguration, he signed into law an amnesty bill, quickly passed by Congress at his request, providing for release of all those in prison on charges of misconduct in political, social, or student activities. He also approved legislation repealing the "Defense Against Communism" law and other antisubversive measures. He followed this action with an announcement that his government was establishing diplomatic relations with Cuba, East Germany, North Korea, and North Vietnam. Mindful of the potential dangers from academic circles, the government quickly took control of the national universities.

On June 20, 1973, Perón returned to Buenos Aires for the second time. His first arrival, during a hard rain the previous November, had been a very restricted affair, with only 300 carefully selected people permitted to greet his plane, behind police barriers, at Ezieza International Airport, which was surrounded by troops and tanks. The Peróns were detained overnight at the airport hotel before being allowed to continue into Buenos Aires. But Perón's second appearance, with his man Cámpora controlling the arrangements, was quite a different show. Reportedly more than 100 people were killed and over 400 injured in clashes of rival Peronist factions among the millions who waited to welcome the Peróns at the same airport and along the highway leading into the city. To swell the crowd, Cámpora's government had provided free transportation for thousands of provincials, who had been enticed to Buenos Aires by a mass media campaign throughout the country. Perón, afraid to land amid such disorder, had his plane diverted to another airport. What was planned as a spectacular welcome turned into a bloody fiasco. But despite the hostile rivalry among his followers, "el Líder" was back; and his nationwide radio and television address the following day made it clear that "Perón in power" was not merely a slogan—it was rapidly becoming a reality.

On July 13, at Perón's insistence, President Cámpora announced that he was resigning to enable Perón to regain the presidency of which he had been "unjustly deprived." The vice president and cabinet also resigned. The following day Raúl Lastiri, Chamber of Deputies president, was sworn in as provisional president of the nation.

Cámpora's resignation was interpreted in Buenos Aires as a victory of the right wing over the left of the now badly factionalized Peronists. By playing to the left, he had alienated the rightists and Perón and not really gained control of the left wingers, who were largely responsible for the growing terrorism. The break between Perón and Cámpora became so serious that the ex-president was not invited to Perón's inauguration. In April 1975 he was expelled from the Justicialist Party for his alleged left-wing connections.

New elections for president and vice president were scheduled for September 23, 1973. In the meantime, Perón reached an agreement with the new military chiefs whereby they would accept him as president in hope of gaining political stability and domestic peace. But privately his physicians warned him that he probably would not survive four years in the presidency.

Perón was the obvious presidential choice of the Justicialist Liberation Front, and he managed to get his forty-two-year-old wife accepted as the Frejuli nominee for vice president. Thus in 1973, with the odds for his survival stacked against him, he succeeded in having Isabelita as his running mate, which he had failed to do with Evita twenty-two years earlier. On election day the Peróns polled 61.8 percent of the total vote. The UCR presidential candidate, once more Ricardo Balbín, trailed with only 25 percent. On October 12 Juan D. Perón, again wearing his uniform of a three-star general, was sworn in as president, and Isabel Martínez de Perón took the oath as vice president. (Christened María Estela Martínez, she had assumed the name Isabel.) She was the first woman in the Western Hemisphere to hold such an office. After eighteen years out of power, Perón had staged a comeback and once more had been confirmed by a large majority of Argentines as their leader. But now he was seventy-eight years old and quite a different Perón— physically and mentally—from what he had been two decades earlier.

In poor health, less aggressive, and apparently content with his vindication by the Argentine electorate, Perón was not inclined to promote any spectacular changes. Economically the balance of 1973 and part of 1974 proved to be a time of relative stability in the cost of living. This stability was due mainly to a "social pact," negotiated by Peronists between business and labor in June 1973, which was designed to freeze wages and prices for two years. It resulted in a decrease in the inflation rate from 60 percent in 1973 to an annual average of about 30 percent by mid-1974. By this time, however, the agreement appeared to be disintegrating because of basic food shortages and pressures for higher wages and prices. The period also witnessed a serious drop in grain production as farmers reduced cultivated areas by about 25 percent. Again, as during his first regime, Perón brought agricultural curtailments by forcing down commodity prices—this time for the purpose of checking inflation.

Meanwhile Argentina was experiencing a new wave of terrorism. Over 500 kidnappings netted ransoms estimated at more than $50 million during 1973; and in early 1974 the Esso Oil Company of Argentina paid $14.2 million for the release of one of its executives. While officials of foreign corporations were some of the most publicized victims, the vast majority were Argentines. Guerrillas and ordinary criminals had found kidnapping safer and more profitable than bank robbery. Assassinations focused principally on the now serious split among Justicialists, and by April 1974 right-wing and left-wing

Peronists reportedly were killing one another almost daily. In January the situation was considered so serious that Congress enacted new antiguerrilla legislation. The battle over this bill revealed and intensified the split in the Peronist congressional bloc. Perón further widened the gap by an attack on Peronist left-wing extremists in a Plaza de Mayo address before a May Day rally of some 100,000 people, about half of whom walked out.

He had promised to heal political discord among the Argentines; but while he succeeded in temporarily calming the Peronist-military feud, Perón actually presided over and intensified violence within his own ranks. Before his return to power, Argentina had been divided between Peronists and non-Peronists. After his arrival the factionalism between left-wing Peronists and right-wing Peronists became more serious. By siding with the older, more conservative politicians and trade union leaders, Perón antagonized the young, left-wing Peronists, who had played a major role in bringing him back in the erroneous belief that he would lead a great social revolution. More deaths resulted from this intraparty strife than the Peronist versus military struggle.

Faced with labor unrest, commodity shortages, black markets, and the escalating terrorism, in a nationwide broadcast on June 12 Perón denounced what he termed a "psychological campaign" to undermine his economic program, and threatened to resign. Nevertheless, as should have been expected, shortly afterward he appeared at a rally of some 50,000 workers in the Plaza de Mayo, reportedly planned beforehand by the CGT, and pledged that he would continue in office. But he had little time left. On July 1, 1974, Juan D. Perón, who had been suffering from circulatory and bronchial ailments, died of a heart attack—and Isabel inherited the presidency.

Isabel Perón was poorly equipped by background and education to become vice president. She had only six years of formal schooling, supplemented by piano and dancing instruction; and subsequently she had appeared with folk music groups and in nightclub acts. Her political training had begun when she met ex-President Perón in Panama in 1956. As his secretary and, after 1961, his wife, she had been involved in answering letters and typing manuscripts of the several books and articles he wrote to extol his accomplishments and keep Peronism alive in Argentina. Distant and introverted, she was quite a contrast to the flashy Evita; and her return to Argentina as Perón's messenger in 1965 revealed a serious lack of skill and finesse in dealing with the Peronists. Her selection as General Perón's running mate in 1973 brought dismay and disbelief to both his supporters and opponents.

As vice president, the conservative Isabel Perón was accepted by the conservative Peronists but not by the left wingers. She did gain valuable experience, though, by presiding over cabinet meetings and some senatorial gatherings and as the leader of Peronist women. She also won respect as a speaker in support of controversial government policies. Then on two occasions, when President Perón made official visits to Paraguay and Uruguay, he granted her full executive powers during his absence. Just before his final illness, she had made a European tour, which included state visits to Spain and Italy, a meeting with the pope, and a major address to the International Labor Organization. On June 29, with her husband under intensive medical care, she again became acting president with full executive authority.

A serious question after her election as vice president was whether Isabel would be permitted to serve as president should Juan Perón not survive the term for which he had been elected. Reportedly, left-wing Peronists and the military accepted her vice presidential candidacy only after reaching an agreement with Perón that she would resign and permit new elections should he die or become incapacitated during his term of office. But she proved to be of a different mind; and once she inherited the presidency, she was determined to keep it. Another question that appropriately could have been raised before his death was whether he would be able to cling to the presidency for his entire four years even if his health permitted. By this time there were fatal cracks in his economic program; and violence, which had claimed more than 200 lives the past year, was growing worse.

Upon her accession to the presidency, Isabel Perón was accorded assurances of support from political, military, business, and labor leaders irrespective of their Peronist or non-Peronist affiliations, including General Lanusse (now retired), the current military chiefs, and UCR leader Ricardo Balbín, who recently had been one of General Perón's close collaborators. Nevertheless, within two weeks a new wave of violence swept the country; and after August 1 assassinations reportedly were averaging one every nineteen hours. Besides some half dozen left-wing terrorist groups, there were several right-wing death squads that specialized in eliminating leftists, including the Argentine Anticommunist Alliance, of which José López Rega, Isabel Perón's private secretary and social welfare minister, was allegedly the mastermind. By this time the power vacuum that had been predicted after Juan Perón's death was obvious, and various Peronist and Marxist elements were in a deadly struggle to gain the ascendancy and fill this void.

For the first time since the military withdrew from power, in mid-August 1974 the army was authorized to join the police in a crackdown on guerrillas. About three weeks later the Montoneros declared "total popular war" on the government. In November President Isabel Perón imposed a state of siege. (A previous state of siege had been lifted shortly after Cámpora became president in May 1973.) In December she asked Congress for broad powers to call up the armed forces to combat subversion; and in mid-February 1975 the military launched an all-out offensive against ERP guerrillas in the northwest provinces, where an estimated half or more were concentrated. At the end of August the commander of this campaign reported at least 800 guerrillas killed, wounded, or captured and definite proof that Cubans and Algerians were their trainers. Guerrillas continued to stage devastating attacks on strategic installations, including army and navy bases, airports, and a federal prison; but the killing of ERP and Montonero commanders and several other terrorist leaders in September and October indicated the increasing effectiveness of the military's antisubversion campaign. Nevertheless, although kidnappings had declined sharply, terrorism took a severe toll. One battle in late December between leftist guerrillas and security forces left more than 100 dead, 85 of them guerrillas. By the end of 1975 over 1,700 people, from all walks of life, were reported to have been killed in political violence in the eighteen months since Isabel Perón became president.

Economically also this second Perón era was a disaster. The Peronist program, instituted in May 1973, to freeze prices, raise wages, and increase public spending simply did not work. The agricultural sector was depressed by government controls on beef and grain production that kept prices low and taxes high to aid urbanites (about 80 percent of the population) and provide funds for public projects. With low beef prices, per capita consumption was up to around 240 pounds a year. After Perón returned to power, a state monopoly of grain exports was reestablished. Even so, in 1974 agricultural products accounted for about 70 percent of exports, although an estimated $500 million worth was smuggled out of the country. But Argentina was no longer one of the world's great grain producers. A sharp drop in industrial production resulted from greatly increased worker absenteeism. This situation was blamed on the return of Peronists to power and the passage of a very liberal labor law that protected workers from dismissal and enabled them to receive their wages while off the job for questionable "illness."

By late 1974 prices were soaring and real income was plummeting. In March 1975 the government announced an across-the-board price freeze and wage increase while formally devaluing the peso to 15 per dollar. Three months later the currency was further devalued to 30 per dollar; and by this time inflation, at an annual rate of 80 percent, was inspiring a series of strikes and walkouts in protest against inadequate wage hikes. In June 1975 Argentina's foreign debt was estimated at about $9.2 billion, with approximately $2.2 billion in interest and finance charges due before the end of the year. Reduced by an unfavorable trade balance, reserves stood at slightly over $750 million. Credits of $1.6 billion, obtained from the International Monetary Fund, Inter-American Development Bank, and other (mainly U.S.) sources, enabled the Argentine government to meet debt-service payments. A government report indicated that at least half of all domestic trade was on the black market, which made the collection of taxes thereon impossible.

In July, with inflation at over 100 percent, President Isabel Perón abandoned Peronist concepts in favor of austerity, which she now recognized as the only cure for Argentina's economic ills. The CGT, in its first move ever against a Peronist government, retaliated with a nationwide strike in opposition to the austerity measures and support of demands for removal of the economy minister and the controversial social welfare minister, José López Rega. (López Rega, considered an extreme rightist, was for several years the Peróns' closest associate and the strong man in Isabel Perón's government.) Shortly thereafter the president succumbed to this pressure by approving wage increases up to 150 percent and dismissing López Rega. During this year there were also farmers' and cattlemen's strikes protesting production quotas, price freezes, and high taxes.

By August 1975, with inflation at an estimated annual rate of about 200 percent, small companies, hard hit by new wage contracts, dismissed some 200,000 workers within a week. But with huge new issues of unsupported paper currency to meet a budget deficit of at least 65 percent, the amount of paper in circulation tripled in one year. (Argentine facilities were not adequate to print all the money the government needed, and a contract was made with a Chilean printing company.) Consequently the peso continued to plunge. A September 15 devaluation brought it down to over 45 per dollar, but at the same time the black market rate was around 90. In January the government announced that in 1975 the cost of living had risen 335 percent. By this time the peso was down to 140 per dollar. Or, translated into old currency, the peso that was worth 4 per dollar in 1946 was now officially 14,000 per dollar!

"Argentina is not just passing through a bad economic situation," a former economy minister stated as the nation faced its worst crisis since the 1930s. "It is witnessing the total destruction of its economic order."[7]

By early 1976 economic reverses and internal warfare had brought Argentina to virtual anarchy with which the government of Isabel Perón was obviously unable to cope. Her identification with a small, right-wing Peronist faction and her tendency to isolate herself and delegate too much authority to two or three cabinet ministers, especially the unpopular López Rega, had deprived her of the wholehearted cooperation of other factions; and she had made little headway in her conscientious attempts to find solutions to Argentina's basic problems. Before the end of 1975 her government had lost its congressional control because of splits among Peronists, and the once solid labor support had crumbled into quarreling segments, some of which were dominated by left-wing extremists. Her control of the news media had not prevented criticism of her administration; and she had resisted many demands that she resign, as well as efforts to impeach her. For over a year and a half the military, not inclined to resume political power, had stood by while the domestic framework deteriorated and the country tore itself apart.

In the meantime, the president's position was not made any easier by charges of misappropriation of public funds, which were leveled at her and used by opponents in trying to force her resignation. Although she was cleared of criminal liability in the initial charge that she had appropriated to her personal use $741,542 from the Justicialist Solidarity Crusade charity, headed by her, with funds from a national lottery, the scandal only temporarily abated. (Eva Perón had never been required to account for the large sums she handled in a similar and questionable operation during the first Perón era.)

In an army shakeup in August 1975, the then commander in chief was forced to step down and Lt. Gen. Jorge Rafael Videla was appointed by President Isabel Perón to this position. A revolt by air force officers in December was a bit premature and failed to set off an uprising by the army and navy as they had hoped. But three months more of spectacular inflation, unbelievable bloodshed, and extreme corruption spurred other military leaders to action. With more than forty people killed in political violence the past week, a new 70 percent currency devaluation, inflation at an estimated annual rate of between 700 and 1,000 percent, and another government austerity attempt countered by strikes and demonstrations, the armed forces moved in. By this time exchange reserves were exhausted and foreign debts totaled around $1 billion. On March 24, 1976, after refusing to resign, Isabel Perón was ousted from the Casa Rosada, taken into "protective custody," and flown to a resort in the Andean lake region, where she was held prisoner. Eight months later she was transferred to a naval base near Buenos Aires. Charged with mishandling public funds and permitting fiscal mismanagement, she admitted that she never had read government financial regulations and had only followed the advice of her aides. After being held under house arrest for over five years, she was permitted to go into exile.

A military junta, headed by General Videla and including the navy and air force chiefs, Adm. Emilio E. Massera and Brig. Gen. Orlando R. Agosti, assumed control of the government. This coup had long been expected and drew little reaction in Buenos Aires or elsewhere in the nation.

"It was such a quick, dull coup," commented one wealthy Argentine. "Such precision—you would have thought they were Germans, not Argentines."[8]

"I returned to the country to unite, not to foment disunion among Argentines," President Juan Perón had said in his last public address.[9] But his feeble efforts had accomplished little. The economic chaos and internal divisions he had fostered during his earlier regime had grown too great to be solved in the last year of his life. And his wife—a political novice—was saddled with a virtually impossible task.

"I am small but I am tough," she had said while promising that nothing could deflect her from the course she and Juan Perón had charted for the country.[10] But although she had the will, she was not able to find the way to stop the bloodshed and bind up Argentina's political and economic wounds.

MILITARY DICTATORSHIP

General Videla was known as a professional soldier, an ardent anti-Communist, and a deeply religious and moralistic leader. He had said the army did not want to be involved again in politics, but he became convinced of the need for military intervention to protect the nation against subversion and eradicate corruption. Although admittedly not an economist, he believed Argentina's economic problems could be solved by reversing Peronist policies and applying moral principles. Having assumed the lead in the anti-guerrilla struggle, he was dedicated to ridding the country of dangerous subversives.

Initially the junta said it would stay in power three years. Within a few days the fifty-year-old Videla was sworn in as Argentina's president, while retaining his position as commander in chief of the army and member of the junta. He appointed a cabinet of six military officers and two civilians. Congress was dismissed and in its place a legislative advisory commission of nine senior officers—three from each service—was created to provide the junta with technical support. Peronist-appointed Supreme Court justices and other judicial officials were replaced by military appointees. Political parties were suspended, and military control was established in the state universities. Censorship of the mass media was imposed by bringing all television and radio stations under government control and carefully regulating the press. Besides Isabel Perón, thirty-five other Peronist political and labor leaders were deprived of their political rights and ordered detained for an indefinite time pending investigations of alleged criminal acts. Shortly after assuming direction of the government, the military stepped up its already vigorous campaign to exterminate the guerrillas and, at the same time, launched far-reaching economic reforms.

With José Martínez de Hoz, a leading industrialist, as minister of economy, the administration began reversing Peronist economic practices. Wages would be regulated by the government, while price controls, which had resulted in shortages and enormous smuggling and illegal trading, were removed. Government restrictions on business enterprises, including the monopoly in beef and grain sales, were abolished. Once again foreign oil companies were invited to assist in exploitation of petroleum resources, and other foreign investments were encouraged. Officially Argentina had returned to private enterprise. But it would be extremely difficult for even a military dictatorship to overcome such built-in resistance as traditional tax evasion by the wealthy and traditional opposition to austerity measures by the highly organized and influential laboring classes, to say nothing of the additional government employees who had swelled the public payrolls by 24 percent during the previous three years. And there was also the ever present ultranationalism. "The government offers no easy or miraculous solutions," warned General Videla. "On the contrary, it asks, and will realize, sacrifices, effort and austerity."[11]

One of the first steps to implement the new economic policies was a decision to dismiss all nonessential government employees. (More than 1.5 million people—a sixth of the total work force—were on government payrolls.) This action was followed by a new set of taxes designed to reverse a serious imbalance in which tax revenues covered only approximately 20 percent of government expenditures. Increased rates for public services and products of state enterprises also were imposed to help relieve the budget deficits. Wages were frozen and strikes banned. With the principal Peronist labor leaders confined on board a ship in Buenos Aires harbor, military managers were placed in key unions. A spectacular stock exchange boom indicated approval of these changes by business and financial interests.

Initially the economic reforms made impressive differences. Inflation, which raised living costs about 50 percent for the month of March 1976 alone, was temporarily reduced to 3 percent for the month of June. This achievement was accompanied by strict wage controls, dismissal of some 60,000 public employees, and a recession that brought a drastic decline in sales of consumer goods. But by October, although the recession seemed to have ended, the government's budget was still far out of balance, with tax revenues sufficient to cover only 44 percent of public spending. And living costs again were rising rapidly. For the entire year the inflation rate was nearly 450 percent.

By March 1977 the revised agricultural policy had paid off with bumper grain crops that permitted the largest grain exports in forty-six years and proved Argentine farmers would respond to economic freedom and better prices. With increased agricultural exports, Argentina returned to a favorable trade balance, and for the twelve months ending in mid-1977 showed a surplus of more than $1 billion—a striking contrast to the trade deficits of the previous three years. But shaken by illegal work stoppages, aware of the influence of labor unions even under military administrators, and fearful of increased unemployment that might produce new guerrillas, the government relaxed its wage controls. Huge budget deficits continued, paid for by huge increases in printing-press money. By August 1977 the official peso exchange rate was 415 per dollar. With subsidies to inefficient state companies the largest single factor in national budget deficits, the administration announced in September 1977 that, with the exception of public utilities, all state-owned companies would be offered for sale. Independent economic studies had shown clearly that inefficiency, mismanagement, and political influence had made state-operated enterprises dependent on costly government handouts. But this proposal to dispose of them subsequently encountered strong opposition.

Continuing high inflation of over 170 percent for 1977 and approximately the same in 1978 and 1979 brought lower living standards for most Argentine families and economic recession in all but the agricultural sector. As usual under serious inflation, it was the elderly on pensions who were in greatest difficulty. By May 1979, after three years of military government, large beef and grain exports together with reduced imports had produced exchange reserves of around $7 billion and restored Argentina's good credit rating among international bankers. But increased military expenditures (primarily because of a border dispute with Chile) and financial losses by state enterprises had boosted the national budget deficits. The 1970 peso was down to about 1,200 per dollar—and still falling. (In terms of the old peso, worth 4 per dollar at the beginning of the first Perón era, the exchange rate was now 120,000 per dollar!) For three years Argentina had held the dubious distinction of experiencing the world's highest inflation.

Suppressing terrorism received top priority in the Videla administration; and soon after assuming power in March 1976, the military intensified its campaign to annihilate the left-wing subversives. Allegedly General Videla and his government sought the destruction of leftist guerrillas, but they did not show the same enthusiasm for exterminating right-wing extremists, who were engaged in anti-leftist terrorism and actually had close ties with national security forces. The drive was directed especially at the two principal guerrilla organizations—the Marxist People's Revolutionary Army (ERP) and the left-wing Peronist Montoneros. Estimates of current ERP strength varied from 500 to more than 2,000 well-trained guerrillas, plus several thousand sympathizers who assisted them. The Montoneros were composed primarily of young Peronists who had fought for General Perón's return, were rebuffed by his and Isabel Perón's governments, and then turned against her. An announced objective of these two groups was a revolutionary army capable of defeating the Argentine security forces, but the latter now numbered about 150,000 well-equipped soldiers and police. By early July the terror and antiterror campaigns were estimated to have claimed about 600 lives since the first of the year, including political exiles from other Latin American countries, several Roman Catholic priests, and 60 members of the federal police. Meanwhile the government decreed death or life imprisonment for anyone convicted of murdering a government official.

In mid-July the security forces scored a major achievement by killing Mario R. Santucho, founder and leader of the ERP, who was also head of a center for international terrorism in Paris. Along with him, his chief lieutenant and other important aides were wiped out. Santucho had been trained in Cuba. His organization had begun operations with a bank robbery in 1969 and had later expanded to large-scale guerrilla activities. By this time the effective anti-insurgency campaign had also taken a heavy toll on the Montoneros. But the death of Santucho and other guerrilla leaders did not stop the violence, and on one day in late July at least ten people were killed. By the end of December 1976, known casualties during the year had reached 1,479.

In October 1977 Argentine security forces estimated that 80 percent of the left-wing guerrillas had been killed or imprisoned. Although terrorist activities were not at an end, with most guerrilla leaders either dead or out of the country, subversive operations had subsided considerably. Relations between Argentina and Mexico deteriorated as a result of Montonero exiles in Mexico allegedly being permitted to carry on political activities against the Argentine junta from there. The problem now was not so much left-wing

guerrillas as right-wing extremists, who continued to operate freely and actually posed a challenge to government authority. During 1977 more than
700 people perished in political violence. By the end of that year several
thousand had been arrested and over 2,000 were reported missing. About
this time the government widened the scope of its war on terrorism. In early
1978 President Videla said, "A terrorist is not just someone with a gun or a
bomb, but also someone who spreads ideas that are contrary to western
civilization."[12] Broadly interpreted, this definition could include anyone critical of government policies.

In 1976 Argentines began complaining of missing relatives, believed under
arrest, about whom they were unable to obtain information; and human
rights issues were being voiced by international organizations, several foreign governments, and the pope over allegedly mysterious deaths and the
disappearance of many people as a result of the antisubversive campaign.
By this time complaints also were being made on behalf of the approximately
15,000 political refugees in Argentina, some of whom had been victims of
assassination or kidnapping. Especially vulnerable were left-wing political
activists who had fled from right-wing dictatorships in surrounding countries.
Of the thousands seized in their homes or elsewhere, many were taken by
government security forces; but others were abducted by left-wing guerrillas
or extreme right-wing, anti-Communist groups who opposed the Videla government's more moderate policies. Some of these victims later reappeared
after being held for days or months and subjected to questioning and various
forms of torture, but many others were never accounted for unless their
mutilated bodies were found.

Investigating teams from Amnesty International, Argentina's Permanent
Assembly for Human Rights, the United States government, and other sources
conducted inquiries and issued reports charging widespread tortures and
executions, which the Videla administration denied. In March 1977 Amnesty
International claimed that from 5,000 to 6,000 political prisoners were being
held and, in the year since the military seized power, between 2,000 and
5,000 people had disappeared without trace. The government denied these
figures and said the report was biased and based on rumors. In December
1977 the interior ministry admitted that 3,607 prisoners were being held under state-of-siege regulations and promised that all names would be made
public. By September 1978 international human rights groups upped their
charges to 8,000 political prisoners and 15,000 *desaparecidos* (disappeared
ones), but the government denied these claims and admitted holding only
3,500 political prisoners.

Mothers and other relatives of *desaparecidos*, many with pictures of missing loved ones, began in April 1976 gathering every Thursday in the Plaza
de Mayo in front of the Casa Rosada. This demonstration became a public
protest to the government for refusing to release the names or provide any
information about people who had disappeared. Although these demonstra-

tions brought retaliation rather than information from government officials and some of the demonstrators themselves reportedly became *desapareci-dos*, the weekly appearances continued.

After assuming office in January 1977, the Jimmy Carter administration in Washington took up the human rights issue and threatened economic sanctions if the Argentine situation did not improve. A cutback in military aid and the withholding of loans for economic development were termed by the Videla government unjustifiable interference in Argentina's internal affairs. An interesting exception was made when President Carter wanted President Videla, along with all other Latin American heads of state, to be in Washington on September 7, 1977, for the signing of the Panama Canal treaties. General Videla, who had stated privately that he disapproved of these treaties, was enticed to Washington by promised State Department approval of the sale to Argentina of eight helicopters that had been withheld for months because of the U.S. administration's objections over the human rights issue. In 1978 the United States suspended sales of any military equipment to Argentina. After that the Videla government purchased arms from Great Britain, Spain, France, and Israel. Late in 1979 it also entered into negotiations with the Soviet Union for military supplies.

Meanwhile abductions continued in Argentina, with the government making only token releases of prisoners and providing minimal information regarding those detained. Mindful of the resurgence of terrorism following amnesty granted prisoners by President Cámpora in 1973, the Videla regime refrained from leniency toward those allegedly involved in recent assassinations, kidnappings, bombings, and attacks on military garrisons. In April 1979 it was estimated that 6,000 people had disappeared in the three years of military rule and an additional 3,000 were admittedly held by the government. By this time President Videla and members of the junta apparently had become quite concerned about the unfavorable image Argentina had acquired as a result of the disappearance of thousands of prisoners and the accounts of torture by many of those who survived in what military leaders were calling the "dirty war." Human rights groups agreed that disappearances had dropped dramatically since the first of the year and a larger number of *desaparecidos* had reappeared. The government's decision to invite inspection by the Inter-American Commission on Human Rights in May indicated relaxation in the antisubversion drive and a belief that there was little to hide. Members of this group, who did not arrive until September, expressed surprise and pleasure over the front-page coverage of their visit by the Argentine press. President Videla was telling visitors, "The war is over, now we must win the peace."[13]

While leading the battle to restore economic sanity and end political terrorism, General Videla was beset by a power struggle between democratic and authoritarian factions within the armed forces. In this conflict he served as a moderator dedicated to maintaining unity. Determined to promote a gradual return to civilian government, he was able to weed out right-wing extremists and gain solid military backing for his moderate position. An early step in this direction was the restoration of civilian administration in the state universities in September 1976, after at least 3,000 leftist professors, administrative officials, and students had been dismissed in an effort to eradicate Marxist indoctrination centers.

By late 1977 the navy, led by junta member Admiral Massera, was challenging General Videla's continuing incumbency as president. Nevertheless, Videla made it clear that he expected to play the central role during a transition period in which a new system of government would be formulated through military and civilian cooperation. After declaring all political parties in recess following the coup of March 1976, military leaders had consistently opposed a revival of party activity. But in March 1978 General Videla set forth his ideas of a political future based on a few well-defined parties. Several weeks later the Radicals accepted what was interpreted as the government's invitation for a "dialogue" aimed at formulating a political plan for restoration of democratic government. Any such hopes were quickly shattered, though, by the junta disqualifying all major political parties from participation and making it clear that, while such parties were essential in representative government, the "dialogue" would be between the military and "capable and virtuous" civilians.

With the curbing of guerrilla activity, the emergency that had promoted unity within the junta diminished and tension rose over future organization of the government. Nevertheless, in May 1978 junta members agreed that upon his retirement from the army on August 1, General Videla would begin a second term as president that would run until March 1981. Admiral Massera, who resigned in September 1978 as commander in chief of the navy, following disagreements with General Videla and other army leaders, appeared to be grooming himself as a potential presidential candidate whenever elected government should be restored. In late 1978 he began building a political base, with strong appeals to various center groups.

After more than four years of rule, with the proposed "dialogue" postponed indefinitely, President Videla and military chiefs, who had reached no accord on a future system of government, appeared in no hurry to return the country to any form of civilian control. Nevertheless, they seemed to agree on the need for a new generation of leaders who could be trusted to combine democracy with common sense in guiding the nation.

With this aim in mind, in October 1980 the junta selected as the next president, for a three-year term beginning March 29, 1981, Lt. Gen. Roberto Eduardo Viola, who had succeeded General Videla as chief of the army. The formal selection of Viola had been delayed due to rivalry among the army, navy, and air force as to their respective roles under the new administration and their determination to preserve the authority of the junta. Considered a strong anti-Communist, political moderate, and shrewd politician, General

Viola was believed to be a logical choice to lead the country back to civilian, democratic government. Having come from a working-class background, he was deemed sympathetic to the demands of labor.

Prior to his inauguration as president, General Viola made a visit to Washington, where he met with President Ronald Reagan and other top officials. It was known that Reagan, who recently assumed office, viewed Argentina in a different light from Carter, and this seemed an opportune time to bring about closer relations between the two countries. Viola claimed the military government had to use harsh measures to defend Argentina from the internal attacks it faced, and he promised that his regime would provide a list of detainees who had died or disappeared during the "dirty war." Reagan emphasized the strategic importance of Argentina and indicated his desire that Congress repeal the ban on military aid that it had imposed in 1978. Viola apparently left Washington with the belief that his visit had contributed to a better understanding and the Reagan administration would respond favorably to Argentina's desire to purchase military equipment in the United States.

On March 29, 1981, with the country facing a serious economic crisis and public support of the military government in eclipse, General Viola was sworn in as president. He took the oath of office in a modest ceremony in the impressive building of the National Congress, surrounded by generals, admirals, and diplomats—but no congressmen, as Congress had been abolished in 1976. A few hundred people had gathered outside. About the only people lining the Avenida de Mayo during President Viola's fourteen-block drive to the Casa Rosada were policemen. When he arrived at the presidential palace, another small crowd of a few hundred was waiting. Members of this group expressed their approval with polite applause. As one attendee commented, "This is not an elected government. There is no reason for people to come out."[14]

In an effort to play down the military aspect, among the thirteen members of the new Cabinet, seven were civilians, including Oscar Camilión as foreign minister. The two major political parties—Peronist and Radical—had instructed their members not to hold public office under this administration.

In spite of his reputation as a shrewd politician, General Viola now found himself in a difficult position. Isabel Perón was still under house arrest at a Perón family estate near Buenos Aires. As long as she remained in Argentina, she posed a problem because, as the last living symbol of Peronism, she was someone the Peronists could rally around. Another problem was closer at hand and more visible—the mothers who demonstrated every Thursday in front of the Casa Rosada. A more serious problem was the economy, which continued to grow worse.

The easiest problem to solve was Isabel. General Viola had wanted her out of the way before he assumed the presidency. Having been acquitted of charges of mishandling public funds and other crimes, in July, after being held more than five years, she was paroled and allowed to go into exile in

Spain. In August 1982 the Supreme Court ruled that she could never again hold public office in Argentina.

The problem of "Las Madres de la Plaza de Mayo," as they were known, was not so easy to solve. Although the disappearances had stopped, with several thousand people still missing, government leaders were in a difficult position to explain what had happened to them and to avoid any blame for their fate. Although while he was in the United States Viola had indicated a willingness to provide a list of the detainees, back in Argentina he insisted he had made no such promise. It also was hard to explain why more than 900 Argentines were still in jail—some for as long as five years—without having been charged with a crime.

With the most pressing problem—the economy—President Viola was unable to make much headway. Although the plan inaugurated by Martínez de Hoz early in the Videla administration had brought considerable economic improvement, it eventually collapsed because the government never made the massive spending cuts that were necessary. During 1980 there was a trade deficit of $2.5 billion and the foreign debt reached $27 billion. In 1981 these figures continued to grow worse. Unemployment, which had been unusual in Argentina, was about 12 percent and resulted in a considerable increase in the already large number of Argentines seeking employment in other countries. The 1970 peso, which officially was down to approximately 2,000 per dollar by the beginning of 1981, plunged to over 5,600 by October of that year.

The economic chaos brought mounting nationwide dissatisfaction with the government and increasing demands for change. Civilians called for a return to civilian rule, while within the military there was rising pressure, led by army chief Lt. Gen. Leopoldo Fortunato Galtieri, to oust Viola. A heart ailment in November brought Viola's temporary replacement by the interior minister. Subsequently the ruling junta announced his permanent replacement on December 22 by General Galtieri, who also retained his post as commander in chief of the army. He and other members of the military opposed an early return to civilian government partly because of a sense of duty in trying to solve Argentina's problems but also because they feared that a future civilian administration might force them to account for the extremes to which they had resorted during the "dirty war."

Galtieri was a vigorous executive who set about to straighten out the economic mess he inherited. But he soon found there was so much opposition to his regime that he became alarmed. Demonstrations were staged in front of the Casa Rosada protesting the deplorable economic conditions, especially the great number of unemployed and the terrific inflation. One of these crowds, on March 30, staged the most violent labor demonstration the military government had experienced. Under these circumstances, with the official exchange rate of the 1970 peso down to 12,000 per dollar, on April 2,

1982, Galtieri ordered the military to seize the Falkland Islands, known in Argentina as the Malvinas Islands.

FALKLAND ISLANDS WAR

There were several reasons for Galtieri's action. One was the extreme spirit of nationalism and widespread frustration over foreign control of territory considered rightfully Argentine. Another reason was to divert people's attention away from troubles at home, an old trick that has been tried time and again in many countries. For a short while it worked. As long as Argentines could believe their armed forces were succeeding and they were going to possess the Malvinas, they worried less about their domestic problems—and Galtieri and his regime were popular. Following announcement of the invasion, thousands of people gathered in the Plaza de Mayo and shouted their approval as Galtieri stood on a balcony in front of the Casa Rosada. So had they done for Juan Perón thirty years earlier. But the 1982 celebrating did not last long.

Argentina had a longstanding claim on the Malvinas, a group of two main and some 200 smaller cold, windswept islands about 250 miles off the Argentine coast, but in 1833 it had negligently allowed the British to gain control. They have ruled them as the Falkland Islands ever since. The total population in 1982 was about 1,800 people, most of them from Scotland and England. The one important industry was sheep raising, with a sheep population of approximately 700,000. The islands had previously been useful as a coaling station for the British fleet. Before the 1982 incident, there had been several attempts by the British government to work out some arrangement to give them up, but nothing had been settled. The people there wanted to remain under British rule. The Falkland Islands Company, part of a corporate empire based in London, actually owned almost half of the land. It was the big element in the sheep business and held a monopoly there in banking and shipping. Also there were a few individuals in the United Kingdom who owned large tracts. Thus considerable British capital was involved and played a significant role in Britain's strong reaction to the Argentine invasion of these "company" islands.

The Argentine navy was especially anxious that Argentina make good its claim to the Malvinas. Allegedly General Galtieri owed his promotion to the presidency in considerable measure to navy backing in the ruling junta based on his promise to push hard to get control of the Malvinas. He and some others in the military also assumed that, since relations with the United States had improved to the extent that Argentina had agreed to assist in its efforts to root out Communist influences in El Salvador and Nicaragua, the United States would support Argentina in the Falklands controversy. But prior to the invasion, President Reagan telephoned General Galtieri, tried to persuade him not to invade, and warned him it would bring military retaliation by the

British and wreck U.S.-Argentine relations. Moreover, Prime Minister Margaret Thatcher's reputation was at stake. The British responded with sufficient force to suppress the rebellion and retain control of the islands. On April 30 the United States officially joined Britain with an announcement of diplomatic, economic, and logistic support.

Although British troops in the Falklands were outnumbered almost two to one, the war lasted only seventy-four days and ended suddenly with an Argentine surrender on June 14. The following day an angry mob of 7,000 to 10,000 people gathered in front of the Casa Rosada, shouting obscenities at Galtieri and demanding his ouster. Initially he refused to accept what the military termed a "cease fire and withdrawal" agreement as admission of defeat, and he blamed the United States for British success. In a grim television address he promised that the Malvinas "will always be within our reach and sooner or later we are going to get them."[15]

The Argentine military reported casualties of more than 1,700, with 712 dead. The British government claimed the taking of 15,000 Argentine prisoners. British losses were reported at 255 dead and 777 wounded. Amid angry dissension in the junta, General Galtieri, who never had fought in a war, was forced to resign both his army command and the presidency. But he insisted Argentina had not lost the war, only a battle.

With the joint military government in a state of collapse, the navy and air force withdrew from the junta and delegated their power to the army, which, after a brief interim, named retired Maj. Gen. Reynaldo B. A. Bignone president for a term ending in March 1984. According to Lt. Gen. Cristino Nicolaides, Galtieri's successor as army commander in chief, this would be a transition administration pledged to return Argentina to democracy in the shortest time possible. With a promise to restore civilian government by the end of his term, General Bignone took the oath of office on July 1 in a ceremony boycotted by the air force chief and some other military leaders. In September the junta was reestablished with the return of the navy and air force chiefs.

In line with his transition intent, General Bignone appointed a cabinet of one military officer and nine civilians. Mindful of the pressing economic problems, he chose as economic minister José M. Dagnino Pastore, a Harvard-educated economist, who had served under a conservative military regime twelve years earlier. His appointment was bitterly opposed by labor leaders and Peronist politicians, who termed him too conservative. The new foreign minister, Juan R. Aguirre Lanari, promised continuation of Argentina's diplomatic battle for the Malvinas.

The economy was miserable before the Falklands invasion, but it was even worse after. In addition to its other serious problems, in the eleven weeks of the Falklands War Argentina had suffered from economic sanctions imposed by Britain, the United States, and the European Community. And in this period the much battered peso had declined in value from 12,000 to over

14,000 per dollar officially. During the balance of the year it continued to fall until by the beginning of 1983 it was down to an official exchange rate of 50,000. In terms of the 1946 peso, the rate was 5 million pesos per dollar! By this time inflation was running at about 450 percent annually. The new economic minister termed the economy in an unprecedented state of destruction. He became so frustrated over his inability to make significant improvements that he resigned less than two months after his appointment. He was replaced by Jorge Wehbe, who had been economy minister in the Frondizi government.

Prior to this time, a greatly expanded and profitable trade had developed with the Soviet Union. Initially it was a result of the embargo imposed by the United States on the USSR following its invasion of Afghanistan in 1979. This Argentine-Soviet trade, principally in grain, continued to expand—under anti-Communist Argentine governments—after the U.S. embargo was lifted in 1981. In this year almost 77 percent of Argentine grain and 28 percent of meat exports went to the USSR. The Argentine-Soviet trade relationship was further enhanced by imposition of economic sanctions on Argentina in protest of its invasion of the Falklands and by Soviet support of Argentina in this war.

Adding to the growing unpopularity of the armed forces were charges of incompetence, cowardice, and corruption leveled at their commanders by soldiers returning from the Falklands. One factor favoring the choice of General Bignone as president was that he had not been involved in the Falklands War. With great unemployment and the overall situation showing little sign of improvement, some military leaders now appeared relieved to step aside and let civilians once more try to solve the nation's problems. But there was increasing fear among politicians that a return to democracy in 1984 might be thwarted by economic calamity. Of even greater concern among certain members of the armed forces was the fact that some politicians were beginning to call for investigations of military officers involved in either the "dirty war" or the Falklands fiasco.

Several days before taking office, General Bignone met with politicians representing fourteen parties. It was the first such meeting between military and civilian leaders and contributed to a better understanding by all. Bignone promised elections in early 1984 to allow the country to return to democratic government by the end of his term.

In mid-July 1982 political parties recovered their legal right to function, and an eight-year ban on political rallies was removed. The next evening some 10,000 cheering fans jammed a boxing arena to hear Raúl Alfonsín, leader of a center-left faction of the Radical Civic Union, the nation's second largest political group. The fifteen now-recognized parties (not including Communists) were split into numerous factions, virtually all of which were left of center, as they would be viewed in the United States. The Peronist

Party, Argentina's largest, comprised factions ranging from extreme left to far right. The titular head of this party was Isabel Perón.

The next several months witnessed increasing popular demands for an early end of military rule. They also brought a more conciliatory policy by the weak Bignone regime, reflecting a desire by members of the armed forces not to offend political leaders with whom they would have to deal after the return to civilian government. These officers were particularly anxious to avoid any investigation of or punishment for their deeds during the "dirty war" or the Falklands conflict that might be imposed by a future civilian administration. This concern led the military rulers to seek an agreement with political leaders to a pact regarding such major issues as responsibility for the Falklands War and the disappearance of thousands of people during the "dirty war." The discovery in late 1982 of some 1,500 bodies in mass, un-marked graves brought increasingly vigorous demonstrations and demands that the military be held accountable for the *desaparecidos*, now estimated at between 6,000 and 15,000. In reply, the military issued an official report in April 1983 denying any blame for alleged human rights violations by term-ing them necessary "acts of service" performed in line of duty while sup-pressing leftist subversion.

On top of these issues was the increasing intensity of the economic dis-tress. It was the crowning reason for the widespread frustration that was expressed by massive protests that culminated in a "March for Democracy" in mid-December 1982. The largest demonstration since the military seized control, it drew an estimated 100,000 people to the Plaza de Mayo. There they shouted their disapproval of the military government and demanded restoration of civilian rule by the following October. This rally, which had been permitted by the Bignone administration in an effort to prevent further violence, was called by five of the leading political parties. But what had been planned as a peaceful, antigovernment demonstration got out of hand and brought a clash between protesters and police that resulted in one per-son being killed and eighty injured. This unrest led to a growing fear of anarchy as the nation tried to move from a now weak military regime to democracy. Subsequently President Bignone, bowing to popular demands for an earlier return to civilian government, scheduled the national elections for October 30, 1983—several weeks prior to the date anticipated.

With a change of government approaching, military officers renewed their efforts to obtain, before yielding power to civilians, a blanket guideline agreement that would protect them. Despite an implied threat that without such an agreement, they might not withdraw from power, it was not forth-coming. Finally in September 1983, only five weeks before the national elec-tions, the military government approved an amnesty measure, called the "Law of National Pacification," granting immunity from prosecution for crimes allegedly committed during the "dirty war." Several weeks before it was issued, rumors of a possible amnesty decree by the military had led to protests against such a step by many thousands of civilians. The amnesty announcement itself was followed immediately by further protests and also rulings by more than a dozen judges declaring it invalid as the military government had no legal right to issue such a decree.

RETURN TO DEMOCRACY

Through mid-1983 the two leading parties, Peronist and Radical, together with several minor parties were maneuvering for advantageous positions. Although the Peronist had long been considered the largest and most influential party, it now became bogged down in intra-party feuds as Peronists tried to promote Peronism without Perón. Many Peronists looked to Isabel to make a dramatic return from her exile in Spain and lend her influence to promote the welfare of the party. In view of an expected pardon which would permit her to hold public office again, some delegates favored considering her for the presidential nomination, although others objected because of her poor performance during her previous term. But Isabel remained a while longer in Spain and showed little interest in being considered.

After ten weeks of provincial primaries to select delegates, the Peronist Party opened its national convention on September 3 to choose its nominees for president and vice president and adopt a national platform. So pronounced was the internal strife that several leaders suggested postponing the convention a few days, but this was not done. Instead, the delegates remained and selected as the party's candidate for president Italo A. Luder, a low-key political moderate, who was a former president of the Senate and had served as provisional president of the nation for a month in 1975 while Isabel Perón was ill. During this time he had signed a significant decree allowing the armed forces to combat leftist terrorism. The Peronist nominee for vice president was Deolindo F. Bittel, who, as first vice president of the party, had been its acting head in the absence of Isabel.

Several weeks earlier the Radicals had nominated as their presidential candidate Raúl Ricardo Alfonsín Foulkes, a former member of Congress, an impressive orator, and a staunch advocate of social justice. As leader of the Permanent Assembly for Human Rights, he had become popular by attacking the military governments on human rights issues. His final Buenos Aires campaign rally drew an estimated 800,000 people.

National elections on October 30 resulted in a sweeping victory for the Radical party. Alfonsín won 52 percent of the popular vote with only 40 percent for Luder. This margin assured him victory in the electoral college. Elected with him as vice-president was Víctor Martínez. Radicals also gained control of the Chamber of Deputies, with 129 of the 254 seats. The Peronists won only 111.

Their crushing defeat caused factional quarrels between members of the

Peronist Party as different groups, especially labor leaders, blamed each other for their misfortune. Most Peronists, however, joined millions of other Argentines in welcoming the demise of military rule and the return to elected, civilian government. The spell of Juan Perón had been broken. Without his charismatic leadership, Peronism without Perón had gone down in defeat.

Following the elections, with the foreign debt now more than $40 billion, the world's highest inflation (running some months at an annual rate of around 1,000 percent), unemployment at 15 percent, increasing popular demonstrations against military rule, and divisions within the armed forces on how to deal with this crisis, President Bignone and the junta consented to a request by Alfonsín that they step down in early December and hand over control to the newly elected officials. Thus the return to civilian democracy was advanced from January 30, 1984, to December 10, 1983—Human Rights Day in Argentina.

In a spectacular inaugural ceremony on December 10, Raúl Alfonsín was sworn in as president for a six-year term. Included in the impressive list of invited guests were the heads of many Latin American democracies as well as representatives from the then military-ruled states of Chile, Uruguay, and Brazil. Also present was another invited guest, Isabel Perón, who returned from Spain in time to attend the inauguration. After the swearing-in ceremony in the Congress building, Alfonsín journeyed to the Casa Rosada in a colorful procession to the accompaniment of enthusiastic cheers and applause from many thousands of well-wishers who lined the Avenida de Mayo.

In an address from a balcony of the Cabildo (at the opposite end of the Plaza de Mayo from the Casa Rosada), he told his listeners, "We know that these are hard and difficult moments, but we do not have a single doubt. We Argentines are going to pull out. We will go forward. We will become the country that we deserve."[16]

"Maybe I am just fired up by the majesty of the moment," commented Vice President George Bush, who attended as United States representative, "but this election, this swearing in, signals a new era for Argentina."[17]

General Bignone, who had skillfully guided the nation through the transition to civilian democracy, was now all but forgotten. Only a few people were present as he quietly terminated his administration by slipping out of the Casa Rosada through a service door. Several days earlier the military junta, composed of General Nicolaides, Adm. Rubén Franco, and Brig. Gen. Augusto Hughes of the air force, disbanded itself, and its members voluntarily retired.

In a speech to Congress, President Alfonsín requested that it annul the amnesty that the military had previously decreed. He had been extremely critical of the anti-terrorist campaign conducted by the military governments, but he said prosecution of military officers allegedly guilty of human rights violations should be left to the courts.

Hoping to strengthen her position as head of the Peronist Party, a few days after the inauguration Isabel Perón met with President Alfonsín. She appeared anxious to resume leadership of her party after being out of politics since 1976.

With the aim of promoting closer relations between the United States and Argentina, Vice President Bush talked with Alfonsín for some thirty minutes in the evening after his inauguration. Their conversation included such issues as Argentine repayment of its foreign debt and its nuclear development program. President Alfonsín, who had admired President Carter for his human rights policy, was a critic of President Reagan, who had just lifted the arms embargo that had been imposed on Argentina because of its human rights abuses. Alfonsín indicated he appreciated this move but did not intend to buy arms. He was interested in getting U.S. assistance in renegotiating the foreign debt, while the United States wanted to bring Argentina under the international safeguard treaties regarding its nuclear program.

Argentina's return to democracy was especially influential in neighboring Chile and Uruguay, where people were anxious to get rid of their military regimes. Alfonsín's inauguration brought demonstrations in both Santiago and Montevideo. He had invited leaders from the principal political parties in these two countries. They attended inaugural events and met privately with Alfonsín. The new Argentine foreign minister, Dante Caputo, promised that Argentina would be a strong proponent of democracy and human rights but would not interfere with the internal affairs of its neighbors. Now Argentina, Uruguay, and Chile were headed in the same direction, with Argentina leading the procession from military dictatorship to civilian democracy.

President Alfonsín lost little time implementing reforms he had promised. Within a few days after he requested it, Congress annulled the amnesty decree the military government had issued the previous September. Less than a week after his inauguration, Alfonsín announced that he had set up a commission to investigate the disappearances of thousands of people during the military regimes. He also ordered that members of the ruling juntas during the "dirty war" be court-martialed on charges of instigating kidnappings, torture, and murder. They would be tried in the Supreme Council of the Armed Forces, the top military court, with its verdicts subject to review by the civil Supreme Court. Among those so designated were Jorge Rafael Videla, Roberto Eduardo Viola and Leopoldo Galtieri. By the end of December court-martial proceedings were under way.

Alfonsín made it clear that henceforth he would be commander in chief of the armed forces. He also began downgrading the military by dismissing from posts of command half the army generals, two-thirds of the navy admirals, and many air force brigadiers. Taking advantage of their demoralized condition, he reduced the grossly overgrown military personnel, which had so expanded during the 1970s that they consumed from 30 to 37 percent of total government expenditures. In line with his determination to make the military a professional, nonpolitical organization, he created a new joint chiefs of staff headed by Brig. Gen. Julio Alfredo Fernández Torres and composed of three new service commanders whom he believed friendly to his administration. The new defense minister, Raúl Borrás, was a civilian, and the three services were placed under civilian secretaries.

Not content with limiting the power of the military, President Alfonsín set out to curb the power and influence of the labor unions, which had been very domineering, especially in the Peronist Party. Legislation introduced in Congress would reduce union power by requiring immediate elections in each one and limiting the terms of union leaders to three years with possible reelection for one additional term. The principal objective was to curb the influence of long-time labor leaders by bringing in new ones to replace them. But with strong Peronist opposition, this measure was defeated in the Senate.

The end of military rule did not bring an end to the activities of several human rights groups. Some of them just changed their focus to the new administration and were loud in their demands that it do more in prosecuting military officers and in attempting to locate any *desaparecidos* who might still be alive. Especially active were the Mothers of the Plaza de Mayo, who not only continued their Thursday demonstrations but, along with other human rights organizations, broadened and intensified their demands on the Alfonsín government.

Argentina's greatest problem at this time, as it had been for many years, was the economy. Alfonsín was destined to spend the rest of his term trying to solve it. When he assumed office the most pressing economic problems were the extremely high inflation and the foreign debt, estimated at close to $45 billion. This debt was exceeded only by those of Brazil and Mexico. Most of it had been accumulated by the previous military regimes, much contracted in order to pay for huge imports under direction of Martínez de Hoz during the Videla administration.

With very poor records from the military rulers, it was difficult to determine Argentina's financial status. Alfonsín wanted to put his fiscal house in order during the early part of his term. He said Argentina would honor its debts but would do so on its own terms and that, in spite of the great inflation, the economy was actually sound. He believed that with proper management it would grow and the debts be paid. But with the government on the brink of financial collapse, his problem was how to pay even the interest on its foreign debts and bring inflation under control.

The new minister of economy, Bernardo Grinspun, began negotiating with international banks that held these loans, seeking delay in payments and better terms. In late 1982 Argentina had agreed to spending cuts in order to obtain a $2 billion loan approval from the International Monetary Fund, but had not lived up to its agreement. Grinspun insisted his government intended to pay all its debts, but at that time could not pay even the interest unless it was granted further loans. In January 1984 he visited the United States and discussed with U.S. officials and officers of the IMF in Washington and commercial bankers in New York plans for overall restructuring of the debt.

Alfonsín believed that Argentina's most serious problem was inflation. He and Grinspun began the very difficult task of finding ways to reduce the budget deficit and finance it by less inflationary means than printing money, as the government had been doing. One way Alfonsín contemplated reducing the budget was by drastically cutting the armed forces. On the other hand, he wanted to increase other outlays such as housing, health, and education. A way of decreasing the deficit, which Grinspun recommended, was to increase tax revenues. Evading taxes was an old game in Argentina. People, especially the wealthy, generally paid about half the taxes they owed, and the government had been reluctant to crack down on tax evaders. Certainly a major drain on the government were the state-owned industries. Much of the financial problem could have been solved by disposing of them, but there were only a few that Alfonsín was willing to sell. Another serious drain had been the flight of private capital to safer investments abroad, estimated at some $40 billion over the years of political instability. If Alfonsín could have found a way to recover it, he would have gone a long distance in solving his problem, but with the economic chaos then existing, it was almost impossible to attract much, if any, of this capital back into the country.

With cash reserves of about $1 billion, a 1983 trade surplus expected to reach $3.5 billion, and additional revenue contemplated from new taxes, Grinspun believed there would be enough income to pay the foreign debt. At this time he was more interested in stimulating the economy than in debt payment.

In 1984, with interest payments far in arrears and approximately $20 billion of the principal due that year, Argentina faced a serious financial crisis. With $100 million from its own reserves; short-term loans from Mexico, Venezuela, Brazil, Colombia, and eleven major U.S. banks; and loan guarantees from the U.S. Treasury, a temporary $500 million bailout was arranged by April 1, which enabled Argentina to survive the crisis by paying the long overdue interest. But in mid-1984, with inflation at an annual rate of about 600 percent, Alfonsín continued to resist austerity measures demanded by the IMF before it would approve further loans. He had promised to keep wages rising faster than prices, and he feared austerity would bring severe recession. Moreover, in the most impressive demonstration since he became president, an estimated 60,000 people voiced their opposition to IMF demands and those of international bankers.

During the next five years Argentina continued to stagger from crisis to crisis. Because the currency had become so unmanageable, on June 1, 1983, with the 1970 peso officially down to more than 78,000 per dollar (100,000 on the black market), the Bignone government had issued a new peso valued at 10,000 of the 1970 ones—an exchange rate of approximately 8 per dollar. By the time Alfonsín was sworn in as president on December 10, this cur-

rency was down to about 20 per dollar. By July 1, 1984, it had dropped to
51 per dollar. But the central bank continued to issue pesos and they continued to fall in value.

With salary increases monthly, usually as soon as a person received his
monthly paycheck he went on a shopping spree to spend his pesos before
they declined in value, and he then tried to convert what was left into dollars.
From time to time labor unions staged strikes in support of their demands
for higher wage increases and in protest of other government economic policies. But despite protest strikes and with weak and divided opposition, Alfonsín remained popular, with ratings considerably above the 52 percent by
which he was elected.

On February 18, 1985, Bernardo Grinspun resigned as minister of economy
and was replaced by Juan Sourrouille, former planning secretary. According
to President Alfonsín, this did not mean a change in economic policy, but
actually it did.

On June 14, 1985, with inflation at an annual rate of over 1,000 percent,
the 1983 peso down to 770 per dollar, and a new agreement with the International Monetary Fund, Alfonsín did an about face and began what he
termed an "economy of war," intended to stop inflation. In a television address to the nation he said, "We do not have any option, we have to reconstruct Argentina."[18] He imposed a freeze on prices and wages, stopped the
indexing of all financial contracts, promised a balanced budget, and announced a new currency—the austral, valued at 1,000 pesos, which would
be pegged to the U.S. dollar at $1.25. To maintain the value of this currency,
he promised that the government would stop printing money to balance its
budget. According to Sourrouille, the additional financial burden would be
covered by more foreign loans and by new taxes and a forced savings program if approved by Congress. As a cushion, the administration already had
commitments of over $5 billion in fresh loans.

Although initially there was strong adverse reaction to this economic
shock, within a few days Alfonsín's popularity shot up and even the General
Confederation of Labor indicated its support. After a one-week bank holiday
period, imposed to help absorb the shock, thousands of people lined up at
banks—not to withdraw money but to buy australes with dollars they had
been hoarding. Two months later, after they had experienced hardships
caused by the austerity program, public opinion polls showed about 65 percent of Argentines supported it. And inflation for the month of August 1985
was only 3.1 percent.

For ten months Alfonsín was able to maintain the austral at its original
value of $1.25, but in April 1986 it started a slow decline. At that time the
government relaxed some controls and began to permit wage and price increases within certain limits. This policy set off a more serious rise in inflation,
which for the first seven months of 1986 amounted to over 33 percent. In
October 1987, after inflation of over 135 percent during the previous twelve

months, Alfonsín devalued the austral by 11.5 percent and reimposed wage and price controls. The government had been experiencing severe deficit problems, and by this time the foreign debt had grown to $54 billion. The return of triple-digit inflation contributed to serious losses by the Radical Party in the congressional and gubernatorial elections of September 1987. With price controls frequently violated and labor unions forcing numerous wage concessions, these regulations had become so ineffective that Alfonsín abolished most of them in April 1988. Inflation for the year 1987 was 175 percent.

By January 1, 1989, the austral had dropped to over 16 per dollar, and by the end of March it was down to 41 per dollar. By June 1 it had plunged to 134 per dollar. In July 1989 it took a real nose dive and on July 17 reached 607 per dollar.

What had caused this resumption of Argentina's wild inflation? The fiscal remedies the government had introduced in 1985 had not worked. While it had imposed additional taxes, it had lowered others, particularly the value-added tax, which was a principal source of revenue. Instead of taxes being collected more efficiently as had been anticipated, tax collections actually declined. There were indications that by 1988 tax evasions were greater than ever and people had learned how to evade the forced-savings law. Also most state industries were still there draining away tax revenue. With insufficient income to meet its budget, the government returned to its old practice of printing money. The only difference was that this time it was australes rather than pesos. With its printing presses running twenty-four hours a day, the national mint ground out australes in increasingly higher denominations to fill orders from the central bank for more and more currency. And the faster the bank issued paper australes, the faster they decreased in value.

In September 1984 the National Commission on the Disappearance of Persons, which President Alfonsín had appointed shortly after he was inaugurated, issued its report. According to this document, at least 8,961 people had disappeared during the "dirty war." Subsequent investigations placed the number at more than 9,000. According to the commission, many of these victims were tortured to death under horrible circumstances. There also were many cases of children being abducted and held by their captors, shipped without identification to orphanages, or just seized and abandoned. The commission concluded its lengthy report with, "We are certain that the military dictatorship produced the greatest and most savage tragedy of our history."[19]

As the Supreme Council of the Armed Forces refused to hear the charges against the nine former members of the three ruling juntas, charges that included murder, torture, illegal search, and robbery, these cases were transferred to a civil court where trials began on April 22, 1985, and continued until August 14. The three former heads of state, Generals Videla, Viola, and Galtieri, chose not to attend the sessions or testify in their own defense. The testimony of many witnesses revealed sordid details of atrocities committed by military and police officers. As a result of these trials, five former military leaders were convicted of crimes committed during the "dirty war." Two of these, General Videla and Admiral Massera, both members of the first junta, were given life prison sentences. Also convicted were General Viola, who was sentenced to seventeen years, Adm. Armando Lambruschini, member of the second junta, who received eight years, and Brig. Gen. Orlando Agosti, head of the air force and member of the first junta, who was given four and a half years. Air force Brig. Gen. Omar Graffigna of the second junta and General Galtieri and other members of the junta he headed were acquitted of "dirty war" crimes. Subsequently, in May 1986, General Galtieri, Adm. Jorge I. Anaya, and Brig. Gen. Basilio Lami Dozo were convicted by the Supreme Council of the Armed Forces of negligence in the Falkland Islands War. Galtieri was sentenced to twelve years in prison, Anaya to fourteen years and Lami Dozo to eight years, and all were stripped of their rank and privileges as retired officers.

The trials by a civilian government of these and other military officers involved in the "dirty war" violated a longstanding tradition and set a precedent in Latin America. They also created uneasiness in the minds of military leaders in Uruguay, Chile, and some other Latin American states.

During the early months of the Alfonsín administration the military, now reduced in size and influence, remained cooperative and apparently glad to be relieved of the problems of managing affairs of state. But with the passing of time there was growing unrest in the armed forces. Between April 1987 and December 1988 there were three army rebellions, all of which were suppressed. All of them grew in part out of military resentment over the trials of military officers for their participation in the "dirty war" or the Falklands conflict. Following the 1987 rebellion, at the request of President Alfonsín, Congress enacted legislation dismissing charges against several hundred middle- and lower-rank officers on the grounds that they had acted under orders, but it did not reverse the convictions of former members of the military juntas and other high-rank officers who had been tried and convicted. This law was upheld by the Supreme Court. But it did not satisfy some officers who insisted that members of the armed forces were carrying out an order of then President Isabel Perón to "annihilate" the guerrillas who were causing so much trouble. Italo A. Luder, who had been provisional president during part of her term, said this order to "annihilate" the guerrilla forces meant to "disassemble the actions of the guerrillas, but did not in any way mean to commit excesses."[20]

Economic influences also played a major role leading to the rebellions. Alfonsín well recognized this fact and insisted that military unrest was largely a result of low salaries and lack of funds to replace or repair equipment, and he promised to seek fiscal improvement. In March 1985 a shake-up within the military had occurred when Fernández Torres, the armed forces chief of staff, resigned in protest over reduction in the military budget. As a result of the December 1988 rebellion, the government granted 20 percent pay raises and small bonuses to members of the armed forces.

The army rebellions had been suppressed partly because of Alfonsín's popularity and his personal intervention to restore order. They had also failed because by that time there was a strong desire among many members of the armed forces to preserve the democracy that had been restored. President Alfonsín had curbed the independence, and won the support, of the military. A result was much popular rejoicing that democracy had prevailed.

During the Alfonsín years the Peronists were in the process of trying to heal rifts within the party and regain their former position as Argentina's most powerful political organization. In response to a special request from Alfonsín, Isabel Perón returned to Buenos Aires from Spain in May 1984. Alfonsín wanted to promote political harmony and thought she might be helpful in healing Peronist wounds. He was anxious to get the Peronists working with him in trying to solve Argentina's economic problems and believed that Isabel, as technically head of the party, would be the logical one to bring this about. But her visit accomplished little toward promoting intraparty harmony. By early 1985 two strong and hostile factions had appeared, each claiming to be the real Peronist Party. Both reelected Isabel Perón as titular head, primarily because she was Juan Perón's widow, but soon thereafter she resigned to prevent either of the quarreling factions from using her name. "I want to be a symbol of peace for the entire country," she said during another visit to Buenos Aires in October 1988.[21]

In 1987 Peronists went through a period of renovation and made an impressive comeback in that year's September elections. They emerged with sixteen governorships and 108 seats in the Chamber of Deputies. They already had 21 Senate seats and there were no Senate elections at that time. Two significant Peronists who won in the 1987 elections were Antonio Cafiero, elected governor of Buenos Aires Province, and Carlos Saúl Menem, reelected governor of the northwest province of La Rioja.

In July 1988 the principal Argentine political parties selected their presidential candidates to run in the May 1989 elections. The nominee of the Radical Civic Union was Eduardo Angeloz, governor of the industrial and politically significant province of Córdoba and one of the few Radical governors to survive the 1987 elections. In the Peronist (Justicialist) Party primary Menem, law school classmate of Angeloz, won an upset victory over Cafiero. A third candidate was Alvaro Alsogaray, nominee of the Union of the Democratic Center. Several other minor parties also chose candidates. As in the United States, Argentines voted for sets of electors, who in turn elected the president. A candidate needed 301 electoral votes to win.

Menem was born in La Rioja of immigrant parents from Syria. Like his father and mother, he was a Muslim, but he converted to Catholicism. His wife, Zulema Yoma, also from a Syrian family, who remained a Muslim, claimed her husband became a Catholic to qualify for the Argentine presidency. (According to the constitution, only a Roman Catholic could be president.) With the Radical Party at a disadvantage because of the serious economic situation, Menem quickly became the front runner in the presidential race, although many Argentines were apprehensive about having another Peronist in the Casa Rosada. His vice presidential running mate was Eduardo Duhalde.

National elections on May 14, 1989, resulted in a sweeping victory for the Peronists. They not only won control of the Chamber of Deputies but also of most provincial legislatures, which in turn elected members of the national Senate. Menem and Duhalde received less than half the popular votes but got 310 of the 600 electoral votes. During his campaign, Menem had promised the people higher incomes and better living conditions while Argentina's creditors and most economists were calling for greater austerity. Now, with extreme inflation, the foreign debt about $60 billion, and interest on this debt approximately a year in arrears, Menem, who had the reputation of never being able to say no, faced the problem of reconciling his promises with reality.

Although elections were held in mid-May, President Alfonsín's term legally ran until December 10, 1989. But near the end of May, food shortages, increasing unemployment, and inflation of 78 percent for the month set off four days of looting and rioting that claimed more than a dozen lives. This crisis brought many demands that Alfonsín terminate his presidency ahead of schedule. Under these circumstances and in view of the apparent impossibility of quickly improving the economic picture, he offered to step down before the end of his six years even though previously he had expressed a strong desire to complete the term for which he had been elected. Initially Menem was not inclined to assume power before December and thus take on sooner than planned the burdens that the Radicals were leaving him, but after some hesitation he agreed to begin his term early. And so it was arranged that Alfonsín would leave office on July 8.

On that morning the Argentine Congress accepted his resignation. Then Carlos Saúl Menem was sworn in as the new president by his brother, Eduardo, president of the Senate. Carlos Menem and his wife rode in the traditional Cadillac convertible amid cheering throngs down the Avenida de Mayo to the Casa Rosada. There they were met by Raúl Alfonsín. After a brief ceremony during which he hung the blue-and-white presidential sash on Menem, Alfonsín was heard to bid the crowd farewell with the words "Hasta luego." One of the guests at this ceremony was Isabel Perón. In his inaugural address, Menem told his audience that Argentina "is broke and in this historic hour its reconstruction begins." He said he was only able to offer the Argentine people "sacrifice, work, and hope."[22]

Before his inauguration, Menem had chosen an eight-member cabinet whose orientation was termed right of center. Two members of this cabinet were not Peronists. One of these was Domingo Cavallo, a Harvard-trained economist, who was appointed foreign minister in the hope that he would be helpful in renegotiating the foreign debt. The other non-Peronist was a retired business executive, Miguel Roig, who was appointed minister of economy. One of the Peronist appointees was Italo Luder, chosen defense minister for the purpose of improving relations with the military. Among significant noncabinet appointees were Alsogaray, founder of the pro-free market Union of the Democratic Center, as an economic adviser, and his daughter, María Julia Alsogaray, a congressional deputy, to lead the privatization of the national telephone company. Menem's cabinet choices brought protests from left-wing Peronists.

President Menem's economic advisers lost no time in tackling what he termed the worst crisis Argentina had ever experienced. With inflation of 114.5 percent for the month of June expected to increase to 200 percent for July, foreign reserves almost exhausted, and various industries closing, they began by dealing with the inflation, which was considered of greatest immediate concern. Among the first steps were devaluation of the austral from 250 down to 615 per dollar, the freezing of prices at the July 3 level, drastic rises of up to 500 percent in public utility rates, and an immediate and substantial increase in July salaries. These measures were aimed primarily at slowing inflation before moving on toward a free-market economy, which would be a reversal of the longstanding Peronist policy of economic domination by the state. Other Menem objectives that were drastic departures from the original Peronist regime were close ties with the United States and more foreign investments. Another important part of the long-range plans was the privatization of government-owned industries. A serious blow to these reforms was the sudden death of the economic minister, Miguel Roig. He was replaced by Néstor Rapanelli, his successor as executive vice president of the prominent Argentine grain and industrial company Bunge and Born. How far Menem had moved from old Peronist policies is indicated by his now close association with this company in shaping his economic reforms. He also came to rely more heavily on his foreign minister, the prominent economist Cavallo.

Six months after Menem was inaugurated president, Argentines were still wallowing in hyperinflation, which hit almost 200 percent for the month of July. During the next four months wage and price controls together with government promises to reduce public expenditures brought monthly inflation down to 38 percent in August and subsequently between 5 and 7 percent. But after replacing the economic minister, Rapanelli, with Antonio Ermán González, former vice president of the central bank, replacing most of his other economic advisers, and terminating his reliance on advice from Bunge and Born, Menem did not yet have a team that came up with a satisfactory solution. With the government apparently unable to reduce spending and collect sufficient taxes, in December inflation was soaring again at

40 percent for the month. For too long Argentines had been addicted to the "free ride" and they still expected it.

In late December, while insisting they continued to support civilian government, commanders of all three branches of the armed forces issued warnings that the economic situation was endangering Argentine democracy. By way of comparing economic growth and efficiency in neighboring Chile with the economic muddling in Argentina, a graffiti artist expressed the feelings of many Argentines when he decorated one side of a building with the words, "¡Viva Pinochet!"

From the time he was inaugurated, President Menem was faced with demands by members of the armed forces to free officers who were in prison or undergoing trial for alleged crimes during the "dirty war." At the same time, he was under much pressure from human rights groups and relatives of "dirty war" victims not to do so. Raúl Alfonsín spoke out, urging Menem not to grant sweeping pardons. In early September 1989 some 30,000 people demonstrated in downtown Buenos Aires in opposition to such pardons. Nevertheless, a few days later Menem stated his intention to pardon eighteen retired generals and admirals who were facing trial and said he would consider later those already sentenced.

On October 7, 1989, the government announced that by decree President Menem had pardoned military officers accused of human rights abuses during the "dirty war" and also those charged with misconduct in the Falkland Islands War and the three military uprisings of 1987 and 1988, as well as alleged subversives who were in prison. Among those released was General Galtieri. Menem said his primary reason for these pardons was to placate members of the armed forces and promote cooperation between them and the civilian government. Not released at this time were top leaders involved in the "dirty war," including General Videla, General Viola, Admiral Massera, and Ramón Camps and Ovidio Ricchieri, former chief and deputy chief of the Buenos Aires police. They, together with Carlos Suárez Mason, former army chief of staff, and Mario Firmenich, cofounder of the Montoneros guerrillas, were released by presidential pardons on December 29, 1990—a carefully chosen holiday weekend to limit media attention and confuse human rights groups that had called for protest demonstrations. Menem said these pardons would "definitely close a sad and black period of Argentine history." But Alfonsín termed December 29 "the saddest day in Argentine history."[23]

With the economy still in deep trouble, the austral, which had been pegged at 655 per dollar, fell to 1,200 when it was freed in mid-December 1989. After that it fluctuated for several weeks between 1,200 and 2,000 before dropping to 5,000 per dollar at the end of February 1990. By this time Argentines were debating whether they should adopt the U.S. dollar as their official currency. One argument in favor of this was that there were enough dollars in circulation or hidden in Argentina (believed to be around 5 billion) and invested abroad (about 50 billion) to support an official dollar economy.

CURBING INFLATION

On January 31, 1991, the austral sank to 9,455 per dollar. Two days earlier President Menem made a significant appointment, shifting his foreign minister, Domingo Felipe Cavallo, to the post of minister of economy. He was Menem's fourth economic minister in a little more than eighteen months, and he was destined to have a profound effect on the Argentine economy. During the preceding year Menem had been reducing government payrolls by selling deficit-ridden state industries to private investors. But inflation for that year was 2,314 percent, and popular discontent was widespread.

Soon after his appointment Cavallo announced that the austral would be kept at an exchange rate of 8,000 to 10,000 per dollar and henceforth the central bank would be independent from the finance ministry. A few days later he presented a plan to eliminate Argentina's deficit. The exchange rate of the currency was firmly set at 10,000 australes per dollar. Supporting this action was a new act of Congress prohibiting the central bank from issuing any more australes that were not backed by gold or hard currency. With 60,000 jobs already eliminated from government payrolls, Cavallo promised to slash employment further if necessary to maintain a balanced budget.

"We are now really committed to budgetary equilibrium," he said, "and I have very strong support from the President on that."[24]

He also advocated selling other costly government businesses and cracking down on tax evaders. With respect to privatization, he said, "The Government is not a businessman, and business should be in the hands of entrepreneurs."[25]

Another part of his plan was to force Argentine industry to become more competitive by reducing import and export duties. "We have to be integrated to the world, not isolated like we were for six decades," Cavallo stated.[26]

Although this plan was similar to others that had failed, it was given a good chance of success because of Cavallo's determination and influence. As Menem's foreign minister, he had made a favorable impression by restoring diplomatic ties with Great Britain, which had been broken since the Falkland Islands War. Now, as economic minister, this devoted advocate of orthodox economics, with a Ph.D. in economics from Harvard and strong support from the Argentine president, was granted so much power that he came to be referred to as the prime minister. He brought with him to the economic ministry over 100 associates from his prestigious consulting firm, Fundación Mediterránea, who proved valuable in formulating various reforms.

Cavallo committed the government to live strictly within its fiscal means, with a currency tied to the dollar and tax laws rigidly enforced. Many of his supporters predicted he would stick by his rules and see his plan succeed because he had a great desire to be the next president.

By the end of May the plan seemed to be working, with inflation down from triple to double digits and continuing to fall, and annual interest rates down from 200 percent to 10 percent. The big question now was whether this government would—or could—abide by its orders and accomplish what its predecessors had not.

By September 1991 the Cavallo plan was proving very popular, with public opinion polls showing at least 62 percent approval. Cavallo's personal approval rating of 52 percent was about the same as that of President Menem. With the currency stabilized, tariffs lowered, and the availability of a $1 billion standby loan from the IMF, Argentina's fiscal position had drastically improved. As a result, significant investments were coming in from various parts of the world. Cavallo now appeared to be emerging as a credible candidate to succeed President Menem at the end of his term, but Menem had begun indicating that he would like to remain in office a second term if he could arrange to have the constitution amended to permit his doing so.

Menem made sincere efforts to reverse the previous strained relations with the United States. Less than three months after becoming president, he visited Washington and began referring to President Bush as his "good friend." In this and subsequent visits to the United States, as well as in other ways, Menem promoted a closer Argentine-U.S. relationship.

In November 1991, a few days prior to another U.S. visit, Menem issued an executive decree providing a broad deregulation of the economy, formulated by Cavallo and his associates in the economic ministry. The purpose of this decree was to abolish many years of economic protection and regulation by the government. Bypassing possible delays in Congress by means of the decree, Menem eliminated all import and export quotas, abolished controls over professional fees as well as critical industries, and ended labor union control over large amounts of retirement funds. These reforms gave Argentina one of the freest economies in Latin America—next to that of Chile. Cavallo now claimed that 150,000 new jobs in private industries had been created since his plan was put into effect the previous March.

In mid-November, with the Argentine currency stable, inflation down to less than 1 percent a month, and the economy growing about 5 percent a year, Menem made a state visit to Washington, where he was accorded a warm welcome. In a ceremony on the south lawn of the White House, which included a twenty-one-gun salute, President Bush said, "Under your leadership, Argentina has become one of the hemisphere's strongest defenders of democracy, both at home and abroad."[27]

In an address to a joint session of Congress, Menem made a plea for free trade between the United States and Argentina and also a trading community embracing the entire Western Hemisphere. He told the members of Congress that his privatization plan would be completed by 1993.

While Menem welcomed the opportunity of a state visit to enhance his image as a Latin American leader, his principal interest was gaining financial assistance in solving Argentina's debt problem and finding investors for its state-run industries. While in Washington he conferred with heads of the

International Monetary Fund, World Bank, and Inter-American Development Bank as well as Secretary of the Treasury Nicholas F. Brady regarding Argentina's international financial arrangements. Also there and in New York and Houston he met with potential investors in Argentina. Overall this United States visit was quite successful and revealed how Argentina's stature had grown since Menem had become president.

During the early days of his administration Menem turned his back on original Peronist doctrine when he began his drive to privatize state-owned industries, many of which had been brought under government control by Perón in the 1940s amid the strong spirit of nationalism that he encouraged. But Argentina's Peronist government of 1989 represented a different philosophy from that of the 1940s, and public sentiment at this time was a contrast to what it had been in the early years of Peronism. Thus a bill for privatization that Menem sent to Congress in July 1989 was approved unanimously by the Senate. Nevertheless, because of the large number of jobs that would be abolished, there was strong opposition to privatization, led by organized labor, the traditional backbone of Peronism.

Industries to be privatized included the state telephone company; railroads; the national airline, Aerolineas Argentinas; the state electric, water, and gas companies; state-owned banks; many industries under military control; and various others, including the "crown jewel" of all, the state oil company, YPF. Another enterprise (which became controversial) was the Buenos Aires zoo and botanical gardens. One of the most successful privatization transactions was the sale of the telephone company in late 1990, which brought almost $3 billion. Sales of stock in the electric company were estimated to produce more than $2 billion, but they also created problems for a company that purchased part of these facilities when it tried to cut power to thousands of Buenos Aires shantytown residents who had been illegally tapping into the electric system when it was government owned. Although buying state-owned industries was not always profitable, many purchasers of these enterprises found that, with good management and minor improvements, they could earn large returns. Two years after sale of the telephone company, which had been a real loser, it was producing profits of almost $400 million a year.

The last big privatization step was sale of 45 percent of YPF. The timing of this sale was determined largely by Menem's desire to be reelected president. With congressional elections scheduled for October 3, 1993, it was very important to him that the Peronist Party gain enough seats to approve constitutional changes that would permit him to run for a second term. With approximately $2.5 billion owed to more than a million retirees in August and September, funds from this sale were essential to pay these obligations. Peronist Party officials feared disaster if they failed to pay them on time. After a major reorganization, including a drastic reduction in the number of employees from approximately 50,000 to about 10,000, YPF, which had lost money in the 1980s, became profitable in the 1990s. In what was considered the largest privatization deal in Latin America, in late June 1993 the government sold 160 million shares of YPF stock for over $3 billion. After this transaction Argentines still owned 72 percent of the company. Only the government—not the nation—had relinquished control.

During this period several other Latin American countries were carrying out privatization programs. Except for that of Mexico, Argentina's was considered the most successful.

Argentina began the year 1992 with a new currency, the peso—old in name but new in value. At 10,000 per dollar, the austral was now stable but inconvenient to use. The new peso, worth 10,000 australes, was on a par with the U.S. dollar. Cavallo and Menem were determined that it remain so. Again Argentina had a peso, but it would take 10 trillion 1946 pesos to equal the value of this one! Thus far had the value of printing-press money declined since 1946 when Perón gained control of the government, then enjoying abundant financial resources, and set it on the road of fiscal irresponsibility.

By July 1993 the government had disposed of most of its industries, tax collection had improved, and unemployment was about 7.8 percent. Since 1991, with an average of almost 9 percent a year, Argentina had one of Latin America's highest rates of economic growth. In spite of loud complaints from thousands of government employees who had lost their jobs, retirees demanding higher pensions, and other people who were feeling the squeeze of Cavallo's cutbacks to balance the budget, he stuck by his economic plan and resisted calls to devalue the peso. He had strong support from President Menem, who said, "with Cavallo we form an indestructible team."[28] In 1992 agreements were reached between Argentina and its creditor banks whereby its debt was reduced and past due interest payments were made. This policy was in line with agreements regarding their debts reached by several other Latin American countries.

One of the chief complaints against Menem's administration was his apparent tolerance of corruption, which became very serious. Early in his regime his wife, Zulema, playing an active public role, was often very critical of her husband's policies. She especially criticized the great amount of corruption she saw in the government. She sought a more active political role and said Carlos needed her to help control corruption.

In early 1994, with prices stable, practically no inflation, a predicted economic growth of 6 percent for the year, and Cavallo still at the helm, the economic picture looked good. President Menem continued his close relations with the United States and made another visit in late June, during which he met with President Bill Clinton in Washington and ex-President Bush at his home in Kennebunkport, Maine. Bowing to U.S. pressure, Menem had dismantled Argentina's ballistic missile and nuclear weapons projects, which had long been a controversial issue between the United States and Argentina. After Clinton became U.S. president, Menem began urging him to approve a free trade agreement between the two countries.

"I did not come to office to put in place a Peronist program, but a program for Argentina," Menem stated.[29] Indeed, the Peronism of free enterprise, balanced budgets, and other sound economic policies which Menem has established since 1989 are radically different from the labor-dominated welfare state with government-owned industries that Perón imposed on Argentina. Theoretically in December 1983 Argentina moved from military dictatorship to civilian democracy. But the democracy of Raúl Alfonsín was eclipsed by the civilian dictatorship of Carlos Saúl Menem, as he ruled by decree and packed the Supreme Court, thus effectively bypassing both Congress and the judiciary.

Although Menem departed very far from most of Perón's policies, the one Perón example he has imitated is the attempt to get himself reelected for a second term. The congressional elections of October 3, 1993, gave the Peronists an overwhelming victory. This result greatly improved Menem's chances of winning approval of constitutional changes that would permit his serving a second consecutive term. Although the Peronists did not gain a two-thirds majority in Congress to assure amendment of the constitution, they did have a working majority. But reforms permitting Menem to run for a second term would not necessarily assure his election. In polls conducted shortly before the October elections, 60 percent of those polled favored the proposed reforms, but only 30 percent indicated they would vote for Menem for a second term.

In mid-November 1993 Menem and former President Alfonsín, leader of the Radical Civic Union, reached an agreement whereby the Radicals would support Menem's proposed constitutional changes in return for his agreement to transfer some executive powers to Congress. Under the proposed reforms the six-year presidential term would be shortened to four years with the right to immediate reelection for one additional term. Also the requirement that the president be a Roman Catholic would be eliminated. There would be more checks on the decree powers of the president, which pleased the Radicals since they were in a very weak position at that time. In December the Menem-Alfonsín agreements were approved by both houses of Congress.

In an April 1994 election for a constituent assembly to amend or rewrite the constitution, the Peronists won by a smaller margin than they expected. One reason for this was widespread concern about corruption in Menem's government. Nevertheless, in the constituent assembly, meeting the following August, these proposed changes were adopted.

In mid-1994, with annual inflation under 5 percent, many billions of dollars in new investments, and economic growth among the world's highest, Ar-

gentina was looked upon as a model of progress. But many Argentines were
dissatisfied. On July 6 more than 40,000 people, mainly from the interior
provinces, arrived in Buenos Aires, assembled in front of the Casa Rosada,
and staged a two-hour, peaceful protest against government economic policies. Contrary to Menem's claim that conditions were improving, demonstrators charged that economic growth had favored the cities and not the
remote regions, where salaries were low and many jobs had been abolished.
But Menem said their protest would "accomplish absolutely nothing."[30]

In November, with elections, scheduled for May 1995, still six months
away, Menem's chance of winning a second term looked good. But with
primaries still to be held by other parties and followed by a lengthy campaign
period, the outcome of the 1995 elections was definitely uncertain. A prime
question was whether Menem, who had departed so far from Perón's economic policies, would match his success in retaining the presidency. A question of even greater significance was whether Argentina will stay on its
present course after Menem and Cavallo cease piloting the ship of state.

NOTES

1. *The Evening Star* (Washington), October 27, 1955.
2. *The New York Times*, July 4, 1966.
3. *The New York Times*, August 26, 1967.
4. *The New York Times*, July 7, 1970.
5. *The New York Times*, March 25, 1971.
6. *The New York Times*, March 11 and 13, 1973.
7. *The New York Times*, August 13, 1975.
8. *The New York Times*, March 28, 1976.
9. *The New York Times*, July 7, 1974.
10. *U.S. News & World Report*, April 5, 1976.
11. *The New York Times*, April 1, 1976.
12. *The Washington Star*, December 17, 1978.
13. *The New York Times*, March 30, 1979.
14. *The New York Times*, March 30, 1981.
15. *The Washington Post*, June 16, 1982.
16. *The New York Times*, December 11, 1983.
17. Ibid.
18. *The New York Times*, June 15, 1985.
19. *The New York Times*, September 23, 1984.
20. *The New York Times*, April 23, 1985.
21. *The New York Times*, November 15, 1988.
22. *The New York Times*, July 9, 1989.
23. *The New York Times*, December 30, 1990; *The Washington Post*, December 30, 1990.
24. *The New York Times*, April 28, 1991.
25. Ibid.
26. Ibid.

27. *The Washington Post*, November 15, 1991.
28. *The New York Times*, November 16, 1992.
29. *The Washington Post*, November 16, 1991.
30. *The New York Times*, July 7, 1994.

Chapter 4

Chile: Democracy That Was

South America has been termed a continent of contrasts, as indeed it is. Within this continent of contrasts there is a land of extremes—the Republic of Chile.

GEOGRAPHIC AND DEMOGRAPHIC INFLUENCES

A quick look at a South American map reveals that Chile is a country extreme at least in shape—more than 2,600 miles long, with an average width of a little over 100 miles. In area it is larger than the state of Texas, which indicates what an outline of Texas might look like if it were stretched entirely across the United States.

Chile's eastern boundary is one of the world's greatest natural barriers, the cordillera of the Andes, including the highest peaks in the Western Hemisphere. On the west are some of the deepest parts of the Pacific Ocean. It is possible to stand on a peak at the eastern border nearly 23,000 feet above sea level and look down on an ocean 26,000 feet deep!

Northern Chile is a desert, one of the driest spots on earth, in parts of which rainfall has never been recorded. Southern Chile is one of the world's wettest regions, where natives say it rains forty days in the month and thirteen months of the year. Between these two extremes—in an area extending from Coquimbo and La Serena south about 800 miles—live some 90 percent of the approximately 14 million Chilean people. Except for earthquakes, which have caused much destruction, it is a very pleasant and fertile land. This is Chile's breadbasket, where from colonial times until the mid-twentieth century Chileans produced not only enough to feed themselves but considerable food for export. The northern desert, most of which was acquired from Bolivia and Peru in the War of the Pacific in the late nineteenth century, is especially important for its mineral deposits. These—first nitrate, and subsequently copper (found here as well as in other parts of the country)—have been the backbone of Chile's economy for more than a century.

"God must be an Argentine," runs a well-known Chilean proverb. "He placed these mountains so far west they almost push Chile into the sea." Actually Chile has certain advantages over most other Latin American states. One is geographic. Although many Chileans consider themselves victims of discrimination by being confined to this narrow land, really it has been a benefit. The Andean cordillera and the Atacama Desert have separated and protected them from their neighbors and permitted them to develop as they wished without serious interference. The concentration of people in the narrow central zone has facilitated political and economic development.

The Chileans enjoy other advantages. During the long colonial period Chile was looked upon by the Spanish crown as one of its less important colonies. It did not have great quantities of gold and silver or a numerous, docile Indian population that could be enslaved; it was established as an agricultural colony of large estates, dominated by a powerful, landholding aristocracy. Being far removed and isolated from the mother country, the Chileans were left more to themselves and had a better opportunity to develop on their own than did the inhabitants of such colonies as Peru and Mexico, which were more important in Spanish eyes and on which Spain concentrated her attention.

Another Chilean advantage has been people. There the Spaniards encountered the fierce, liberty-loving Araucanians, who inhabited the territory from middle Chile southward and had maintained their independence against attempted Inca encroachments from the north. Subsequently many immigrants arrived from northern Spain and, after independence, from northern Europe. Clashes between the Europeans and the Indians, as well as the mingling of these two racial groups, produced a compatible society noted for independence and endurance. Often termed the "Yankees of South America" (a term also applied to the Argentines), modern Chileans are products of a civilization based on values and customs different from those of most other Latin Americans. While there have been pronounced caste differences, a considerably larger middle class appeared, even in the colonial era and just after, than in most other Spanish colonies. Today's annual population growth of about 1.6 percent is reasonable.

EARLY DEMOCRACY

With these advantages, after achieving independence in 1818, Chile was able to move quickly through the turbulent period that normally beset other newly independent Spanish American states. By the early 1830s it settled down to a stable but progressive existence, and within two decades it came to be recognized as the leading Latin American republic. Its long record of democracy, broken only by military intervention in 1924–32 and again in the 1970s and 1980s, has been unequaled in Latin America.

The 1833 Constitution, under which Chile lived until 1925, established an aristocratic republic, similar in many respects to that of the early United States, except that it was highly centralized, as appropriate for the background and environment. With indirect election of the president and members of the Senate, and literacy and property qualifications for voting, it was controlled by a landholding aristocracy. After the 1830s, however, this government gradually evolved into something more democratic and more liberal—a process that also occurred in the United States.

It is convenient to trace the history of Chile through the nineteenth and much of the twentieth century as is customary in the United States—namely, by administrations, because they follow in regular order. During the first forty years, beginning in 1831, there were only four presidents, each serving two five-year terms. (They were Joaquín Prieto, 1831–41; Manuel Bulnes, 1841–51; Manuel Montt, 1851–61; José Joaquín Pérez, 1861–71.) After a constitutional amendment in the late 1860s prohibited two successive terms, there were five-year presidents but still in regular order of succession with little political turmoil until 1924, except in 1891.

Chile's orderly political development began in the 1830s as a two-party system. The Conservative and Liberal Parties, as they were known, became exceedingly well established, and for several decades in the early- and mid-nineteenth century Chile governed itself peacefully and progressively under this arrangement. But gradually both of these parties split—first into two factions and subsequently into more—until by the latter part of the century Chile was operating under a multiparty system. In this process, government had become considerably more democratic but also more complicated and inefficient. The trend had been from conservative to liberal, with the Conservative Party in power until 1871, when the Liberals took over.

This trend was due in no small measure to an increasing middle-class influence, resulting in part from the rising level of education. Chile today enjoys a high degree of literacy—estimated at over 90 percent. It was carefully planned that way in the early years of independence. Bernardo O'Higgins, first ruler of independent Chile, who governed with dictatorial powers, said that Chileans were not ready then to govern themselves because most were uneducated. He and other political leaders agreed that a comprehensive educational program was needed, and they set about to provide it. Because of the large middle class and consequent demand for mass education, rather consistently over the nineteenth and twentieth centuries the school system has been extended, and gradually there has appeared a numerous, literate electorate. Education to govern themselves led Chileans to more democracy but also, in time, to some serious problems.

Along with proliferation of political parties and the liberal trend, the mid- and late nineteenth century also witnessed the rising power of Congress.

This reached a climax toward the latter part of the century and resulted in a civil war in 1891. It was a war between Congress and the president over the respective powers of the chief executive and the legislative body, particularly with regard to cabinet appointments and budgetary matters. The military was divided, with the regular army remaining loyal to the president and the navy, reinforced by a hastily recruited but well-equipped revolutionary army, supporting Congress. The devastating struggle, which cost some 10,000 lives, ended in a congressional victory and President José Manuel Balmaceda's suicide. It resulted in a modified parliamentary system of government in which Congress was the dominant factor.

Parliamentary government did not work well in Chile. From a system with the president all-powerful, in national as well as local affairs, Chile moved into one in which the Congress was supreme and the president subject to the whims of the legislative body. Gone was the former power of the chief executive and his party to control national elections and appoint municipal officials. In his appointment of cabinet members as well as in other matters, the president was forced to act according to the will of the congressional majority, over which he had no control. Parliamentary government can operate effectively in a country of two main parties where the head of state is backed by the party with a majority in the legislature. But in Chile the president was not assured of such support. Moreover, in a multiparty system, where it is virtually impossible for one party to gain a congressional majority, government is necessarily by coalition. This situation presents serious difficulties. The composition of a coalition can change quickly and its power may shift accordingly. Under these circumstances, Chile's parliamentary experiment resulted in frequent cabinet reformations, a breakdown of effective administrative leadership, and general political stagnation.

Because of the widespread prosperity of the 1890s and early twentieth century, the country was able to muddle through. It was in the midst of impressive economic growth; and until the competition of synthetic nitrate after World War I, the income from nitrate duties alone was so large that the government did not have to worry much about other revenue. The influx of foreign capital and the arrival of new immigrants from Europe also contributed to the overall development.

Nevertheless, the governmental system seemed to breed corruption. Bribery was prevalent from the highest to the lowest levels. The composition of Congress deteriorated and this body became topheavy with members who appeared more interested in their own welfare than that of the nation. The office of president had, in effect, been repudiated; and after 1891 the chief executive often was ignored by congressional leaders. In the absence of any strict regulation, political parties continued to increase in number as politicians recognized the advantages of heading even a small party rather than merely belonging to a large one. Under these circumstances, most parties became personal rather than ideological in orientation. Along with administrative disorganization went serious fiscal irresponsibility and waste. From a responsible, aristocratic republic, Chile was transformed into a corrupt democracy.

Until 1920 the landholding aristocracy managed to remain rather securely in control; but the rise of mining, manufacturing, and international trade had brought a new, wealthy class, which had little or no connection with the old oligarchy. These economic leaders were now exerting an increasing political influence. Also, by this time many of Chile's masses, who felt they had not shared in the nation's prosperity, were making themselves heard. In previous years there had been pleas for labor protection and social welfare legislation, and the few concessions that had been granted only served to stimulate a more vocal demand for others. Labor unrest in urban and mining areas continued to grow and was intensified by effects of the economic depression resulting primarily from collapse of the nitrate market after World War I. In addition to these elements, a new, educated middle class, faced with very limited employment opportunities, was now quite influential.

A combination of such groups led to the election in 1920 of Chile's first "man of the people," Arturo Alessandri, candidate of the Liberal Alliance, composed of some fifteen liberal parties or factions. Alessandri's elevation to the presidency was a result of the rising influence of the forgotten masses and his promise to them of profound social, fiscal, and political reforms, including a new constitution to restore the power of the president, extend voting privileges to all adult citizens, including women, and separate church and state. What happened in Chile in 1920 was also a reflection of a similar political turnabout in Argentina four years earlier.

POLITICAL INSTABILITY

Although as president Alessandri appeared more moderate than he had as a candidate, he encountered serious difficulties in obtaining congressional approval of any of his proposed reforms. For more than three years, with a liberal majority only in the Chamber of Deputies, Congress was unresponsive, even in raising revenue. Moreover, the conservative Senate forced Alessandri to make frequent cabinet changes. After the Liberal Alliance won control of both chambers in the elections of early 1924, the legislative body still remained uncooperative. Within a few months this attitude led to a political crisis and military intervention.

The Chilean armed forces have quite a different history from those of virtually every other Latin American republic. Since the early nineteenth century, they have been composed of very professional, well-organized, efficient units. The policy of the military has been to support civilian, constitutional government, protect the duly elected administration, defend the country, preserve order, and stay out of politics. With rare exceptions, it has stuck to this policy. It has already been noted that in 1891 the military became involved in the struggle between the president and Congress, with the army and navy divided over the issue. But this clash was of relatively short duration and did not result in military control of the government. Twice since then, however, the armed forces have been drawn into political strife, and on both occasions they have assumed an administrative role. The first of these incidents was in 1924.

By September the endless debates and inaction in Congress, together with increasing demands for reforms and the fact that their own salaries were in arrears, spurred the army to intervene. Under military pressure, Congress quickly passed several reform bills and the president signed them. Included was an act inaugurating a social security system. Then, by way of more clearly voicing his objections to the chaotic political situation and military intervention, President Alessandri departed from the country after being granted a leave of absence by Congress. Thereupon the military took complete control, dismissed Congress, and appointed a junta to run the government—all apparently with popular approval. The junta, which proved more conservative than the initiators of the military coup, remained in power until late January 1925, when it was pushed out by an ambitious group of younger and more liberal officers, led by Col. Carlos Ibáñez del Campo. One of their first acts was to recall Alessandri from his self-imposed exile in Europe. He returned in March, received an enthusiastic welcome, and resumed his duties as president.

A result of this turn of events was the assembling of a convention that formulated a new constitution, as Alessandri had promised during his campaign for the presidency. It deprived Congress of the right to force the resignation of cabinet ministers, forbade members of Congress to serve in the cabinet, and limited the power of the legislative body in budgetary matters. It provided for direct election of the president for a six-year term, with no immediate reelection. Suffrage was granted to all literate males over twenty-one years of age. Church and state were separated and freedom of religion was guaranteed. The political influence of the Roman Catholic Church, established as the state religion by the 1833 Constitution, had been curbed gradually over the intervening years; now the effects of complete separation were eased by permitting the church to retain its extensive real estate holdings and granting it government financial support for an additional five years.

The Constitution of 1925, ratified by national plebiscite in August, repudiated parliamentary government, which admittedly had not been a success. Officially it restored the authority of the president. But tradition is difficult to eradicate, and by 1925 a strong legislative body had become traditional. As became quite evident in later years, the power of Congress, although never as great as between 1891 and 1924, had been curbed more in theory than in practice.

The return of Alessandri and the promulgation of a new constitution had not brought an end to military interference in government. Politically ambitious Carlos Ibáñez was now minister of war, and with a presidential election scheduled for October, he pressed his candidacy while at the same time refusing to relinquish his cabinet portfolio. Unable to persuade Ibáñez to leave, and fearing a military crisis and possible bloodshed should he dismiss him, Alessandri resigned a few months before his term as president was due to expire and again left the country.

Although Ibáñez subsequently agreed to step aside and permit a free election, it was now clear that he was the political strongman. From December 1925 until May 1927 Chile had an elected, civilian chief executive, Emiliano Figueroa Larraín, but Ibáñez really was in control. In the meantime, he managed to shift his position to become minister of the interior, which placed him next in line for the presidency. Thereupon, when the ineffectual president was pressured into resigning, Ibáñez assumed the office temporarily. He then hastily called an election and, without giving any potential opponent reasonable time to campaign, got himself confirmed for a six-year term. Through such a maneuver, Chilean voters were induced to elect a dictator.

The time was right for a dictatorial president. Many people were weary of the recent instability and welcomed a chief executive who appeared capable of restoring order in government. Moreover, the current economic prosperity helped create an environment in which a diminution of political liberty might be more readily overlooked by the general public than under less favorable circumstances.

By jailing political opponents, muzzling the press, and suppressing existing political parties, Ibáñez achieved firm control over the country. Having thus gained political supremacy, he instituted a sweeping administrative reorganization and set about the task of remaking Chile with far-reaching and much-needed developments. His vast public works program included extensive construction of highways, railroads, irrigation canals, and port facilities. There were also some agrarian reforms. In line with the long-recognized need for better educational opportunities, he began erecting several hundred new school buildings, mostly in rural areas, hired many additional teachers, and greatly expanded teacher-training programs. These and other projects were designed in part to provide jobs for the unemployed, and for a time they succeeded in doing so. Mindful that it was necessary to retain his military support, he did not neglect favors to the armed forces.

In order to finance these lavish expenditures, Ibáñez resorted to unbalanced budgets and heavy borrowing from abroad, as was the practice of many other Latin American heads of state during the prosperous era of the mid- and late 1920s. By that time copper had replaced nitrate as Chile's chief export, and rapidly increasing sales of copper contributed to the national treasury as well as to the overall economic boom. As long as prosperity continued, the Chilean people appeared content and little concerned with the government's method of operation. But these programs were expensive and there was much bureaucratic extravagance.

The coming of the worldwide Great Depression in late 1929 brought a drastic change. With foreign loans no longer available, the money supply dried up and Ibáñez was forced to halt his public works projects, leaving many unfinished. Economic collapse and unemployment spawned popular dissatisfaction, and the national administration was blamed for the difficulties that now beset the nation. Under these circumstances, many people began to demand the return of their freedom and democracy, which had been curtailed under the dictatorship. The situation became so tense that in July 1931 Ibáñez was persuaded to resign. He, like several other Latin American rulers, was a victim of the depression and accompanying popular reaction. But in this case the lever that pried him out of office was not a military coup, for the armed forces supported him. It was a more widespread manifestation—a civilian strike.

The strike began as a peaceful protest by students at the University of Chile, in downtown Santiago. After attempts to suppress it had resulted in bloodshed, the protest spread throughout the city. Shopkeepers, lawyers, doctors, teachers, and laborers joined in a general strike, which soon paralyzed the capital. Since Ibáñez had no means of forcing these people to return to work, his only recourse, as he saw it, was to leave the country, which he did. Chileans had found a way to overturn a government even when the military supported it.

But they had only ousted the president. Apparently, as has happened elsewhere in popular uprisings, the leaders had given little thought to where the country would go from there. The result was another year and a half of turmoil before political stability was restored. In the meantime, due to the depression and lack of a strong leader, governments succeeded each other rapidly, with the military calling the shots. Indeed, in view of the very serious economic crisis in Chile, it would have been extremely difficult for any administration to survive very long.

The effects of the Great Depression, which were more severe in Chile than in most countries, focused attention on Chile's economic disadvantages. On the one hand, it had become too much oriented toward one export product—copper instead of nitrate—and thus was drastically affected by fluctuations in the world demand and price of this commodity. In the nineteenth century and earlier, Chile had been quite productive agriculturally and, before the nitrate era, farm products were among its chief exports, along with copper and other minerals. Agricultural production had not kept pace with population increase, however, and by mid-twentieth century the nation reached the point where it no longer could feed itself and became an importer of food. In the meantime, the decline in the nitrate market had left copper the one great item of export. On the other hand, with abundant hydroelectric power and mineral resources, Chile was one of the first countries in Latin America to turn toward industrialization; but after its initial head start, labor and other internal difficulties caused it to fall behind some other Latin American republics in this area.

The turbulent era that had begun in 1924 was finally brought to a close by elections in October 1932, resulting in a return of Arturo Alessandri to the presidency for a six-year term beginning in late December. Chile then settled down once more to democratic stability—at least for a while. The military faded into the background and for the next forty years followed its more traditional role of aloofness from political affairs.

DRIFT TO THE LEFT

During the preceding, chaotic decade, the increasingly restless masses had for the first time succeeded in making themselves heard. The power of the landed aristocracy, which had ruled the country for a century, was now effectively challenged. But the reforms of 1924, constitutional revisions of 1925, and various material improvements during the Ibáñez administration only partially satisfied the rising demands of the urban proletariat. In the rural areas Chile was still a land of large estates controlled by a few land-owners; and, except for improvements in the school system, virtually nothing had been done to solve the plight of the impoverished, landless masses. The rural laborers and tenant farmers were still too remote and disorganized to agitate meaningfully for changes.

In spite of the prosperity of a considerable portion of this decade, the 1920s saw Ibáñez point the government down the path of extravagant spending, unbalanced budgets, and excessive borrowing, resulting in further devaluation of the currency and consequent inflation. Although after Ibáñez the pace was slowed for a time, it was destined to accelerate in later years, as politicians tried to meet the soaring demands of their constituents, and reach a wild climax in the early 1970s.

Politically the 1920s and early 1930s witnessed a further drift to the left. Especially significant for the future was the appearance of well-organized Communist and Socialist parties, which were to play increasingly influential roles in succeeding decades.

During his second term, Alessandri, although elected with primarily liberal support, turned considerably more conservative than in his earlier years as president. Apparently shaken by events of the previous decade, he shied away from policies advocated by the extreme Left, which he feared were dangerous to orderly government. He was particularly worried by the rising influence of the Communists and Socialists and took drastic steps to curb these as well as other agitators. While he provided additional schools, much low-cost housing, and other public works, his chief interest seemed to be maintaining order and preventing a return to the instability the country had experienced recently. But the disastrous economic situation, widespread unemployment, and rising expectations of an ever more vocal populace promoted a further leftward trend despite the efforts of Alessandri and the conservatives to offset it. Chile had already begun a rough journey down the road to Welfare State.

COMMUNISTS AND SOCIALISTS

In this environment the Communists, Socialists, and other extreme Left groups flourished. By 1936 they had succeeded in joining with the Radical (actually moderate) Party and organized labor to form a Popular Front, even though this combination was a strange one and it was known that the Communist Party was directed from Moscow. In view of the multiplicity of Chilean parties, such an arrangement provided the Communists considerably greater influence than they would have had as a small, independent group.

The principal announced objective of the Popular Front was social reform. With the Radical Party as the moderating influence, this coalition elected the president in 1938. Although a split between Communists, Socialists, and Radicals led to the breakup of the Popular Front in early 1941, in the next two presidential elections (1942 and 1946) candidates of the Radical Party were elected with Communist, Socialist, and other left-wing support. There was no provision for an elected vice president. In case of death or incapacity of the president, the minister of the interior served as chief executive until a new president was elected, within sixty days. Pedro Aguirre Cerda, elected president in 1938 for a six-year term, died in 1941, necessitating an election in 1942. Juan Antonio Ríos, elected then, also died before completing his term, making another election necessary in 1946.

As a further reflection of contemporary world ideological influences, a Chilean Nazi Party appeared in the 1930s. This group, known as Nacistas, denied any connection with Nazi Germany but was looked upon by many Chileans with suspicion because of the large German element in the population. In 1938 the Nacistas supported for the presidency Carlos Ibáñez, who had returned from exile the previous year. Without waiting for the scheduled election, however, a small group of Nacistas made an ill-fated attempt to seize the presidential palace by force, which resulted in their execution.

The late 1930s and early 1940s was a time of chaotic political conditions, caused in part by party realignments. The inability of the president to realize significant accomplishments was due in large measure to the lack of united support in Congress. This situation also emphasized the fact that, in spite of the theoretical revisions provided by the 1925 Constitution, the Chilean Congress was still a very powerful and independent body.

The victory of Gabriel González Videla in the special presidential election of 1946 brought into sharp focus Communist influence in Chile, riding the crest of Soviet popularity right after World War II. González Videla was a member of the Radical Party but welcomed Communist support. As a reward for this help, which he believed had been crucial in his victory, he appointed three Communists to his cabinet. It was the second instance in Latin America of formal Communist participation in a national government. (Previously in Cuba, Fulgencio Batista had appointed two Communists to cabinet posts without portfolio.) But the Communists soon made themselves so obnoxious by their demands and their efforts to promote strikes among organized labor that within a few months these members were dismissed. The strange Radical-Communist political alignment had ended—for a time. Subsequently González Videla broke diplomatic relations with the USSR and other Soviet bloc countries, and in 1948 Congress outlawed the Communist Party. Its members were forbidden to vote or hold public office.

For ten years thereafter the Communists operated underground. Although illegal, they wielded considerable influence. They controlled a bloc of votes, and there were politicians who were willing to cooperate with them in return for Communist support in elections. The late 1940s and early 1950s, years that witnessed a continuing rise in the cost of living, brought more strikes and labor violence, for much of which the Communists were blamed. González Videla sought and obtained from Congress drastic legislation to cope with such subversive acts, but labor unrest, like the inflation, continued unabated.

The inflation and frequent strikes were chief issues in the presidential election of 1952. It resulted in the return to power of Carlos Ibáñez, who had been overthrown in 1931, had twice since then run unsuccessfully for the presidency, and on two other occasions had tried to seize power. Why, after repudiating him these five times, did the Chileans bring back in 1952 this strongman, now almost seventy-five years old? It was primarily a protest against the ever increasing cost of living (up 150 percent in five years) and the ineffectuality of the González Videla administration in solving the economic problems. As in the case of the election of Getulio Vargas in Brazil in 1950, amid a crisis of inflation, Chilean voters in 1952 turned to a candidate they remembered as a man of action. During his campaign, Ibáñez had gone about the country reminding people of the cost of bread when he was president as contrasted with the inflated price in 1952. Also of the four candidates, he was the best known. In addition to support by the conservative Agrarian Labor Party, factions of certain other parties, and a large percentage of women, who voted for the first time in a presidential election, Ibáñez profited from the numerous protest ballots, which cut across party lines. With 47 percent of the total vote, he ran far ahead of any other candidate and subsequently was approved by Congress, which had to make the final choice when no one gained a majority. Bringing up the rear, with less than 6 percent of the total, was Salvador Allende Gossens, a medical doctor who was candidate of the Socialists, Communists, and other left-wing groups.

Hardly had the results of the 1952 election been announced, when numerous Chileans, including many who had voted for Ibáñez, began expressing fear that he might revert to the dictatorial policies he had followed in

1927–31. Worry among the upper classes, most of whom had not supported him, was reflected in a sharp decline in the stock market, a drop in the value of the peso, and a rumor that money was being shipped out of the country to Uruguay and Switzerland. Strong expressions of nationalism emanating from the Ibáñez camp caused concern, especially in the United States, over possible seizure of the copper mining industry, which was almost entirely U.S. owned. As time passed, however, it became apparent that these fears of harsh and repressive actions by Ibáñez were groundless. Indeed, although still very active physically, he appeared to be at an age where he was willing to let the nation drift along rather than take firm stands as had been expected. Under these circumstances, inflation continued unabated and the Communists had a field day.

With a membership estimated at 40,000, the Chilean Communist Party, although illegal since 1948, was the largest in proportion to population and probably the best organized in Latin America. By controlling a few well-placed members in the Chamber of Deputies, who operated skillfully through a coalition of parties and fellow travelers and played effectively upon the themes of nationalism and opposition to "Yankee imperialism," the Communists were able for a time to wield great influence in Congress and tie the hands of Ibáñez in his attempts to deal with the economic crisis. They took advantage of frequent strikes in virtually every major industry in the mid-1950s to spread propaganda and extend their influence among organized labor. In attempts to deal more effectively with Communist-led violence, several times Ibáñez imposed a state of siege, only to have it annulled by Congress. During his six years in office, however, he failed to follow a consistent policy.

Although previously Ibáñez had appeared strongly anti-Communist, the Communist Party hurriedly rallied to his support when his victory became obvious. He responded then by indicating a desire to restore the party to legal status and renew diplomatic and economic ties with the Soviet Union. He soon reversed this position, and over the next several years, as the Communists became more militant in provoking violence, he tried to weaken their power, but at times showed tolerance toward them. By May 1958, having previously restored trade with the USSR, he was asking Congress to legalize the Communist Party, but he was also calling for drastic penalties against anyone spreading foreign ideologies aimed at overthrowing the government. In July 1958 about 10,000 Communists staged a mass meeting and parade in Santiago, with government permission. Before the September presidential election, the Communist Party had regained its legality. In November delegates to the party's eleventh national convention met in the Hall of Honor of Chile's National Congress building—their right as a legal party under the Chilean democratic system. There, in a room revered by Chileans as a symbol of their representative democracy, before a capacity crowd of wildly cheering, card-carrying Communists, the delegates vowed to wage relentless war against the free-enterprise policies of Chile's new president and reaffirmed their ultimate goal: the destruction of Chilean democracy!

DRASTIC INFLATION

At the base of labor agitation and strikes was the continually rising cost of living. Despite Ibáñez's mandate in 1952 to solve this problem, little was accomplished. Although the country was no longer producing enough food and other consumer goods to supply domestic demands, the mid-1950s was a time of high copper and nitrate prices, relatively good industrial production, and virtually no unemployment. Under these circumstances, politicians were inclined to ignore the inflation rather than turn to any program of austerity. Of the nineteen political parties represented in Congress, President Ibáñez could count on the support of only the Agrarian Labor Party, with merely 25 of the 147 seats in the Chamber of Deputies. Congressional elections of March 1957 further weakened his support there. With an overwhelming majority against him, there was little he could do short of reverting to dictatorial methods, which he carefully avoided. The cost of government continued to rise along with the cost of living, and the administration made up budget deficits by issuing increasing amounts of paper money.

Of course, this policy resulted in further depreciating the currency and thus feeding the inflation. When Ibáñez was elected in September 1952, the exchange rate of the peso, which had declined drastically in previous years, stood at 133 to the dollar. A rise of 78 percent in Chile's cost of living in 1954 was termed the highest increase in the world for that year. The next year it rose 85 percent. This continuing rise brought other paralyzing strikes, cost-of-living wage increases—and more inflation. By early 1956, following the advice of Klein and Saks, prominent Washington economic consultants, Ibáñez was able to prevail upon Congress to adopt part of an austerity plan, which temporarily halted the inflationary spiral. The following year, however, with elections approaching, Congress refused to follow through. This and other setbacks revived the inflation and stimulated new waves of violence. By the time Ibáñez left office in November 1958, the free-market value of the peso had dropped to approximately 1,200 to the dollar. In the meantime, as a consequence, living standards of most Chileans had declined.

In this environment, with a 10 percent slump in industrial production, unemployment at approximately 8.5 percent, and a foreign debt of over $700 million, Chile held a presidential election in September 1958. In a field of five candidates, the victor was Jorge Alessandri, prominent, conservative businessman and son of former President Arturo Alessandri. He ran as an independent, with backing of the conservative parties. As finance minister in 1948–50, he had produced an almost unheard of phenomenon in Chile—a budget surplus. Considered completely honest and exceptionally capable, he now promised to lead the country back to economic soundness through a no-nonsense policy of hard work, honesty, and patriotism. A friend of the United States, he advocated close economic ties with the West and a soundly managed system of free enterprise. Close runner-up in this election was Salvador Allende, supported by a coalition known as Frente de Acción Popular (FRAP), composed of his own Socialist Party, the Communists, and other left-wing groups. He had based his campaign on a repudiation of "capitalistic imperialism" and the transformation of Chile into a welfare state, supported by trade with the Soviet bloc.

After being approved by Congress (necessary because he had not received a majority of all votes cast), Alessandri was inaugurated on November 3 in a ceremony noted for its simplicity. With a nonpolitical cabinet composed of businessmen and technical experts, he set out to cope with inflation, unemployment, agrarian reform, and other problems that beset the nation. Basic causes of the continuing inflation were budget deficits and increasing importation of food, which Chileans should have been producing themselves. Early in 1959 President Alessandri asked Congress for special powers to halt inflation, increase production, and reduce unemployment. Congress responded by giving him absolute control of the economy for one year. He was also authorized to reorganize government agencies, reduce the number of employees, reform the tax structure, modify the banking system, and establish a new monetary unit. Soon thereafter Chile was granted credits and loans totaling more than $135 million by the United States government, international lending institutions, and private U.S. banks, to be used for economic development and currency stabilization. In addition to these funds, a sudden rise in the price of copper provided the treasury with unexpected additional revenue.

Initially Alessandri's policies worked so well that before the end of his first year in office the budget had been balanced and the currency stabilized at 1,052 pesos to the dollar. Industrial production increased 10 percent and copper output rose 37 percent. During this time substantial new credits from Europe as well as the United States aided the economy. Alessandri reduced the government staff by 5 percent, significantly improved tax collection, and paid off overdue government obligations. These months also witnessed a dramatic decline in the number of strikes. By 1960 the annual inflation rate, which stood at 73 percent in 1958, had been reduced to only 5.4 percent.

Unfortunately, the economic stabilization program received a serious setback by a very disastrous series of earthquakes and tidal waves that struck southern Chile over a period of several weeks in May and June 1960. They took a toll of approximately 5,000 lives, rendered more than 350,000 people homeless, and caused property damage estimated at over $500 million. Nevertheless, with considerable foreign assistance, the administration set about the task of rebuilding the devastated areas while, at the same time, continuing the fight against inflation and formulating an impressive ten-year, $10 billion economic development plan.

After four years of pressure by Alessandri, in November 1962 Congress passed an agrarian reform act. By providing for expropriation of unused and inadequately utilized agricultural lands, it initiated a system that in time could transform Chile's semi-feudal rural society by making available more land for peasant farmers. The immediate need, though, was a substantial increase in agricultural production. Imported foods, now costing $75 million annually, not only were expensive to the consumer but were largely responsible for the balance-of-payments deficit, which in turn fed the inflation. In order to boost production, there were plans to create efficient, medium-size farms from inefficient haciendas and combine the very small plots into cooperatives. But this plan would take time—and time was running out.

On January 1, 1960, a new monetary unit, the escudo, worth 1,000 pesos, was issued to replace the old currency. The exchange rate was 1 escudo for 95 U.S. cents. The peso had first been put into circulation in 1812 (six years before Chile won its independence). Initially the silver peso was approximately on a par with the U.S. dollar. The inconvertible paper peso, which appeared in 1878 as result of a monetary crisis, lost value as increasing amounts were issued until by 1960 more than a 1,000 were required to equal a dollar. Despite growing pressures, President Alessandri was able to maintain the 1960 ratio and prevent devaluation of the currency until October 1962.

For nearly four years he was rather successful in holding down inflation and coping with the other serious problems. Congress, controlled by a conservative-moderate coalition, was reasonably responsive. Also Chile was particularly fortunate in receiving foreign financial assistance, especially from the United States. By early 1962 large quantities of Alliance for Progress development aid were pouring in to support the ten-year plan. On the theory that Communist advances could be counteracted by impressive economic and social developments, during the next few years the United States provided more aid per capita to Chile than to any other Latin American country. But in spite of this financial assistance and the constructive programs being carried out by the Alessandri government, by late 1962 there was growing dissatisfaction.

Due primarily to a return to deficit financing for reconstruction in the devastated areas and continued economic development, by October Alessandri had lost control of the inflation. In less than a year the free market value of the escudo plunged from 95 to 34 U.S. cents; and the cost of living rose 45 percent during 1963 and 39 percent in 1964. Now there was much criticism of the administration's unpopular austerity measures and their failure to check rising prices. An alleged slow pace in social reforms also brought increasing restlessness. The Communists and other left wingers took advantage of every opportunity to exploit these difficulties and to discredit the Alliance for Progress as a way out for Chile. Both the menacing leftist strength and worsening inflation contributed toward weakening the economy by frightening off many potential investors. Of major significance by late 1963 was the presidential election due the following September. Political maneuvers aimed at improving party positions prior to the election led to a breakdown of the conservative-moderate coalition that had provided Alessandri's chief support in both his cabinet and Congress.

LEFTIST THREATS

As September 1964 approached, a potential danger, long recognized not only in Chile but throughout the Western Hemisphere, came more sharply into focus. There was the disturbing possibility that Chileans, in a free election, might choose as president an avowed Marxist. In what promised to be a three-way race, one of the leading candidates was Senator Salvador Allende, founder of the extreme leftist Socialist Party, who had come close to victory six years earlier. (Ideologically Allende's pro-Peking Socialist Party was more militant and leftist than Chile's Moscow-oriented Communist Party.) Again in 1964 he was supported by FRAP, the coalition composed of Socialists, Communists, and four other small, far-Left parties. Declaring that Chileans were being strangled by U.S. imperialism, Allende promised, if elected, to transform Chile into a socialist state, with nationalization of all public utilities, mining and other major industries, and even a large part of agriculture.

His leading opponent was Senator Eduardo Frei Montalva, whose Christian Democratic Party had experienced a remarkable growth since its organization in 1957 from a slightly left-of-center Christian Social group and had emerged from municipal elections in early 1964 with 23 percent of the total vote, the largest amount accumulated by any single party. Although there was no overt connection between the Christian Democratic Party and the Catholic Church, the party's organization and ideology were significantly affected by Catholic doctrine, the teachings and influence of several liberal members of the Chilean clergy, and especially a Jesuit sociological research complex in Chile known as the Centro Bellarmino.

Frei promised a "revolution with liberty," including extensive agrarian reform, increased and more diversified industry to create at least 50,000 new jobs, more government participation in and regulation of mining (but not nationalization), and a doubling of copper production over the next six years.[1] Because of his advocacy of sweeping land reforms, many of Chile's landholding conservatives considered him as serious a threat as Allende. Actually both Frei and Allende charged that the Alessandri administration had preserved upper-class privileges and neglected the poor.

The third candidate, Senator Julio Durán, member of the moderate Radical Party, was sponsored by the Democratic Front, composed of Radicals and the right-wing Conservatives and Liberals, which had supported President Alessandri. Durán withdrew from the race after his coalition suffered defeat in a key special congressional election, but he later returned as candidate of the Radical Party. This move weakened his position and left Frei and Allende the two principal contenders.

Over a period of several months prior to September 1964, there was a growing fear in Chile that an Allende victory would usher in a Marxist government, which in turn might bring military intervention and the loss of democracy. Many Chileans were so worried over the prospect of a Communist regime that they began sending out of the country several million dollars monthly and were quietly making arrangements for voluntary exile if Allende should win. In other Latin American capitals and especially in Washington there was great concern over this election. It was believed that an Allende triumph would be a serious defeat for democracy, would quickly place Chile in a position of hostility toward the United States, and would significantly boost Soviet influence in South America.

President Alessandri maintained an impartial position in this contest, although the Conservative and Liberal Parties turned their support to Frei after Durán's temporary withdrawal. One thing was certain—no matter whether pro-Marxist Allende or anti-Marxist Frei should be elected, Chile would move to the left.

Fears of Chile "going Communist" in 1964 proved groundless. The September 4 election resulted in a sweeping victory for Frei, who won approximately 56 percent of the total vote to become the first Christian Democrat ever elected president of an American nation. Allende polled about 39 percent and Durán only 5 percent. An estimated 50 percent of Chilean men and 65 percent of the women cast ballots for Frei, including not only Christian Democrats, Conservatives, and Liberals but an impressive majority of independents (who outnumbered party affiliates) and even numerous Radicals, who saw no chance for their own candidate. Many of these voters were more against Allende than for Frei, and the latter's victory brought sighs of relief and enthusiastic celebrations throughout the country.

Although a reform-minded leftist, Frei was reservedly pro-United States; and his triumph assured continued Chilean cooperation with the U.S. and the Alliance for Progress. A former economics professor who had promised to build homes and schools and provide jobs for all Chileans, he expressed a desire for more U.S. investment and outlined a plan to push ahead rapidly with economic and social improvements, but he cautioned his people not to expect miracles.

How quickly and effectively Frei could bring about "profound transformations and rapid advances in the social and economic order," as he pledged after his inauguration on November 3, would depend largely on Congress, now dominated by moderates and rightists.[2] Since his party held only a small minority of seats, he had to have the cooperation of others. But the rightist parties, although they had supported him for president, opposed extensive reforms; and the FRAP members, who favored reforms but were so angry

over Allende's defeat that they boycotted Frei's inaugural ceremony, announced their role as opposition to the Christian Democrats. With these hur-
dles, Frei's progress was bound to be slow—at least until new congressional
elections in March.

Nevertheless, in an effort to get his program on the way without delay, he
plunged ahead with measures aimed at land redistribution, more low-cost
housing, educational improvements, restructuring the central bank, imposition of new taxes on capital and property, and the "Chileanization," by purchase, of major public utilities and the largely U.S.-owned copper industry.
But the Liberals and Conservatives in Congress charged him with trying to
create an unwarranted crisis atmosphere, and the Communists and Socialists
branded his program too general and vague. As a result, very few of his
measures were approved.

On March 7, 1965, however, Chilean voters came to the rescue in congressional elections, which were termed a struggle between reform and tradition. They resulted in a landslide that increased Christian Democratic
representation in the Chamber of Deputies from 28 to 82, producing a miracle
of Chilean politics—a single party in firm control of this 147-member body.
With only 20 of the 45 Senate seats up for election, all Christian Democratic
candidates won, increasing the party's total from 1 to 13; but since this number was considerably short of a majority, for the next four years Frei could
not count on unqualified support from this legislative branch. And the situation became more complicated in early 1967 with the election of Salvador
Allende as president of the Senate. Under the Chilean system, however, it
was possible for one house to override the other by a two-thirds vote and
passage of a measure three times. Thus Frei occasionally was able to bypass
the Senate and gain enactment of desired legislation.

Evaluating the 1965 election results as "a magnificent vote of confidence,"
President Frei now promised that his government would not hesitate to
"move ahead energetically."[3] On this note of self-confidence, he renewed
his attempt to gain approval of his various reform measures while, at the
same time, trying to impose a painful and unpopular austerity program to
retard inflation, which had brought a rise of approximately 39 percent in
living costs in 1964. Fortunately for Frei, the world price of copper continued
to climb, providing his administration with increased revenue. Also large
amounts of foreign financial assistance still poured in, principally from the
United States.

U.S. aid to Chile continued in spite of Frei's independent and at times
critical attitude toward the United States. His outspoken condemnation of
U.S. intervention in the Dominican Republic in April 1965 aroused fear within
his own administration that he might be jeopardizing U.S.-Chilean cooperation. Two months later he departed on a tour of four European countries,
a journey that appeared to many as a slap at the United States since he
had not previously visited Washington, as was customary among other Latin

American heads of state. Moreover, in November 1964, only a few weeks after his inauguration, the Frei government had reestablished diplomatic relations with the Soviet Union, which had been broken in 1947, and subsequently renewed ties with Bulgaria, Czechoslovakia, Hungary, and Poland. Later, in 1968, Chile became the first South American country to conclude an aid agreement with the USSR. In January 1967, as Frei was about to embark on an official visit to the United States, the Chilean Senate, asserting its right under an outdated law, refused him permission to leave the country—an act attributed primarily to the influence of his rival, Salvador Allende, now president of this body. (The Senate action could have been overturned by a two-thirds vote of the Chamber of Deputies, but that appeared impossible to obtain.) This situation was an internal political matter in which senators of the far Right joined with those of the extreme Left to embarrass President Frei and the Christian Democrats, as well as the United States.

For the most part, however, relations between Santiago and Washington remained cordial. As should have been expected, in Chile, Frei's independent foreign policy, designed to prove he was no Yankee puppet, was generally approved, not only by the avowedly anti-United States Left but among many moderates and conservatives as well. In the United States the Christian Democratic reform program was seen as right in line with aims of the then popular Alliance for Progress. Indeed, U.S. officials shared the view of many Chileans who felt there was no alternative to supporting the Frei government because if it should not succeed, Chile likely would go Communist.

Frei's presidential term was a time of continuing political intrigue in which he and the Christian Democrats were caught in the middle between rightists, who wanted no reforms, and leftists, who demanded more drastic reforms. The Liberals and Conservatives, who united in 1966 to form the National Party, represented the conservative aristocracy, and throughout these years their objective was to maintain the status quo. By impeding legislation, provoking strikes through the Communist-controlled labor unions, and demanding unreasonable spending and taxation, the Marxist parties sought to handicap Frei and the Christian Democrats in the hope that failure of their reform program would pave the way for election of a Marxist president in 1970. The Radicals (moderates), who held the balance of power in the Senate after 1965, were declining as a political force and often opposed the Christian Democrats because they feared them as political rivals.

Successive elections after 1965 brought a decline in Christian Democratic power. Unwisely, as a reaction to his humiliation by the Senate in January, Frei chose to make the April 1967 municipal elections a test of his popularity; but they resulted in losses by his party and gains by the Nationals, Radicals, Socialists, and Communists. The Communists fared especially well as result of a massive campaign believed to have been heavily financed by funds channeled through the Soviet embassy. In congressional elections of March 1969, the Christian Democrats suffered a severe setback while the Nationals were the most successful. Christian Democratic representation in the Chamber of Deputies dropped to 56, with the Nationals holding 34 seats, the Radicals 22, Communists 24, and Socialists 14. (The number of congressional seats had been increased to 150 in the Chamber of Deputies and 50 in the Senate.) The 30 percent of the total vote retained by the Christian Democrats was less than they had hoped for, although considerably greater than that of any other party. One significant Senate race resulted in the reelection of Salvador Allende and boosted his candidacy for the presidency in 1970.

By this time the Christian Democrats were badly split into three factions, with a left wing which often coincided ideologically with the Marxists. It now seemed clear that the Christian Democrats were too weak to win another presidential election. Chile was back to its normal political state, with wide gulfs between its numerous parties and no party strong enough to elect a president or control a legislative body.

Although the accomplishments of the Frei government fell considerably short of his announced aims, by the end of his term he could point to a number of substantial achievements. The goals of the extensive agrarian reform program were to settle at least 100,000 landless families on plots of approximately 200 acres, which it was believed would stimulate agriculture and return Chile to its former self-sufficiency in food production by breaking up the large estates that were not being effectively utilized into farms of practical size for efficient cultivation. Land redistribution actually had begun under Jorge Alessandri; and until Congress finally passed Frei's sweeping land-reform measures in July 1967, it was implemented under the Alessandri law of 1962. By late 1970, however, only about 30,000 of the estimated 300,000 landless families had been provided land—at enormous expense to the government in land costs and administrative bureaucracy. This shortfall created dissatisfaction among those who did not receive land; and, prodded by Marxist agitators, many of them seized property illegally. These acts emphasized the overall inadequacy of Frei's land reforms and the growing militancy of Marxist political leaders. In spite of efforts to stimulate agricultural production, by the end of Frei's term, Chile was spending about $200 million annually to import food—double the cost when he became president. While this need to import was due in part to the worst drought in a century, it was primarily a result of lingering deficiencies and instability in the agrarian sector.

As part of his slum-clearance program, during the first two years of the Frei administration some 87,000 permanent, low-cost homes and 48,000 temporary dwellings were built; but it was discovered that thousands of the families who moved into them could not afford to pay for them. The government then cut back on such projects and instead encouraged self-help housing, with groups of people working together to construct their own homes. In May 1970 Frei claimed that approximately 2.5 million people had occupied new houses during his term.

Impressive improvements were made in the educational system, and by the end of his second year in office, Frei could boast that his administration had built 10,000 classrooms, trained several thousand new teachers, added an eighth year of free, compulsory education, and increased enrollment in primary, secondary, and technical schools from 1.8 million to 2.3 million students. Also in these two years government expenditures for higher education almost doubled and enrollment in universities increased from 74,000 to 82,000.

During his six years as president, Frei went a long way toward "Chileanizing" copper production. Initially the government bought a controlling interest in the Kennecott Corporation's El Teniente, the largest underground copper mine in the world, and a part interest in some other major U.S.-owned mines in Chile. Later, in 1969, it reached an agreement whereby the Anaconda Company would sell to the government its Chilean properties, including the huge Chuquicamata open-pit mine, the world's largest and responsible for more than half of Chile's total copper production. Frei avoided outright expropriation, which the Marxists wanted, but acquired controlling shares on the best possible terms. For them he paid what his opponents charged were excessive prices, guaranteed lower taxes and freedom from expropriation, and concluded agreements whereby new investments would be made by the companies to increase output. In this way the private companies continued to handle mining and marketing operations with the government able to intervene when it deemed necessary. While production was expanded considerably, it was not doubled by the end of Frei's term as he had contemplated. The real question remained whether in the long run Chileanization would result in greater or less prosperity for the nation. Frei recognized this doubt when he said, "To pronounce the word nationalization is easy and may be a good banner for political agitation. . . . We have countless examples of nationalizing processes that have resulted in chaos and precipitated the different countries backward into confusion for long years."[4]

Obviously unsuccessful were the efforts to curb inflation. New levies on capital and property, which increased tax revenue from 13 to 17 percent of gross national product between 1964 and 1966, gave Chile the highest effective land tax in Latin America. The rise of copper prices from 34 cents per pound in late 1964 to 70 cents by 1970 also provided greatly increased funds in the treasury. (Each additional cent per pound brought about $8 million more in foreign-exchange earnings per year.) A result was favorable international trade balances in some of these years despite the large food imports. In 1969 Chile registered the highest trade surplus in its history—$182.3 million. In addition there was massive Alliance for Progress aid, totaling more than $1 billion during this period. Nevertheless, the enormous cost of the government's programs and burgeoning bureaucracy outpaced the enlarged revenues; and throughout Frei's term the cost of living rose at between 23 and 30 percent annually, resulting in frequent demands and strikes for wage hikes. The escudo, which was worth 27 U.S. cents at the time of Frei's inauguration, was down to 7 cents when he left office. Moreover, by late 1967 it was estimated that private Chilean capital was being exported to safer havens outside the country at the rate of about $200,000 per day—more than the United States and the Alliance for Progress were providing.

Frei and the Christian Democrats were perpetuating an unworkable practice engaged in by previous Chilean administrations, as well as those in a number of other countries—granting greater social and economic reforms than the treasury could stand. They refused to recognize the fact that, no matter how desirable these might be, they were too expensive. Thus one of the most serious problems Frei encountered in his determination to carry out his "revolution with liberty" was how to continue reforms amid the continuing inflation to which he was contributing by his vast expenditures.

Ironically, some of the most sweeping changes advocated by Frei were not approved by Congress until late December 1969, to go into effect at the beginning of the next presidential term in November 1970. The president was given greater independence from the legislative body, especially in the economic field where he was granted more power to control public expenditures and taxation. Should Congress block him on an issue of national importance, he would be able to present the matter to the people in a nationwide referendum. He also would be permitted to leave the country for as much as fifteen days without congressional approval. Another provision lowered the voting age from twenty-one to eighteen. These were reforms Frei had long requested, but they came so late that only his successor stood to benefit from them.

In 1964 many Chileans who voted against Allende did so because they feared losing their democracy to military dictatorship. By 1973 they were begging the military to take over. Why?

In the September 4, 1970, presidential election there were three principal candidates. One was the conservative former president, Jorge Alessandri, running again as an independent. Another was Christian Democrat candidate Radomiro Tomic, recently ambassador to the United States, whose political philosophy was to the left of Frei. The third was Salvador Allende, supported by a coalition known as Popular Unity (Unidad Popular), composed of his Socialists, the Communists, many Radicals, and three small, far Left parties. The well-organized, Moscow-backed Communist Party apparently played the major role in assembling this 1970 combination; and Fidel Castro, through television and leftist publications, effectively campaigned for Allende in Chile. (In recent months the Frei government, although not reestablishing diplomatic relations with Cuba, had made contacts that provided ample communication channels between the two countries.) In composition Popular Unity was similar to FRAP, which had backed Allende in 1958 and 1964. But this time, in a rather close, three-way race, he came out with approximately 36 percent of the vote, slightly ahead of Alessandri, the runner-up.

Lacking a majority of popular votes, Allende could become president only if Congress approved; but in order to gain approval, he needed the support of the Christian Democrats, who, with seventy-five members, held the largest bloc of seats. Despite his assurances to the contrary, it appeared that his campaign platform, if carried out, would take the country down the road to a complete socialist state and virtually destroy the democratic system that Chileans had long cherished. Indeed, one of the greatest fears of the day was that under an Allende administration, democratic, constitutional government would disappear. In order to secure sufficient support in Congress, he was forced to renounce some of the principles he formerly had espoused and agree to certain constitutional amendments that supposedly guaranteed civil liberties and the continuance of multiparty democracy. With these question-able safeguards, and after Allende had threatened a popular uprising if he was not approved, Congress confirmed his election and he was inaugurated president on November 3.

A MARXIST REGIME

The prospect of a Marxist president, who promised to nationalize numer-ous businesses and create a state-controlled economy, spread panic among many Chileans and resulted in a run on the banks and mass exodus from the country, beginning right after the September election. Most of these ref-ugees fled to neighboring Argentina, where their number was estimated at tens of thousands of families. (In Chile estimates of the total number of peo-ple who left the country ran all the way from 30,000 to 100,000.) They packed hotel rooms and strained Argentine banking facilities by converting as much Chilean currency as possible into dollars. Many of the really wealthy Chileans were believed to have banked or invested their money abroad before this crisis. The September election also halted the inflow of foreign capital as well as domestic private investment, which forced the economy from expansion to recession almost overnight.

Initially Allende moved cautiously. Without a majority in Congress, he was quite limited in obtaining favorable legislation. As long as this situation ex-isted, the opposition could at least apply some restraints should he go too far. And congressional elections were not due until March 1973.

Allende was also aware of potential danger from the military. Being tra-ditionally nonpolitical, however, military leaders tended to wait and hope that matters would work themselves out under the constitutional system. From his inauguration until mid-1973, they were saying, "We support dem-ocratic, constitutional government." (Such statements were made to me by several high-ranking military officers during visits to Chile in April 1971 and May 1973.) What they were really saying was, "We support Allende only as long as his government remains democratic and constitutional." Thus the specter of possible military intervention always lurked in the background. For this reason, Allende was very careful not to offend the armed forces. Actually he courted their support by granting them considerably more favors than had preceding administrations.

Although Allende vigorously denied it, from the beginning of his administration he was allowing numerous Marxist subversives from various countries to slip into Chile. The bulk of them, along with large quantities of arms and other equipment, were from Cuba, but many individuals and supplies came directly from behind the Iron Curtain. On November 12, 1970, only a few days after taking office, Allende announced resumption of full diplomatic relations with Cuba. Subsequently relations were established with Communist China, East Germany, Albania, North Vietnam, North Korea, and the Congo Republic. In November–December 1971 Castro made an official visit to Chile and remained twenty-five days. The magnitude of this subversive infiltration was not realized until after Allende was overthrown. With these arms and men he was building up a personal army with which he hoped to counteract any opposition that might arise from the established military. As later events revealed, apparently he and some of his advisers were also mindful of a possible offensive use for this force.

Allende used the municipal elections of April 4, 1971, as a test of his strength. Although elections of municipal council members should not seriously affect the national government, he believed his position would be materially enhanced if candidates of Popular Unity parties would gain 51 percent or more of the total vote. This figure would indicate that a majority of Chileans were behind the government. The president then would feel free to move ahead with various reform measures; and if Congress should turn him down on some important issue, it might safely be taken to the people in a referendum.

With these ends in mind, Allende launched an extensive campaign to win the elections. Strict price controls held inflation to about 2 percent from November to April—a remarkable accomplishment in Chile. At the same time, wages were permitted to rise about 35 percent, approximately the inflation rate of the previous year. This policy gained Allende much support, especially among the laboring classes. Another effective vote-getting technique was an appeal to the poor with large donations of food and milk. Also for the first time Chileans in the eighteen-to-twenty-one year age bracket were eligible to vote and went rather heavily for leftist candidates. Even with these advantages, however, Popular Unity parties won slightly less than 50 percent of the ballots. Thus Allende failed to obtain the mandate he wanted to move forward rapidly with his reform program. Moreover, three subsequent special congressional elections went definitely against the administration, revealing that the opposition, which had been divided, was now united.

Despite these and other limiting factors, shortly after his inauguration Allende initiated a far-reaching program aimed at creating a socialist state. Bowing to pressures about him, he actually moved faster than probably he would have otherwise. There were peasants and farm laborers who demanded—and in many cases were seizing—land; there were urban workers who demanded—and many who seized—houses. Ostensibly to satisfy peasant demands but also to destroy the economic base of the conservative landholders, Allende instituted a vast extension of the agrarian-reform efforts of the previous administration—but with a new twist. Under the guise of providing more land for the landless, many additional rural properties were expropriated. But this move soon brought loud complaints not only from those losing land but also from many who theoretically were receiving land. Instead of being deeded to individuals, most of the expropriated tracts were retained by the state in so-called cooperatives, which were just state farms. Here Allende was following a pattern set by Castro in Cuba, which was based on practice in the Soviet Union. Many farmers who had expected to get a piece of land found themselves merely employees of the state as part of a cooperative. They simply had changed masters. This agrarian-reform program, together with private seizures of property, also had the very disturbing effect of further retarding agricultural production and thus necessitating the importation of greater quantities of food. The importation of food and other essential commodities soon virtually wiped out the approximately $400 million in foreign exchange the Allende administration had inherited.

"We are going to expropriate those investments that fundamentally and essentially influence national economic development. . . . We are going to nationalize those companies that we believe to be fundamental for the economic development of the country."[5] So stated Allende shortly before his inauguration. After becoming president, he set about to take over what he termed the "basic industries," including mining, other heavy industries, banking, and all transportation and communication facilities. Many Chileans feared his government would go much further—and it did.

Because of Chile's strong spirit of nationalism, expropriation of foreign-owned properties, especially minerals, was popular, and Allende was able to induce Congress to go along with him 100 percent in approving seizure of the copper mines. The Frei administration had bought controlling interest in the principal U.S.-owned mines, but now Allende took over everything—without further remuneration. The nationalization law, passed by Congress in July 1971, called for indemnification at the December 31, 1970, book value, less equipment depreciation, outstanding taxes, and "excessive profits." With a free hand in applying the last provision, Allende claimed such "excessive profits" as to more than wipe out any compensation due Anaconda or Kennecott. The government also failed to pay compensation as previously agreed with Cerro Corporation for its Río Blanco mine, which had just begun production.

Popular support for expropriation of foreign-owned mining properties did not extend to seizure of other industries, however, especially those owned by Chileans. Within a few months there was so much opposition to the speed with which the government was moving and the methods being used that Congress stepped in and tried to put on the brakes. Laws were passed requiring congressional approval before Allende could take other properties. But, with questionable interpretations of laws already on the statute books, he had been careful to operate by executive decree within the framework of the constitution, and his legal advisers found ways around even the new congressional restrictions. (Allende admitted privately that his pretended respect for the constitutional system was merely for the purpose of gaining power.) Many takeovers occurred as result of close cooperation between the administration and labor unions, most of which were Communist controlled. In some cases, workers seized industrial plants and then the government stepped in "to maintain production." In others it was a matter of the industry becoming so handicapped by government and/or labor that it could not continue independently. Wage increases, which had to be absorbed by the employer, frequently forced businesses to the verge of bankruptcy, thus inviting takeover by the government, which did not permit their being closed. Control of most private banks was acquired by a combination of stock purchases and coercive measures. There were still other instances of more direct seizure by the administration. Also Allende managed to extend his grasp considerably beyond what were generally considered "basic" industries. Such steps, which seemed to indicate that eventually his government would take over everything, stimulated the opposition to greater resistance.

As has been noted, during the first few months of his term, until the April 1971 municipal elections, President Allende managed to hold prices down, grant large wage increases, and keep the economic situation generally under control. But, as should have been obvious, this state was only temporary. After the elections, the lid soon blew off, as a result in part of the shortages that occurred in agricultural production and in the various industries that were taken over by the government. It was also due to the greatly increased cost of operating these industries under government control. Initially Allende partially solved the unemployment problem he had inherited by giving many people jobs in the now state-run plants; but this measure, of course, added significantly to the cost of operation. The fact that employees could not be fired led to a degree of absenteeism that even Allende termed "incredible"; and workers' objections to sacrificial contributions to the "construction of socialism," which the government demanded, resulted in costly strikes. Also in many industries, particularly copper, a large percentage of the skilled managerial personnel left, and little consideration was given to the expertise of new appointees. Thus, as should have been expected, in the government industries, production declined as payrolls increased.

Allende had promised that state ownership of the copper mines would finance economic development and social reform. What he did not tell the people was that under arrangements made by his predecessor, the government already was receiving, through joint ownership and taxes, approximately 85 percent of gross profits from copper and that the Frei administration had attracted about $500 million additional U.S. capital, which had nearly doubled the productive capacity of Chile's copper mines. Due to mismanagement and labor difficulties, under the Allende government's control, production seriously declined. For these and other reasons, government expenses skyrocketed and income decreased.

From the beginning of his administration, Allende had clashed with Congress and the Supreme Court. By mid-1971 political and economic problems were reaching crisis proportions. In the midst of this disaster, a dozen Radical Party supporters in Congress broke away, claiming the administration was becoming "too Marxist." This departure was followed by the resignation of five non-Marxist cabinet members, including the minister of defense. What Allende really wanted was to abolish both Congress and the Supreme Court, which stood in the way of his revolutionary changes, and substitute a unicameral "Assembly of the People," which he hoped to control, and a Supreme Court elected by this body. In September 1971 he announced that such a proposal would be submitted to the people in a plebiscite, but it never materialized as its approval was very doubtful. For all their economic and political woes, Allende and his Marxist supporters blamed an "international conspiracy" organized by the United States.

What quickly became a very costly operation was piled on top of the annual deficits and continuing inflation that Chile had experienced for many years. The burden was compounded by policies of the Allende administration. He made up the deficits, as Chilean governments had done in the past, by printing more money—but on a much larger scale than ever before. The result was the highest rate of inflation the nation ever had experienced. According to the government's own figures, during the year 1972 the cost of living rose over 163 percent. The following year it grew much worse. By September 1973 it was soaring at 50 percent per month. After the military took over in September, controls were lifted, thus permitting a drastic rise in prices that destroyed the black market. The overall cost of living increase for 1973 was 700 to 1,000 percent, depending on how one figured it. For many years Chileans had been accustomed to living with inflation but not that great an inflation.

Efforts to control the value of the escudo led to a serious black market in currency. By April 1973 the official exchange rate had dropped to 70 per dollar, but shopkeepers in Santiago who had items to sell were offering from 650 to 900 escudos per dollar. By early September the official rate had plummeted to 300 and the black market exchange to around 3,000 per dollar.

Along with the inflation, there were shortages in most basic commodities, which grew more severe as time went on. People who could not afford to buy on the black market queued up in long lines very early each morning, or even the night before, at shops that sold meat, groceries, and other staple products to obtain—at the increasingly high prices—small amounts of the little that was there. Beef, which quickly became very scarce, was strictly rationed. Finally, in January 1973, rationing of other foods was imposed for the first time in Chile's history. After Allende's downfall, it was discovered that he and close associates had been hoarding huge quantities of food and other scarce items. Many other affluent Chileans who had access to dollars and the black market had fared quite well.

Before the end of 1971, the scarcity and high prices of food brought violent protests. On December 1, 1971, at least 5,000 women, from all walks of life, marched through the streets of Santiago beating on pots and pans and shouting slogans against the government and Fidel Castro in protest of food shortages and the visit of the Cuban dictator to Chile. This demonstration, which led to clashes with pro-Allende forces and intervention by riot police, was the largest and most violent since Allende had taken office a year earlier; but it was only a prelude to more massive protests later. In October 1972 tens of thousands of Santiago housewives, further enraged by chronic shortages and rising prices, again marched through the streets to the tune of pots and pans. This protest drew an estimated hundreds of thousands of people and was considerably larger than a pro-Allende rally staged the night before. Prior to this demonstration, on August 21, protests against government economic policies had resulted in a twenty-four-hour shopkeepers' strike, which closed practically all of Chile's stores for a day. It was followed by three weeks of political demonstrations, including acts of violence. Throughout the Allende era, such events frequently brought serious clashes between paramilitary extremist units—Marxist and anti-Marxist. Extreme leftists were trying to promote a violent revolution; extreme rightists hoped for a military coup.

A fatal move that helped bring on Allende's downfall was his attempt to gain control of the trucking industry, a very important business in Chile. Most of the people involved were small operators, men who owned one or maybe a few trucks. By mid-1972 the administration began to put a squeeze on these truckers by withholding spare parts and in other ways trying to force them into a position where the state could take over this branch of the transportation system. A reaction to this effort was a nationwide truckers' strike in October, which became quite effective. It soon embraced many businesses and professions as shopkeepers, lawyers, doctors, dentists, teachers, students, and others joined. Mindful of the effectiveness of a widespread strike such as had toppled President Ibáñez in 1931, Allende became alarmed and backed down. At this juncture he took a step he had not dared take before— he brought three of the top military leaders into his cabinet, including Gen. Carlos Prats, head of the army, who was made minister of the interior. (These military officers remained in the cabinet until March 27, 1973.) Prats in effect became the second man in the government, next to Allende. Within a few days he arranged a settlement of the strike and announced there would be no nationalization of the trucking industry. Shortly thereafter Allende departed on a two-weeks overseas trip, leaving Prats in control. (Allende visited Mexico, U.N. headquarters in New York, the Soviet Union, and Cuba.)

Allende's departure relieved the tense situation momentarily and created a standoff, which continued until the March 1973 congressional elections. Both administration and antiadministration forces decided to wait for these elections in the hope that they would provide a solution. The political opposition, now united, hoped to gain a two-thirds majority in Congress, which would be enough to impeach Allende or at least stop his program. The Allende group was hoping to win a majority of congressional seats. As they turned out, however, the elections did not really prove decisive. Allende's parties gained a few seats, which the opposition claimed was by fraud. (Subsequent investigations, which uncovered numerous cases of fraudulent voting, helped bring on Allende's overthrow by convincing the military that it would be impossible to hold a fair election in 1976.) With a division of 30 to 20 in the Senate and 87 to 63 in the Chamber of Deputies, the opposition, composed mainly of Christian Democrats, the conservative National Party, and factions of the Radicals, still retained a large majority in Congress. There were not enough anti-Allende members to impeach him, but there were enough to maintain some restraints.

By this time it was clear that while some people had profited from the Allende regime, the population as a whole had not. Many of the laboring classes who formerly were unemployed had jobs and certain other benefits. Many people had larger incomes than before, but these were offset by increased living costs unless they had ready access to dollars. Allende had promised to create "a republic of the working class." What he actually did was pit the poorer sectors of the population against the affluent middle and upper classes, thus promoting class hatred. Moreover, his favors to the downtrodden were more apparent and temporary than real and lasting; and he ignored the fact that in Chile the well-to-do middle class is large and influential. Even among leftists themselves there was dissatisfaction; and frequently Allende was attacked by extremists, who, not content with a peaceful revolution, charged that he was not making changes rapidly enough. In view of the worsening inflation, decreasing supplies of basic commodities, and increasing unrest among so many people, after the 1973 elections it was obvious that unless he quickly did an about face, which seemed very unlikely, Allende and his government probably would not last through the approaching winter.

On September 4, 1973, thousands of people marched through the streets of Santiago celebrating the third anniversary of Allende's election to the presidency. By late afternoon an estimated 18,000 had massed in front of the Moneda (the presidential palace) where the president addressed them. (This number is the police estimate. It was greatly exaggerated by some writers.)

Exactly one week later the Moneda was the scene of a very different demonstration. On that day, as the Chilean air force strafed and bombed the palace, the army gained control amid bloody fighting and Allende committed suicide. Obviously the September 4 rally had revealed only one side of the picture.

This show of support for Allende had come during the worst political and economic crisis he had faced in his thirty-four turbulent months as president. That morning the Confederation of Professional Employees, with membership of more than 90,000 white-collar workers, and the National Confederation of Retailers, representing 440,000 small businessmen, joined a renewed strike of approximately 45,000 truckers, then in its fortieth day. Previously other farm, business, and professional groups opposing Allende's policies had joined in sympathy walkouts. For more than three weeks most business establishments in the provinces south of Santiago had been closed in response to calls for a "total eradication of Marxism in government." During two weeks medical services had been very limited as a large majority of doctors and nurses refused to work. One reason for the doctors' strike was a shortage of necessary medical supplies. After the military overthrew Allende's government, they reported finding eight well-equipped underground hospitals, which had been prepared for the civil war leftist extremists considered necessary to consolidate Marxist rule.

This now virtually complete nationwide strike was the culmination of many months of increasingly loud protests against the economic and political chaos that had resulted from the determination of Allende and his associates to carry out their objective of "total, scientific Marxist socialism." An earlier strike by employees of the big, state-owned El Teniente copper mine had lasted more than ten weeks from late April until July. It had pitted Chile's copper miners, whose wages were from three to six times those of the average industrial workers, against the "government of the workers," inspired many sympathy strikers, resulted in several bloody clashes, and cost the country over $50 million in foreign exchange. By August street battles between Allende's foes and supporters were occurring almost daily; and riot police, armed with water cannon trucks and tear gas grenades, were a common sight in downtown Santiago. From the provinces came reports of sabotage of highways, railways, and power lines.

"I think it is up to the politicians to solve the country's political problems, and I believe the armed forces agree," President Allende had stated in a news conference on August 3, 1973, by way of explaining his decision not to include military officers in his cabinet.[6] Nevertheless, six days later, in a desperate attempt to stop the strikes and violence aimed at overthrowing his government, he had again turned to the military. On August 9 he had brought into his cabinet the commanders of the army, navy, air force, and carabineros (national police), including General Prats as minister of defense. The move had been termed by Allende a "last ditch" attempt to avoid civil war. Opposition groups, including Christian Democrats, had demanded military members in the cabinet to protect Chile's democratic institutions. This time, however, the military presence had provided no solution. Opposition leaders in Congress had charged that the military officers had not been given sufficient powers and were merely being used by the president as political weapons, an evaluation with which some generals and admirals agreed. Within two weeks all four commanders had resigned from both their cabinet and military posts. General Prats was replaced as head of the army by the chief of the army general staff, Gen. Augusto Pinochet Ugarte.

As early as September 1972, General Prats had admitted that the armed forces were under mounting pressure to overthrow President Allende's Marxist government. In succeeding months this pressure had increased. Initially demands for military intervention had come primarily from the Nationals, but later the Christian Democrats joined in. Ideas as to the form and extent of this proposed intervention changed with time.

"What we demand is sufficient military presence to be an effective guarantee of the Constitution and the laws of the country," the chairman of the Christian Democratic Party had declared.[7] For a while this "presence" was conceived as an effectual participation by the military in the Allende government; but after failure of such an arrangement in August, opposition groups had finally united in demanding Allende's replacement by a military government to restore law and order. On August 22, 1973, the Chamber of Deputies, controlled by Nationals and Christian Democrats, had adopted a resolution accusing the Allende administration of violating the Constitution and calling on the armed forces "to end immediately all the situations caused by violation of the Constitution and the law with the aim of directing governmental actions through legal channels."[8] Allende had responded by charging that the opposition parties were "trying to promote a coup d'état."[9]

Messages from the Supreme Court had also encouraged a drastic change in administration. An October 1972 letter from this body demanding that Allende, his cabinet, and the police enforce judicial decisions, together with subsequent complaints that court orders were being ignored, had supported charges that the president was violating the Constitution. Just a few weeks before the September 1973 coup, the president of the Supreme Court, Enrique Urrutia Manzano, had stated that the Allende government had "lost its legality by acting on the margin of the law."[10] These and other Supreme Court remarks had been interpreted as pleas for military intervention. After the coup, when asked about its legal basis, Urrutia replied, "The oldest legal basis in the world—self-defense." He added his belief that the military revolt had prevented a "countercoup" planned by the Marxists, and said he thought "the good-will of the military leaders" would permit an eventual return to legal government.[11]

Pressure for military action had also come from many professional associations, labor representatives, and private individuals. Members of the armed services had been especially disturbed by laborers' reports of heavily armed gangs of Marxist terrorists stationed in or near many factories and public utilities as a threat to workers and equipment.

By mid-1973 military officers were being taunted frequently by people on the streets who greeted them with clucking sounds and hurled "chicken" and similar epithets at them for not intervening. General Prats's association with the Allende government had been so strongly resented that, while he was in the cabinet in August, several hundred women had marched to his home and stoned it.

The presence of military officers in the cabinet apparently had prolonged Allende's administration. After resigning, General Prats said his role as defense minister had sparked a left-right split in the army. Prats had been quite influential in keeping the armed forces neutral, and he personally had led loyalist troops in crushing a June 29 attack on the presidential palace by part of an armed regiment. His departure from the cabinet had inspired warnings by leftist labor leaders of alleged plots to overthrow the government; and sources in the defense ministry had stated that unrest in the military was reaching "uncontrollable proportions."

At the end of August 1973 the military had still appeared divided on the advisability of intervention. This indecision within military circles reflected the division that lingered among political opposition leaders as to whether Allende should be allowed to remain in the presidency. It also was influenced by propaganda, long promoted by Allende, that an armed attack on his government would provoke a civil war. (After his fall from power, investigations uncovered large quantities of war materials, which had been collected and stored in several places in preparation for armed conflict.) By September 4, however, the military position had been believed to be crystallizing, and that day's anniversary rally had seemed inspired in part by fear that the armed forces might soon abandon their traditional neutrality.

On September 5, the day after the pro-Allende rally, Santiago had witnessed another massive demonstration, led by approximately 100,000 women, demanding that Allende resign. It had drawn several hundred thousand people and set off three hours of rioting. It had been a final barrage delivered by Chilean women who had played prominent roles in many protests during the struggle over socialism. On September 9 Christian Democratic party leaders had called for resignation of the president and members of Congress, to be followed by new elections; but Allende had refused to compromise. These events no doubt had helped arouse the military to action. By that time, as one admiral put it, "The generals reached the conclusion that democracy does not have the right to commit suicide."[12]

Since the truckers' strike in late 1972, middle-rank army, navy, and air force officers had been plotting a coup, but the generals and admirals had not been included because it was feared some of them would object. After the coup, Gen. Gustavo Leigh, a member of the junta, stated that the decision to overthrow Allende had been made on September 9. General Pinochet said the coup had been decided on "when the military intelligence services verified the existence of large arsenals in the power of the Marxist elements."[13]

Of special significance in uniting the armed forces and determining the date they would move against the government was an alleged discovery that Allende was planning a coup of his own, with the personal army he had quietly assembled, a coup that would include assassination of the nation's top military commanders and other officials considered dangerous to his government. This coup was believed to be scheduled for September 18–19, during Chilean independence celebrations.

COUP D'ÉTAT OF SEPTEMBER 1973

On the morning of September 11—one week before the date for the alleged Marxist coup—the military struck. The first blow was by the navy, which seized the port of Valparaíso. Unfortunately, early that morning Allende received word of what was taking place and hurried down to the Moneda before the armed forces could arrest him at his residence. Otherwise, the bloody attack on the palace that followed probably would not have occurred.

In the Moneda Allende made use of its radio communication facilities to broadcast an appeal: "Workers and students, come to the Moneda and defend your government against the armed forces."[14] He hoped to protect himself and those with him by surrounding the building with thousands of people on the theory that the armed forces would not attack unarmed citizens. But this strategy did not work because the military had blocked all roads into Santiago and imposed rigid controls within the city. Allende broadcast two messages—the first at 8:30 A.M. in which he sounded confident and another at 9:45 in which he sounded desperate. Shortly after, the air force put a stop to further broadcasts by locating and destroying the antenna.

With large quantities of arms and ammunition that had been stored there since he became president, Allende, his guards, and associates who had managed to enter the Moneda with him determined to defend themselves. Supporting forces also took positions in and on top of government buildings facing the palace. From these various points they directed their fire in an attempt to turn back the attack.

Initially Allende was offered a helicopter to take him out of the Moneda, along with any others who wanted to leave, and he and his family were promised safe conduct out of the country, but he declined. Several times he was given a chance to surrender, but each time he refused. According to high-ranking military officers who were trying to arrange a surrender, the president and those around him were drinking heavily and Allende became quite drunk. One of these officers also told me that for several months before this, Allende had appeared to be deteriorating mentally, and frequently in security council meetings, where this officer was present, he would become very despondent over the current state of affairs, begin crying, and have to leave the room.

The battle continued throughout the morning and into the afternoon, during which the palace was bombed and strafed and many people were killed. (The military placed the number of casualties at 1,250, most of whom were people on the streets.) Finally, with the situation obviously hopeless, Allende agreed to surrender. But as he and his associates were filing out of the palace, with Allende bringing up the rear, he turned and ran back, sat down on a sofa, and with an automatic rifle given him by Castro, shot himself.

Several times previously, as well as on this particular morning, Allende had stated that should his government be overthrown, he would never leave the palace alive. After his death, some of his supporters claimed he had been murdered; but there is abundant evidence, including testimony by his personal physician, Dr. Patricio Guijon Klein, who witnessed the suicide, and several reporters and photographers who were admitted to the scene after the incident, that he placed the gun between his legs and shot himself in the mouth. Parts of his brains spattered on the wall behind him indicated clearly the direction and proximity from which the shot was fired. Examination of the body when it was removed from a temporary resting place and reburied in a Santiago cemetery in September 1990 confirmed suicide.

According to a Reuters dispatch, shortly after the coup Mrs. Allende stated, "He always said he would never abandon the Moneda as president and he would kill himself rather than betray all his ideals."[15]

During his lengthy visit to Chile in late 1971, Castro had warned Marxist leaders there that they would lose their revolution because they insisted on playing by the old democratic rules. But Castro never seemed to comprehend the differences between Chile and Cuba. Marxist forces in Chile could not realistically have hoped to seize power in their country as Castro had done in his. Allende's greatest blunder was not recognizing that he was a minority Chilean president who did not have a popular mandate to grab lands and industries and bring about the sweeping changes he attempted. By blindly rushing down the revolutionary road as he did, he ignored the barricades ahead. By refusing to slow down or turn back, he destroyed his chances for survival.

In 1973 Chileans had to make a choice between allowing the country to plunge on toward a complete Marxist dictatorship, with permanent destruction of democracy, or persuading the military to take over, in the belief that eventually democracy would be restored. In this crisis they chose the military—the only force of sufficient strength and organization to step in and assume control. The armed forces accepted this mandate only after it became clear that the Marxist march to total power could not be restrained by constitutional means.

Former President Eduardo Frei, who was out of the country during the coup, subsequently commented, "The military have saved Chile and all of us. . . . A civil war was being well prepared by the Marxists. And that is what the world does not know, refuses to know."[16]

Several times during a visit to Chile, in April 1974, I was asked by prominent officials of the military government, "Do you think we did right? Do you believe we should have taken control?" The Chilean armed forces had been so professional and nonpolitical that they were still questioning whether they should have become involved in governing and wondering if perhaps there was some other way out they had overlooked.

Charges by Allende sympathizers that he was overthrown because of United States pressure have been proved groundless. Chile had been the one country in the world to approve a Marxist regime in a free election. Now enough Chileans exercised their right of protest to force it out. It was an unusual situation, but Chile is an unusual Latin American country.

Following the September coup, the news media carried many stories bemoaning the "loss of democracy" in Chile, grossly exaggerating the number of people killed and wounded, and overplaying alleged atrocities by the military. To be sure, democracy was destroyed for the time being; but it already was being destroyed by the Allende government before the armed forces moved in. Gradually, over many years, the Chilean people, by demanding too much from their government, had also contributed to destruction of the democracy they had so carefully cultivated. Then in 1970, under a system that permitted a minority to win the presidency, enough of them had supported the Allende coalition—in the hope of getting more out of the government—to bring about his election. They found out too late that, for Allende and those about him, their platform was merely a way to power. But the Marxists had not been satisfied with winning the presidency. Their aim was total power, and to attain it they had set out to destroy the constitutional system. Only after the military took over and made a thorough investigation was it revealed how much Allende and leaders of the Communist and Socialist Parties had accumulated for themselves—fine houses, numerous automobiles, vast storehouses of food and other commodities—and how much they had forgotten about the masses of people they were supposed to be helping and who initially had helped them gain control.

One of the most disturbing revelations was the degree to which Soviet influence had penetrated Chile before and especially during the Allende years. Most of his supplies and financial support had come from the USSR and eastern Europe, principally through Cuba. Of special worry to the Chilean military were the tens of thousands of armed subversives, most Cuban trained, who had been admitted. After the September revolution, many of these and much of their supplies were captured, but many were believed still at large in the country. It was also known that numerous others had slipped across the Argentine border and from time to time tried to make their way back into Chile. By mid-1974 it was estimated that at least 40,000 people had left the country since the military coup. Of course, not all of them would be classified as subversives.

This danger, posing a threat of armed revolt, was of particular concern to the military rulers. It accounted in large measure for a feeling of insecurity, which propelled them to extremes in trying to round up all leftists who might engage in an attempt to reestablish by force a Marxist regime.

MILITARY DICTATORSHIP

Upon seizing power, the military set up an administration headed by a junta composed of Gen. Augusto Pinochet as chairman; Adm. José Toribio Merino, commander of the navy; Gen. Gustavo Leigh, commander of the air force; and Gen. César Mendoza, commander of the carabineros. Congress was dissolved and martial law imposed. The same day the junta announced that diplomatic ties with Cuba had been broken and relations with all Communist countries would be terminated. Two days later General Pinochet, who had vowed to "exterminate Marxism," was proclaimed president of the junta, with the other three members sharing in decision making. Initially the four junta members were supposed to share power equally and the presidency would rotate between them; but Pinochet, who in the past had carefully avoided politics, quickly emerged as the leading figure in the government and the idea of a rotating presidency disappeared. In June 1974 he became "supreme chief of the nation," and the other junta members were transformed into a kind of legislative body, with the day-to-day decisions to be made by Pinochet. The following December he was officially named "president of the republic." He formed a cabinet composed of thirteen military officers and two civilians.

The government broke Chile's long tradition of political freedom by declaring all leftist parties illegal and non-Marxist parties in recess. In contrast to the dissolution of Congress and disqualification of political parties, the junta preserved the autonomy of the Supreme Court and other branches of the judicial system.

It is one thing for the armed forces to take over a government but quite another matter for them to run a government. This they have not been trained to do. In September members of the Chilean military began the process of trying to straighten out the mess they had inherited. They appeared dedicated to an eventual restoration of freedom and democracy and determined to make sure that what had happened during the previous few years would never happen again. They promised a new constitution with provisions to prohibit a minority candidate from becoming president, which, they hoped, would prevent another Marxist era. They also set out to reconstruct a society in which, once again, the people would produce more than they consumed rather than trying to live off the government, as so many had been doing.

Within a few days after assuming power, the military junta informed creditors that it intended to pay all debts that had been legally incurred by Chile. Subsequently it signified a willingness to discuss with the copper companies their claims for compensation, and before the end of 1974 agreements were reached. It also began returning to their former owners numerous other businesses that had been expropriated by Allende. At the same time, the new rulers promised to preserve many of the reforms that were in progress, and they assured those who had gained land or other benefits under previous regimes that, except properties illegally seized, these would not be taken away from them. They committed themselves to a continuation of agrarian reform and improvements along many lines. In this process, however, they encountered numerous difficulties. It was obvious from the beginning that such an undertaking would require time—probably several years before the military could permit free elections and a return to democratic, constitutional government. President Pinochet stated that political activity would be banned for five years and military control of the government was envisaged beyond that.

The most difficult problems for the new administration appeared to be economic. The military had gained control amid utter economic chaos. The Allende regime had brought decline in agricultural and industrial production and a huge balance-of-payments deficit. The treasury was empty and the budget deficit for 1973 was at least 50 percent. Because of strikes and shortages, the entire economy was virtually at a standstill.

The junta members soon found that the cure for such an economic disaster would be long and difficult. To meet the problem head on, they instituted an austerity program. In order to eliminate the black market and provide more normal supplies of commodities, within a few weeks most price controls were lifted, permitting goods and currency to seek their real values. But the easing of controls also brought drastic price increases for most articles and contributed to at least a 700 percent overall cost-of-living rise for the year 1973. During 1974 the junta managed to cut inflation approximately in half, but it still reached 376 percent. In May 1975 the administration began to implement a "shock treatment" to stem the inflationary spiral. This treatment included a 15 to 25 percent cut in government spending; substantial increases in property, income, and commercial transaction taxes; a drastic reduction in printing of new money; and elimination of subsidies on many necessities. By this time unemployment was about 15 percent and reached 20 percent during the following year. There also was a further decline in industrial production. Under the shock treatment, inflation dropped slightly to 340 percent for 1975.

"Temporarily we have lost our democracy," remarked a Santiago merchant to me in April 1974, "but at least I have my store back."

In less than three weeks after assuming power, the military government returned approximately 350 business firms. Chile's austerity policy, the return of most businesses to their former owners, encouragement of private enterprise, and a liberal investment code resulted in an influx of new foreign capital. Nevertheless, by the end of 1976 labor leaders were pleading for a resumption of public investment and farmers were demanding government subsidies. But President Pinochet, pointing to an inflation of only 180 percent for the year, claimed the worst was over and stood firm. The country now showed a balance-of-payments surplus, and the foreign debt had been reduced slightly to $4.5 billion. In order to combat the continuing rise in consumer prices and with the aim of stimulating more competitive domestic production, the government relaxed restrictions on foreign imports. There was increasing discontent, however, not only in the working classes but also among some middle-class business and professional people, and many of the latter were migrating to other countries. Finally, by the end of 1977, with the inflation rate below 70 percent, reserves of $700 million, exports at record levels, and unemployment down to 12 percent, austerity seemed to be paying off. The tight economic squeeze, which had imposed serious hardships on much of the population, was beginning to ease.

After the September 1973 coup, with exchange adjusted to more realistic rates, the currency black market soon disappeared; but the value of Chilean currency continued to slide. One problem the junta faced was an increasing money supply due to the return of many people who had fled with their cash after Allende's election. By August 1975 the system of multilevel rates, in effect during the Allende regime, was reduced to a single-level exchange at 6,000 escudos per U.S. dollar. The following month the escudo was replaced by the peso, valued at 1,000 escudos. At the time of its launching, the exchange rate of the new peso was 6.40 per dollar; but within two days it began to decline and has suffered many subsequent devaluations. In mid-1946 the exchange rate of the peso was approximately 30 per dollar. In April 1978 the rate was also about 30 per dollar. But it was not the same peso—nor the same dollar. The Chilean peso of 1978 was worth 1 million of the 1946 pesos! Thus had the Chilean currency deteriorated during a little over three decades.

"The government believes that social conquests ought not to be stopped. These and other changes ought to be carried out on a legal basis. . . . This military action is not a step back, but one for legality and order. We seek only to carry out advances in a rational form."[17] So stated General Pinochet a few days after the September coup, in reply to a question as to the new government's policy regarding social and economic reforms. When asked about elections, his answer was, "the sooner the better."[18] But in a ceremony marking the first month of military rule, he declared the armed forces would withdraw from the government "only when the country has achieved the social peace necessary for progress and economic development."[19]

"We will return to the barracks when all violence has disappeared, when we have discovered all the hidden arms and guerrilla schools, and when we have changed the mentality of the people," remarked Gen. Oscar Bonilla, minister of the interior, a few days later.[20]

"We do not like it, but we concede that a period of dictatorship is necessary," said Patricio Aylwin, president of the Christian Democratic Party in February 1974. He added that party leaders wanted this period "to be as brief as possible, but we understand that it cannot be too brief, that it can last two, three or maybe five years."[21] At the same time, Sergio Jarpa, president of the National Party, was calling for the junta to govern for a "generation."[22]

"I never said this was a transition government," declared Pinochet on the first anniversary of the September coup. "It may last ten years, twenty years, or maybe only five."[23] Popular demonstrations throughout Chile at this time indicated strong support for the military regime, but there were continuing complaints of arbitrary arrests and various forms of torture.

A year later Pinochet, while leveling sharp criticism at the politicians, indicated military rule might last for a generation. About the same time, however, General Leigh, following lengthy debates among junta members, predicted a new period of liberalization.

By early 1976 there were rumblings of discontent in high military ranks, including demands for radical policy changes and the resignation of President Pinochet. About the same time, former President Eduardo Frei launched a campaign to oust Pinochet and the junta. Although only a few months earlier the Catholic hierarchy had endorsed the government with an assertion that the military had saved the nation "from a Marxist dictatorship that seemed inevitable and would have been irreversible," by this time the church was voicing more criticism of alleged human rights violations.[24] Nevertheless, Pinochet held firm to the path of economic austerity and military dictatorship. In March 1977 the remaining political parties were outlawed.

In April 1977 General Pinochet indicated that eventually Chile would move toward an "authoritarian democracy."[25] In July he surprised the country with an announcement that democratic government would be restored, with a possible presidential election in 1984. He proposed to arrive at this restoration by stages, through a unicameral legislative body, initially chosen by the military, which would evolve into a more popularly elected congress that would in turn select the president. He warned, however, that this progression would depend on a continuation of "the positive signs that have permitted us to advance up to now."[26] Subsequently he indicated this future government would contain a "security power" through which the armed forces would "represent the permanent interests of the nation."[27]

The outlawed Christian Democratic Party rejected Pinochet's plan, demanded termination of the state of siege, and called for election, within a year, of a constituent assembly to revise the 1925 Constitution and prepare the way for an elected government. Pinochet's reply was that it probably would be ten years before a new constitution, which the junta was in process of formulating, would be ready for public ratification.

A few weeks later the president scheduled a plebiscite for January 4, 1978, in which Chileans would be asked to express approval or disapproval of his administration. The vote was prompted by a United Nations General Assembly resolution accusing his government of human rights abuses. In announcing the plebiscite, Pinochet asked voters to support him against "unjust international aggression."

The ballot stated, "In the face of the international aggression unleashed against the government of the homeland, I support President Pinochet in his defense of the dignity of Chile, and reaffirm the legitimacy of the government of the republic to conduct, in a sovereign way, the process of institutionalization of the country."[28] He also indicated that if the vote went against him, he would consider stepping aside in favor of a civilian government.

This call for a referendum produced a crisis in the junta, where two members, General Leigh and Admiral Merino, declared their services opposed to it on legal and political grounds. They were joined in opposition by the Roman Catholic bishops. Former President Frei termed the plebiscite a "trap" because at issue was more than the UN resolution. Two of the banned political parties—Christian Democrat and Socialist—called on the people to vote against the president. From his exile in Moscow, the secretary general of the Chilean Communist Party instructed its members to vote negative or abstain. With the country still under a state of siege and President Pinochet presenting the plebiscite on patriotic, anti-Communist lines, there were serious questions as to how free the election could be. Nevertheless, on the appointed day in 1978 voting was conducted smoothly and, as predicted, resulted in an overwhelming victory for Pinochet. According to an official report, about 75 percent voted *sí*, 20.4 percent *no* and 4.6 percent cast blank ballots.

"There are no divisions within the military junta because we remain united. But now I lead the way and the other three follow." Thus did the president summarize the effect of his election victory on Chile's military power structure. This consultation with the people, he added, "allowed Chile and the government to continue with plans to recover an authoritarian democracy."[29] But the outcome also hardened his opposition to political parties.

Two months later, impressed by his apparently popular support and bowing to demands for relaxation of controls, Pinochet announced termination of the state of siege that had been in effect since September 11, 1973. "This is not a threat," he commented, "but I am testing how the people will behave." "The reality is that we are living in a tranquil period and there is support for the government."[30]

After overturning the Allende government in 1973, the military junta began seizing those considered dangerous supporters of the Marxist regime. In a television broadcast a week after the coup, General Bonilla, the military government's interior minister, said 5,200 Chileans had been arrested. He stated, "The majority of the prisoners are innocent, but we cannot afford the luxury of making any mistakes." He promised the innocent would be freed "once they have been sufficiently interrogated."[31]

It was reported that prisoners were being held in Santiago's National Soccer Stadium and also on navy vessels anchored near Valparaíso. By September 22 the government placed the number of prisoners in the National Stadium at around 7,000 and announced that about 30 top aides of the Allende administration were being kept on Dawson Island in the Strait of Magellan. Other accounts of the number of prisoners in the stadium varied from 3,500 to 15,000. On October 14 General Bonilla announced that 3,700 prisoners were still in the stadium and 2,935 had been freed. He stated on October 24 that only 1,900 remained there and the stadium would be completely evacuated by the end of the month.

Reportedly about 500 Chileans sought political asylum in foreign embassies in Santiago. On September 23 the embassies were notified that no longer would Chilean citizens be given safe conduct passes to leave the country; but following a change of policy, on October 17 the government announced it had granted 4,761 safe conduct passes, mostly to Chileans, but many of them did not yet have a place to go.

A special problem was how to handle the more than 13,000 foreign refugees in Chile. Most of them were leftist exiles from other Latin American countries who had gained asylum in Chile during the Allende regime. By October the government was establishing reception centers and sanctuaries to assist those wishing to leave the country or whose lives were believed to be in danger. On October 23 it was announced that the National Committee for Help to Refugees, organized by Roman Catholic and Protestant churches after the September coup, had received safe conduct passes for 1,665 refugees. Most of these were from Uruguay, Bolivia, and Brazil.

For the purpose of countering exaggerated reports which had been published, on October 3 the military junta announced that 476 persons had been killed in fighting since the September coup. A government report five days later placed the death toll at 513, in contrast to some claims as high as 2,500. A *New York Times* summary, taking into account many unreported incidents, indicated a probability of around 2,000 deaths during the month following the coup, including "many senseless killings and much unwarranted brutality in the arrests of suspected leftists."[32] Amnesty International claimed on January 19, 1974, that political arrests and executions in Chile were continuing. While conceding fewer killings and less torture than in the weeks immediately following the September coup, it claimed hundreds of people were still held in prison without trial.

In an effort to wipe out all Marxist influences, the military government embarked on a campaign of book burning. Homes were searched for Marxist books and pamphlets, which were collected and burned in piles on Santiago streets. The government also attempted to counteract the influence of left-wing intellectuals by replacing all university rectors with military appointees.

During the latter part of 1973 and early 1974 the military junta was in the process of strengthening its hold throughout Chile. It particularly directed attention to the slum areas around Santiago and other large cities because it was there that much of Allende's influence had been concentrated. By the end of March these areas appeared to be under firm control. The government also was focusing attention on the Argentine border, where General Pinochet claimed there were some 14,000 leftist extremists planning terrorist attacks.

There were numerous reports of torture by military officials in their drive to round up all former members or principal supporters of the Allende government. According to a Catholic Church report in late April 1974, the government was still holding more than 6,000 political prisoners, many of whom had not been charged with a crime. Well before this time all prisoners had been removed from the National Stadium and placed in detention centers in several parts of the country.

In May 1974 leading religious groups, including the Committee of Cooperation for Peace in Chile, composed of Roman Catholic, Protestant, and Jewish clergy, issued complaints alleging widespread torture of political prisoners. They were joined by political groups that had supported the military government, including leaders of the Christian Democratic Party, who charged the junta with torture and other violations of human rights. In reply, General Leigh, member of the junta, promised the government would "adopt drastic measures against those responsible for proved abuses."[33]

In June 72 Chileans, including some officials of the Allende government, who since the coup had been in the Mexican embassy in Santiago, were granted safe conduct and flown to freedom in Mexico. In return Mexico resumed full diplomatic and commercial relations, which had been strained since the 1973 coup. By this time approximately 1,000 Latin Americans had left Chile under protection of the Mexican embassy.

As part of the government's "war on crime," it continued arresting thousands of people, and in late July 1974 approximately 6,000 Allende sympathizers were still held as prisoners.

On the first anniversary of the coup d'état the Chilean government placed the number of political prisoners at 2,200, but unofficial figures ran as high as 8,000. At the same time General Pinochet announced that with the exception of some especially serious cases, his government would allow all political prisoners to leave the country, provided Cuba and the Soviet Union would release an equal number of prisoners they were holding. Subsequently the USSR denied a report that it was considering releasing any political prisoners under such an arrangement.

In October 1974 the International Commission of Jurists, a forty-member private organization based in Geneva, recognized by the United Nations and describing itself as "strictly nonpolitical," following investigations in Chile charged that political repression there was more widespread than at any time since Allende was overthrown and that "for every detainee who has been released in recent months at least two new arrests have been made."[34]

In December an OAS report by its Inter-American Commission on Human

Rights charged the Chilean government with very serious violations of human rights, including extensive torture of political prisoners. This charge was based on a twelve-day tour of Chile by an investigating team a few months earlier. But the Pinochet government issued a rebuttal claiming the report contained "manifest errors." By March 1975 some independent observers reported conditions in Chile considerably improved. In May the government indicated that since September 11, 1973, over 41,000 people had been arrested for political reasons and held at least temporarily. Religious sources claimed the number was more than twice this figure. There seemed to be general agreement that about 5,000 such prisoners were still being held. Although it was believed at this time there was less torture, it had not ceased; and the UN, OAS, and other human rights organizations claimed numerous and serious violations. One unanswered question was what happened to more than 1,000 people who had disappeared after being arrested. Two years since the coup there was no satisfactory answer. The junta denied any knowledge of their fate.

There were increasing complaints about the growing power of secret police organizations. Of five principal government intelligence services, the most powerful and notorious was the National Intelligence Administration (Dirección de Inteligencia Nacional), familiarly known as DINA, which was created by decree in early 1974. It soon became a dreaded, secret police force responsible only to the junta. It was replaced in 1977 by the National Information Center (Centro Nacional de Informaciones).

In a report of October 1975, the United Nations charged that eleven "torture centers" were being operated in several parts of the country in which prisoners were being questioned "by methods amounting to torture." It also claimed that many people were "detained incommunicado" or actually had been "eliminated."[35]

In mid-December 1975 President Pinochet branded a UN resolution accusing his government of torturing prisoners as "false, artificial, slanderous and deeply unfair."[36] On December 18 he ordered the release of 165 political prisoners, including five priests, "because of the proximity of Christmas."[37] Also in January 1976 the junta, reflecting the international pressure against alleged violations of human rights, issued a decree establishing legal guarantees for persons arrested by security forces. But in February a special UN committee charged the Chilean government with using tactics of torture that "stagger the imagination." It claimed that various persons were continuing to "disappear."[38] In reply to the UN charges, the Chilean government filed a protest claiming the UN analysis of the Chilean situation was "neither objective nor serious." It further claimed the UN report contained "unconfirmed assertions, obvious contradictions and flagrant exaggerations."[39]

By late 1975 disputes over human rights issues brought strained relations between the United States and Chile. In an attempt to improve its image, the Chilean government in early 1976 drastically reduced the number of arrests.

In May U.S. Secretary of the Treasury William E. Simon warned it that United States aid to Chile would be linked to its progress in restoring political and social freedoms. As a result of a short visit by Simon to Chile that month, more than 300 political prisoners were released and Pinochet rescinded his opposition to a visit by the United Nations Human Rights Commission to investigate allegations of torture and other human rights violations, which he had prohibited a year previously.

In June 1976 the Organization of American States general assembly of foreign ministers was held in Santiago. In an address at the opening session, President Pinochet called on all Latin American states to join with the United States in an "ideological war" against Communism. He condemned "peaceful coexistence" and said "there is no room for comfortable neutralism" in the Americas.[40]

Hosting this OAS conference brought to the Chilean military government a degree of international respectability it had not enjoyed previously, and reflected an improved relationship between the Pinochet regime and other American states. This meeting also provided an opportunity for U.S. Secretary of State Henry A. Kissinger and other foreign ministers to discuss with Chilean representatives human rights issues. Kissinger warned the junta that U.S.-Chilean relations would remain cool unless it improved its human rights policy. Subsequently, while avoiding harsh criticism of previous acts, the OAS adopted a mild resolution asking Chile to protect human rights.

General Pinochet told the visiting foreign ministers that Chile soon would officially announce human rights legislation "which will constitute one of the most advanced and complete juridical documents in the world regarding this subject."[41]

But shortly before this OAS meeting, while the Chilean government was releasing hundreds of political prisoners, a major increase in the number of arrests was reported. A majority of these were by agents of DINA.

Also attributed to DINA was the controversial car bomb assassination in Washington, September 1976, of Orlando Letelier and his secretary, Ronni K. Moffitt. Previously Letelier had served as ambassador to Washington and foreign minister in the Allende cabinet. He had been arrested along with other Allende officials after the 1973 coup. Following release from prison, he had been permitted to go into exile and had returned to Washington, where he was one of the most outspoken critics of the Pinochet regime. At the time of his assassination, he was pushing for U.S. sanctions against Chile. He and his secretary were killed by a remote-control bomb as they drove along Washington's Embassy Row (Massachusetts Avenue). Her husband, who was in the rear of the car, escaped with minor injuries. DINA was blamed for this crime. Twice the Chilean Supreme Court rejected U.S. government requests for extradition of Gen. Manuel Contreras, head of DINA at the time of the assassination, and his deputy, Brig. Gen. Pedro Espinoza. During the democratic administration of Patricio Aylwin, a law was passed permitting the case to be tried in Chile. This law led to their being convicted of ordering the assassination of Letelier. On November 12, 1993, Contreras and Espinoza were sentenced to prison for seven and six years respectively, but their sentences were held up by appeal to the Supreme Court.

In November 1976, after the U.S. Congress had cut off military aid to Chile and limited economic assistance to $30 million annually, the Chilean government responded it no longer wanted U.S. aid because of the pressures involved. Nevertheless, it announced it was freeing all but 20 of the 300 political prisoners it still held and that all Chileans would be allowed to return home from remote parts of their country to which they had been banished. The 20 were considered especially dangerous to internal security. One of them, Luis Corvalán, head of Chile's outlawed Communist Party, was exchanged in late December for a Soviet dissident and exiled to the Soviet Union. He had been held more than three years without formal charges.

Contrary to Chilean claims that virtually all political prisoners had been freed, a report by Amnesty International, together with statements of others who had been in Chile recently, claimed there were numerous detainees in provincial prisons and some 1,500 or more "disappeared persons." In February 1977 a special United Nations panel reported that although the number of people involved had decreased, the Chilean government was continuing to torture those it detained. In a statement by six Roman Catholic Church leaders published in Santiago newspapers March 26, 1977, they asked Chilean authorities to help find hundreds of detainees reported missing after arrest. This source placed the number of disappearances at about 900 in contrast to the 1,500 figure and said none had been reported since December.

In June 1977 the Chilean junta released Jorge Montes, a former Communist senator, the last political prisoner it admitted holding, in exchange for eleven political prisoners held by East Germany. In January 1978 the International Commission of Jurists claimed violations of human rights continued.

The following April President Pinochet announced he would pardon all sentenced political prisoners or commute their sentences to foreign exile. A few days later the Chilean government decreed a general amnesty for people being held for violating state-of-siege laws in effect between September 11, 1973, and March 10, 1978, but who had not been sentenced. These steps brought expressions of approval from the U.S. State Department.

In June 1978 Sergio Fernández, new civilian interior minister, promised there would be no more illegal arrests, disappearances, torture, or assassinations. "I cannot be responsible for what happened before me," he said, "but I can promise that anyone who violates the human rights of another will be swiftly punished."[42]

Nevertheless, according to Catholic Church officials and other human rights groups, abuses continued. By December 1982 opposition to the Pinochet government had become more vocal and those who were very loud in their complaints were dealt with by the secret police. Allegedly these punishments included imprisonment and torture to about the same degree as in the previous three or four years. Most punishments were for violating the ban on antigovernment political activity. Many political opponents were sent into relatively short-term exile in remote parts of Chile. Thousands considered more dangerous were expelled from the country.

Step by step after the military assumed power in 1973, General Pinochet had tightened his control over Chile. What had begun as government by a four-man junta evolved into the Pinochet dictatorship. From a politically inexperienced army general he had developed into a skillful politician and a popular president with a large and loyal following. His support was especially impressive among Chilean conservatives who looked upon him as their protector against Communist aggressors who had threatened to take over the country and still were a dangerous menace. Nevertheless, he had aroused strong opposition not only from the numerous leftists but also from more moderate political leaders anxious to regain their control.

Although relations between Pinochet and the Jimmy Carter administration were strained over human rights issues, he, along with other Latin American heads of state, was invited to Washington by Carter in September 1977 for the signing of the Panama Canal treaties. He received a triumphal welcome upon his return to Santiago on September 9. This journey enhanced his political prestige in Chile. The appointment soon thereafter of a distinguished career diplomat, George W. Landau, as U.S. ambassador to Chile, a post that had been vacant since Carter became president, confirmed the success of Pinochet's Washington visit.

Pinochet's hand was strengthened by the January 1978 plebiscite from which he emerged as the popularly approved leader of the country and unquestionably the top member of the junta. Bearing in mind Chile's long history of civilian democracy, during 1978 he was taking steps to modify the appearance of his government to conform more closely with Chilean tradition. A part of this process was repeal in March of the state of siege and accompanying curfew. Pardon or amnesty for many political prisoners and permission for hundreds of those in exile to return to Chile also contributed to the government's more moderate appearance. Mindful of Chileans' great desire for constitutional government, in April Pinochet announced that he would have a new constitution ready by the end of the year and it would be submitted to the voters in a plebiscite.

These reforms also included appointment of a new cabinet in April 1978 in which civilians were in the majority. With this act Pinochet appeared to be speeding up the timetable of return to more civilian influence in government.

It was another member of the junta, General Leigh, who had stood out in calling for return to constitutional government with "participation by the people in political decisions." Meanwhile, his increasing criticism of Pinochet's policies led to a crisis within the military in which Leigh was dismissed from his posts as member of the junta and commander of the air force. This step was taken by General Pinochet with approval of the other two junta members. During the past year Leigh had been expressing more openly his moderate views as contrasted with Pinochet's conservative policies. He also had opposed measures adopted by Pinochet and accepted by Merino and Mendoza that strengthened Pinochet's personal power. Gen. Fernando Matthei was appointed to Leigh's former positions as commander in chief of the air force and member of the junta. Leigh's removal also brought the departure of eighteen of the twenty members of the air force general staff who were passed over with the appointment of General Matthei. These changes gave General Pinochet more complete power and opened the way for constitutional reform, which he desired in order to prolong his term in office until at least 1989. Thus this maneuver was a significant victory for him.

President Pinochet continued his firm resistance to increasing demands that he restore civilian government. Time and again he met criticisms of his regime with charges that the country was not ready for traditional democracy. "Under no circumstance can we accept the return to professional politicians and political parties . . . because the parties would allow the Marxists to penetrate and return again to power," Pinochet stated in May 1980.[43]

On several occasions he was able to turn aside a heavy attack with a firm stand and a change of focus. He met increasing criticism in mid-1980 with a new constitution, which was rushed to completion and scheduled for approval in a plebiscite to be held on September 11, anniversary of the 1973 coup.

The scheduling of this plebiscite resulted in the first major political demonstration since the downfall of Allende. On an evening in late August tens of thousands of people congregated in downtown Santiago and staged loud protests against President Pinochet. These occurred during and after a speech by ex-President Eduardo Frei in which he criticized the proposed constitution that would extend Pinochet's term in office. The government had authorized the meeting to permit discussion of the plebiscite. During the demonstrations, which were broken up by police, several people were arrested and at least two injured. Estimates of the size of the crowd ran as high as 50,000.

The proposed constitution was criticized because it would grant to Pinochet eight more years that would keep him in office until 1989, at the end of which he could be approved by the junta for another eight years carrying him to 1997. This constitution, which replaced the one of 1925, provided for a powerful chief executive but no elected congress. In the plebiscite the only choice voters were given was *sí* or *no* on the new constitution; but those who voted *sí* would be approving the additional years for Pinochet. Should this constitution now be approved, the military would continue to govern the country.

Pinochet had permitted public expressions of opposition because he felt confident of the support of a majority of voters. Although people questioned the necessity of the military government remaining in power until 1989, the social and economic chaos of the Allende period still haunted many and contributed significantly to the continuing popularity of Pinochet. Thus a majority of Chileans supported the argument of military leaders that the new constitution and eight-year transition were necessary to complete the very successful economic development program and assure that Communism would not return to Chile. Although opponents of the constitution were hampered in their efforts to campaign against it, the voting appeared to be free and fair with ballot boxes being opened and votes counted at each polling table in front of the general public as was customary in Chile. Under these circumstances, approximately two-thirds of the more than 6 million Chileans who went to the polls voted *sí*.

The outcome of this plebiscite reflected in part the booming economy and internal peace Chileans were enjoying under the Pinochet regime. It also expressed the memories, especially among women, of food shortages and bread lines during the Allende years. Although unemployment was still almost 13 percent, it had been decreasing slowly; and inflation, now at an annual rate of nearly 30 percent, was far below that under Allende. Moreover, there had been a significant decline in human rights abuses since the mid-1970s.

A majority of Chileans did not look upon the Pinochet administration as a harsh dictatorship but as an efficient and honest government that was enabling them to enjoy a comfortable life. And so by ballot in 1980 they confirmed and extended the term of President Pinochet, whom they had brought to power by invitation in 1973.

In response to criticism of the plebiscite by the U.S. State Department, Pinochet replied that he had "just one" message for the United States: "We have always had good relations and I would say only one thing—leave us alone. Let us work peacefully because that way we can serve the United States more than it imagines. It did not cost the United States one single dollar, one bullet or one life to kick the Communists out of Chile. . . . So the only thing we ask is that they leave us alone."[44]

Certainly a primary reason for Pinochet's success in the 1980 plebiscite was the economic prosperity that the country had been enjoying. It stood in extreme contrast to the chaos at the end of the Allende regime. In seven years the Pinochet government had brought Chile to the point where it was recognized as the most prosperous country in Latin America. Its economic growth of more than 8 percent in each of the last three years was one of the highest rates in the world. From practically empty shops in 1973 with long lines of people waiting outside to purchase what little goods were available, Chilean stores were now filled with merchandise and shoppers. How had the country moved so far so quickly?

Despite attempts at an austerity program and a "shock treatment," by the end of 1976 the Pinochet government had only partly solved the economic mess it had inherited. Inflation for that year, although far below the figures for 1973–75, stood at 180 percent. The government had not gone far enough in implementing the free enterprise advice of Milton Friedman, prominent economist at the University of Chicago, who had recommended drastic cuts in government spending and printing money. But with an economic team including several of Friedman's former students or disciples—the so-called "Chicago boys"—the government began following his philosophy more faithfully, with amazing results.

By 1978 new Chilean investments by major United States and other foreign corporations together with nearly $1 billion in loans from private U.S. banks stimulated impressive economic developments. At this time U.S. government and multilateral loans to Chile were withheld because of alleged human rights violations. The year 1978 saw annual inflation down to 30 percent and an increase in exports that raised reserves to more than $2 billion. New investments went into various industries. Especially significant was the revival of agriculture and the production of fruits and vegetables to levels where Chile was not only able to satisfy its domestic market but also export large quantities to the Northern Hemisphere during the winter months there. The lowering of tariffs to a near uniform 10 percent, as contrasted with 200 percent and over previously levied, led to a great increase in imports, which found ready markets in Chile. This competition resulted in considerable improvement in quality and decrease in cost of Chilean-made items.

With approximately 13 percent of the labor force unemployed, many thousands of others underemployed, and wages for numerous skilled workers at only subsistence levels, the government undertook to help the poor through its minimum employment program. It also operated a vocational education project for the purpose of training workers for jobs created by new investments. In an effort to raise living standards, the government undertook impressive public housing projects. These efforts were effective in creating greater employment and higher wages.

Through such methods, by 1979 Minister of Finance Sergio de Castro and his fellow "Chicago boys" brought a favorable balance of trade and significantly increased production, with manufacturing rising since 1976 at the rate of 10 percent a year. They also claimed to be devoting a larger percentage of the budget to social welfare than was done by the Allende regime. This fact was confirmed in a study by the U.S. embassy in Santiago, which reported the Chilean government spent 59.5 percent of its budget in 1982 on welfare programs.

In early 1980, with copper prices over $1.40 per pound, contrasted with an average of 90 cents during the previous year and as low as 55 cents two years earlier, the economic picture appeared better than at any time since Pinochet assumed control. A highly favorable report on the Chilean economy published by the U.S. embassy confirmed Chile's bright economic prospects.

Under these circumstances, de Castro extended the fixed exchange rate of 39 pesos per dollar for the remainder of the year.

General Pinochet's new eight-year presidential term began March 11, 1981. Previously he had requested and received the resignations of all his cabinet members to give him freedom to name new ones. Seven of the posts were filled by new members, but in this reshuffle the interior, finance, and foreign affairs ministries remained unchanged.

The arrival of the Ronald Reagan administration in Washington in January 1981 brought significant changes in U.S. policy toward Uruguay, Argentina, and Chile. In a reversal of the Carter policy, U.S. delegates to international development banks were instructed to support loans to these three countries. With regard to Chile, this reversal of policy was in line with an official State Department statement that "there have been no disappearances in Chile since 1977" and "almost all political prisoners had been released by early 1978."[45]

By late 1981 Chile was experiencing a recession brought on in part by a worldwide downturn and an overvalued Chilean peso but largely by its own "economic miracle," which had produced a growth rate averaging 8 percent annually over the previous four years. During this period, production outran demand and the increasing cost of Chilean labor discouraged foreign investments. Partly as a result of the recession, inflation for 1981 was less than 10 percent.

By the end of the year, some businessmen who had profited from the free-enterprise policy were begging for government protection, while more-extreme nationalists were clamoring for a return of state-owned corporations. Amid increasing criticism of his economic policies, in April 1982 Pinochet dismissed all his cabinet members but said he would not change his economic policy or devalue the peso as demanded by critics, who claimed the fixed exchange rate had discouraged foreign investments and decreased Chilean exports. Nevertheless, on June 14 he devalued the peso from 39 to 46 per U.S. dollar. A further shift on August 6 permitted the currency to float freely on the world market. Subsequently the exchange rate fluctuated for a time between 55 and 65 per dollar.

Especially serious for Chile was a drastic drop in the price of copper, which in mid-1982 reached its lowest level in thirty years. At the same time, the costs of imported items remained about the same or actually increased because of the decline in value of the Chilean peso.

With more than 800 business firms in bankruptcy and industrial production down 22 percent during the past year, before the end of 1982 unemployment reached nearly 30 percent. Chile's economic problems at this time resulted partly from borrowing too heavily at high interest rates during the prosperous 1977–81 era and neglecting to convert enough of these funds into industries that would produce profits in the future. By 1983 it was stuck with an approximately $18 billion foreign debt, reportedly the world's highest per capita.

Along with several changes in economic advisers, the government backed away from its free-enterprise policy and began intervening more in the economy. Pinochet's cabinet shakeups brought in as finance minister Rolf Lüders, prominent businessman with a Harvard Ph.D. in economics, who was less rigid than the "Chicago boys" in adhering to a free-market policy. For the purpose of helping revive the economy, he budgeted a small deficit for 1983.

Dissatisfaction over the economic hardships brought loud public criticism, but it was directed primarily at government economic officials and at banks rather than at Pinochet himself. He was still regarded by many as an honest man who was trying to promote the nation's welfare. Confronting increasing criticism of the government's economic policies, he began touring the country more frequently to promote a closer relationship with the people and better understand their problems.

In a desperate effort to solve the economic crisis, Pinochet appointed and dismissed four finance ministers over a period of a year. In late April 1983 the finance minister, Carlos Cáceres, who had replaced Lüders, announced a new economic plan. It went even further than other emergency plans of the past year in moving away from free-enterprise theories to more state intervention. While insisting that the government remained committed to free enterprise, this economic team claimed its plan was conceived to permit greater flexibility.

By mid-1985 Chile was still suffering from three years of recession. It lacked sufficient economic diversification; and although there had been considerable success in expanding the exports of fruits and vegetables, profits from these were offset by the low prices of copper and other major exports. During the previous four years, exports had increased in volume approximately 25 percent, but prices had fallen about the same amount. Actually Chile's continued economic growth of 3 to 4 percent in 1983–85 and about 5.7 annually during the next three years was better than that of other Latin American countries. In these years the government had continued payments on its foreign debt, which now stood at around $20 billion. These payments had further retarded its economic development.

According to the head of the central bank, the budget remained approximately in balance despite the serious recession. The government was rather successful in resisting the temptation to prop up the economy with printing-press money. By late 1985 economic discontent appeared to be increasing, but it was generally believed that this did not seriously threaten Pinochet's tenure in office. Despite strong objections from human rights groups, in late 1986 Chile still was receiving multilateral bank loans.

Through the mid- and late 1980s the Pinochet regime continued disposing of government-owned industries, which it had begun right after assuming power in 1973. During the intervening years some of the industries that were not salable in the mid-1970s were reorganized and made profitable and their offers of sale in the late 1980s met with popular response. These years also brought a rapid growth in the Chilean economy, including the production of new foods and forest products for export. In 1987, 11 percent of Chile's exports were forestry products. By 1989 fresh fruit had become the second most important item next to copper, which had fallen to 40 percent of total exports from about 80 percent ten years earlier.

The late 1980s witnessed a considerable increase in Chile's trans-Pacific trade and in Asian, Australian, and New Zealand investments in Chile. By 1988 Japan had become Chile's second most important trading partner, next to the United States. At this time Pinochet was being criticized by opposition political groups for what they termed "foreignization" of the economy.

In October 1982 Pinochet announced the creation of a special commission to study requests by exiles who wanted to return to Chile. He promised quick action to approve up to 30,000 Chileans, including children, provided they recognized the legitimacy of his government under the Constitution of 1980. But he dissolved this commission shortly after it delivered its report in December, and its recommendations were kept secret. In early 1983 it became known that the reentry plan had been modified significantly. By March only 309 persons had been authorized to return. Over the next few months limited numbers of exiles were admitted until by July 10 the number of returnees reached 648. By mid-September 1983 the announced total was 1,835.

Many of them joined an anti-Pinochet movement. Indeed, a primary reason for forcing people into exile and preventing their return was to bring political stability by keeping out opponents who might cause trouble. Apparently this policy had served its intended purpose and permitted Chile to avoid serious political unrest for a decade. But now, ten years after the 1973 coup, many returning politicians added their influence to a group calling for Pinochet to resign. His firm control had been weakened by the economic recession, and from month to month in 1983 demands for his resignation were voiced in increasingly violent public protests. Nevertheless, he refused to be pushed out, and was supported by loyal followers and pro-Pinochet demonstrations. He assured the people that, as provided by the 1980 Constitution, elections would be held in 1989—but no sooner.

In the belief that a more conciliatory policy might discourage a mass protest movement, in September 1983 the Pinochet government was considering permitting all exiles to return except a few believed to be terrorists. But although the principal leftist party leaders were still outside the country, there was growing uneasiness over the presence of many exiles who had come back. During the next year there was increasing pressure by many left-wing leaders to get into Chile, but Pinochet consistently refused to permit their return, especially those who had been prominently associated with the Allende government. In September 1984 the total number of political exiles was estimated at between 10,000 and 20,000, but the government claimed that less than 2,000 were actually banned from the country.

By early 1984, due in part to factionalism among the opposition as well as to Pinochet's skillful maneuvers, protests against his government had lost their vigor and mass demonstrations largely disappeared. Under these circumstances, he restated his determination not to hasten Chile's return to a more democratic administration. But within a few months increasing antigovernment agitation reappeared and led to a nationwide strike on October 29 that resulted in the deaths of eight people and, according to the interior ministry, the banishment of 477 to internal exile. This strike caused Pinochet to resume a harder line against the opposition. On November 6 he reimposed a state of siege for the first time in six years to combat what he termed a Marxist insurgency. It remained in effect until June 1985. A more limited nationwide state of emergency, imposed after the 1973 coup and renewed every three months, continued.

The government appeared to use its state of siege especially to muzzle the news media, which it did more extensively now than at any time since the month following its assumption of power. Six opposition magazines were closed; and from day to day newspapers and radio and television stations were told how they should cover the news. The result was almost complete disappearance of information regarding political opposition, human rights, and adverse economic developments. But in mid-June, along with ending the state of siege, the government lifted the strict censorship, claiming a significant decline in terrorism and a desire to restore "greater freedom of information and opinion."

Antigovernment demonstrations in September 1985 resulted in ten people killed and more than three dozen wounded. Some political leaders claimed these protests, led by the outlawed Communist Party, showed the continuing ability of Marxists to stage successful demonstrations. Nearly 600 arrests were reported.

In a reversal of policy, in early 1986 the Reagan administration in Washington emphatically criticized human rights abuses in Chile. It joined the United Nations Human Rights Commission in a resolution urging the Chilean government to cease torture and other human rights violations and reestablish "democratic institutions." Contrary to its 1981 evaluation, the State Department now viewed the Pinochet regime as more violent in dealing with political opponents. But demonstrations against Pinochet had become more violent amid increasing efforts to get him out of office.

In late August 1985 eleven political parties, although still formally suspended, joined in a National Accord for the Transition to Full Democracy, sponsored by the Roman Catholic Church. This agreement was signed by all major opposition parties except the Communist, including the rightist National Party, which had consistently supported Pinochet. It was reached after secret meetings between political leaders and church representatives extending over a period of several months. The accord called for general elections for a president and Congress to be held on a date to be negotiated.

Pinochet replied to this in his annual address on the anniversary of the 1973 coup. While not completely rejecting the national accord, he said of his critics, "Their anxiety for reaching power at any price makes them try to destabilize the government."[46] He claimed Chile would achieve "true democracy" only by staying within the 1980 Constitution. It called for members of the military junta to nominate a presidential candidate, with their choice being subject to approval or disapproval in a referendum not later than February 11, 1989. The candidate could be Pinochet himself. Congressional elections would be held in 1990. In an address in July 1986, Pinochet said he expected to remain president until 1997 and was "convinced that the people will support this government for a new presidential term" beginning in 1989.[47]

Pinochet's firm hold on the presidency was due not only to his still strong popular support but also to the lack of a significant opponent. The extreme rivalry and jealousy between the political parties made it virtually impossible for them to agree on any one leader. Also because many prominent politicians had supported the military coup in 1973, they were in an awkward position to oppose the military government. Pinochet's skill in manipulating opposition groups enabled him to use their rivalry to his advantage.

By the end of April 1986 three branches of the armed forces had expressed their desires that a plebiscite scheduled for early 1989 be converted into a free and open presidential election. The army, however, the most powerful branch, had not indicated its position. Army leaders, desiring to avoid a split within military ranks, preferred to try to convince Pinochet to decide himself to step aside, but no one in the army seemed in a position to approach him on this subject. A strong feeling existed among political opponents that there should be a transition before 1989; but Pinochet refused to discuss the issue and appeared unshaken by the demonstrations, strikes, and violence over the past few years. United States efforts to nudge him toward an earlier departure from power also proved unsuccessful. He still had many loyal defenders who believed he had saved Chile from Communism and feared a Marxist takeover should he and his fellow military officers retire from political control.

Another public protest against the Pinochet regime took the form of a two-day general strike in July 1986. It was started by an organization calling itself the Assembly of Civility, composed of eighteen labor, professional, student, and other groups, for the purpose of persuading Pinochet to negotiate with them for ending his control. This strike resulted in six deaths and approximately 50 people injured. It was only partly successful in closing stores, schools, and transportation facilities, and did not accomplish its mission of bringing negotiations with the military government.

In September 1986 there was an attempt to kill Pinochet in an ambush of his motorcade by guerrillas of the Communist-created Manuel Rodríguez Patriotic Front. This resulted in the deaths of five of his bodyguards. It also apparently gained for Pinochet sympathy and support from the public and other military leaders.

In one of the most politically sensitive journeys of his career, Pope John Paul II visited Uruguay, Argentina, and Chile in late March and early April 1987. He labeled the government of President Pinochet "dictatorial" and insisted that the church try to bring democracy to Chile. Pinochet greeted the pope in Santiago with a reminder that his government had faced "the most extreme materialistic and atheistic ideology ever known to man."[48]

The pope's trip originally was planned to celebrate his successful mediation of the Beagle Channel dispute between Chile and Argentina that was inaugurated by treaties signed in Montevideo in 1979. For this reason, his first stop was Montevideo. This dispute involved a conflict over three islands, Picton, Nueva, and Lennox, at the Atlantic end of the Beagle Channel just south of Tierra del Fuego. It grew out of undefined boundaries at the termination of Spanish colonial rule in the early nineteenth century. After a border treaty in 1881, which gave all islands south of the Beagle Channel to Chile, it was discovered that the first maps, which had been drawn some fifty years earlier, contained errors. This discovery resulted in disputes between Argentina and Chile that continued off and on for approximately one hundred years. In 1902 the two countries agreed to arbitration; but a subsequent decision by the British crown, which gave the islands to Chile, was rejected by Argentina. Direct negotiations between Chile and Argentina also did not succeed. Argentina refused to accept an award in 1977 by Queen Elizabeth II, which confirmed Chile's control over the islands. This refusal led to threats of war with military buildups on both sides and large purchases of military equipment, especially by Argentina.

The three small islands were of minor significance themselves; but Argentine nationalists were anxious to preserve Argentina's claim to sovereignty over the south Atlantic coast, important for fish and other marine products and potentially rich oil and gas deposits. Contrary to the relative size and strength of the two countries, President Pinochet's strong position in Chile and determination not to back down gave him an advantage over President Videla of Argentina, whose tenure there was less secure.

In the midst of this tension, with thousands of troops posted on the long Argentine-Chilean border and vessels of both fleets stationed near the Beagle Channel, first Chile and then Argentina accepted an offer by Pope John Paul II to mediate the quarrel. The pope then dispatched Antonio Cardinal Samore, a Vatican expert on Latin America, to undertake peacemaking efforts. Agreements providing for mediation and no further aggression were signed in Montevideo January 8, 1979. After lengthy negotiations, on November 29, 1984, representatives of Chile and Argentina signed in Rome a treaty settling the Beagle Channel dispute. According to this agreement, Picton, Nueva, and

Lennox went to Chile; but Chile's maritime jurisdiction was limited to the area west of the Cape Horn meridian and it relinquished all claims outside the eastern end of the Strait of Magellan.

The treaty was ratified by the Argentine Congress, the Argentine people in a plebiscite, and the Chilean junta. President Raúl Alfonsín, who had led the campaign for approval in Argentina, claimed it preserved "the essential interest of the nation." President Pinochet reminded Chileans that papal intervention had saved Chile from a war with Argentina, which had military superiority. Pope John Paul II had succeeded in the first papal intervention in a territorial dispute since 1885.

In 1987–88 President Pinochet was campaigning to win election for another eight-year term. Along with other political maneuvers, he increased his already extensive travels about the country and extended his numerous personal contacts with the Chilean people.

On the assumption that Pinochet would be the one candidate in the forthcoming plebiscite, opposition political leaders believed the only way to defeat him was by enlarging the electorate and persuading enough people to vote *no*. For this purpose, they were busily engaged in trying to expand the rather short registration list. In this effort politicians were aided by Roman Catholic bishops, who urged all Catholics to register. A complicated registration system helped Pinochet in limiting the number of voters, which apparently would work to his advantage. According to government figures, in June 1987 there were only about 1 million registered out of a total voting-age population expected to reach 8.5 million by mid-1988. By the end of August 1988 the estimated number of registrants stood at 7.3 million. Sixteen political parties, headed by the Christian Democrats, Chile's largest party, had formed a coalition called the Command for the No, which hoped to persuade a majority to vote against Pinochet.

The three other military commanders favored choosing a civilian candidate for the plebiscite as a means of easing the nation into democratic government. Because of the still vivid and horrible memories of the Allende regime, there were many civilians, especially business executives, who were hesitant about returning to a free political system. Pinochet played upon these fears by telling people they had to choose between him and the chaos brought on by politicians in the past.

On August 30, 1988, Pinochet was formally nominated for a new term as president. In their desire to avoid confrontation with the army, which consistently supported him, the commanders of the navy, air force, and carabineros joined in approving his nomination, although they really preferred someone else. They did insist that, should Pinochet win in the plebiscite, he retire from the army and begin his new term in March 1989 as a civilian. He promised to do so.

In conformity with a constitutional requirement that the plebiscite be held within sixty days of this nomination, the voting was set for October 5, 1988.

If Pinochet should win then, he was expected to conduct a democratic government during his new term. This would be part of a transition to democracy, with a congress elected in late 1989 or early 1990 and free presidential election in 1996 or early 1997. If Pinochet should not win, the term that he was then serving would be extended one year. During this time he would be required to call free elections by December 1989 and relinquish power to the victorious presidential candidate in March 1990.

Prior to Pinochet's nomination, the government withdrew all states of emergency for the first time since the military assumed power in 1973. This action was in line with the increasing degree of freedom permitted during the past year. On September 1 Pinochet announced that all remaining Chilean political exiles were free to return.

The lifting of the emergency decrees opened the way for political parties to campaign legally. As October 5 approached, opposition leaders were trying to convince voters that Pinochet's defeat would not lead to chaos as he claimed. The first major test of campaign freedom was an anti-Pinochet rally on September 4 attended by more than 100,000 people.

In this campaign Pinochet had the advantage of the most efficient national infrastructure in Latin America. He could point to renewed economic prosperity and other advantages that had come with his free-enterprise economic system. He could also claim significant physical and social improvements during his administration. His political opponents, however, had the advantage of Chile's long history of parliamentary democracy and the desires of millions of Chileans to recapture the freedoms they had enjoyed before the Allende era.

Chile had a traditionally honest voting system; but as a further guarantee against fraud in the plebiscite, the Command for the No set up an elaborate network including thousands of volunteers to serve as poll watchers. They expected to have at least two watchers at each voting site.

Political opponents climaxed their anti-Pinochet campaign on October 1 with a huge rally in Santiago staged by the Command for the No. The crowd, estimated at hundreds of thousands, was made up of people from all over the country, many of whom had traveled long distances to express their opposition to another term for Pinochet. This rally resulted from the freedom to campaign he had granted. He also had allowed his opponents fifteen minutes of free television time each evening on the government-controlled channels to present their views. On October 2, the last day of legal campaigning before the plebiscite, Pinochet supporters paraded through Santiago in some 30,000 vehicles with horns blowing and occupants shouting for people to vote *sí*. Although the majority of pre-plebiscite polls showed Pinochet losing, he seemed to believe that the good luck that he felt had seen him through other crises would still prevail and he would win.

On October 5, 1988, voting proceeded peacefully with a turnout of over 7 million of the 7.4 million registered voters. By a margin of 54.7 percent to

43 percent, with the remaining ballots voided, the opposition won and President Pinochet lost his bid for another term. He accepted his defeat gracefully and pledged to abide by the results of the plebiscite. In 1973 he and his fellow military officers had been persuaded by public demand to take over the government when the political system failed. Now, fifteen years later, Pinochet was dismissed from the presidency by the voters, who expressed themselves in a fairly conducted plebiscite.

The opposition, led by Patricio Aylwin, head of the Christian Democratic Party and spokesman of the Command for the No, called for a reconciliation with the armed forces to agree on "a road of transition to an authentic democracy that includes us all."[49] He proposed selection of a "consensus" candidate to run in the free elections to be held the following year. Aylwin himself had already emerged as a logical choice for such a candidate. Several months earlier, in a consideration for leadership of the parties composing the Command for the No, he was termed the "first among equals." While denying any ambition to be president, he was already prominently mentioned as a possible nominee by the Christian Democrats and several other parties. Aylwin was a former member of the Senate and a staunch opponent of Salvador Allende. He was one of the founders of the Christian Democratic Party and had served as its president six times. His affiliation with the party's center-right wing made him acceptable to the armed forces.

As he did not win the plebiscite, under the 1980 Constitution Pinochet's term of office was extended an additional year. He was required to call presidential and congressional elections to be held in late December 1989 and the new president would be inaugurated March 11, 1990. Opposition leaders tried to persuade the military commanders to shorten the timetable, but they firmly stated after the plebiscite that they intended to abide by the terms of the Constitution, which permitted General Pinochet to retain his position as commander in chief of the army for eight more years after his presidential term ended. The opposition also wanted to amend some articles in the Constitution that they thought gave the military too much power.

In what was termed the Festival of Democracy and Reconciliation, hundreds of thousands of people gathered in a large park in Santiago on October 7 and demanded Pinochet's early resignation. This demonstration, notwithstanding, in a nationwide address the evening after the plebiscite, President Pinochet acknowledged his defeat but promised to uphold the 1980 Constitution.

On October 14 Aylwin announced an accord between the sixteen parties that made up the Command for the No whereby they would support a single candidate in the 1989 presidential election. "We will work together to assure an effective transition to democracy, to guarantee the stability of the democratic regime and to give broad backing to the government that the people will soon elect," Aylwin said.[50] There already were indications that the nominee would come from the Christian Democratic Party—probably Aylwin himself. The accord appeared to unite the Christian Democrats with the most moderate faction of the Socialists, headed by Ricardo Lagos. This faction, now also part of the Command for the No, was an offshoot of the old Socialist Party of Salvador Allende, formerly bitter enemies of the Christian Democrats. These and some other Socialists appeared willing to support a Christian Democrat as the coalition candidate because they realized there still was so much anti-Allende sentiment that it would be virtually impossible for a Socialist to be elected.

With a presidential election now scheduled for December 14, 1989, by the end of January 1989 politicians who had led the successful campaign to overthrow Pinochet were quarreling among themselves over a nominee for the presidency. Within the Christian Democratic Party a struggle developed among Aylwin; Andrés Zaldívar, a vice president of the party and former cabinet member; Eduardo Frei Ruiz-Tagle, son of former President Eduardo Frei Montalva; Gabriel Valdés, foreign minister under President Frei; and Sergio Molina, also a member of President Frei's cabinet. At the same time, other parties in the anti-Pinochet coalition grew rebellious over the Christian Democratic domination in choosing a "consensus" candidate. Nevertheless, in February 1989 the Christian Democrats nominated Patricio Aylwin to run for president in the December election against the candidate or candidates nominated by pro-Pinochet parties.

Pinochet's defeat on October 5 had brought quick assurances from opposition leaders that demise of the military regime would not end its successful policies, formulated by skillful advisers, which had resulted in very impressive economic growth and prosperity. In answer to Pinochet's warning that his defeat would bring economic chaos, they promised that Chile's economic growth of approximately 5.7 percent a year would be maintained or improved and that inflation, down to about 15 percent annually, would continue to decline as would the unemployment rate then estimated at only 7.5 percent. Political opposition leaders were especially concerned with gaining the support of businessmen who had benefitted from Pinochet's economic policies and had backed him in the plebiscite. While stressing his party's approval of private enterprise and praising the sound fiscal policies and steady growth of the economy over the past three years, Aylwin claimed the economic prosperity had been of little benefit to the poor classes of society. "We have to make important changes in social justice," he said.[51]

During the months following the October 1988 plebiscite, Chile remained calm and continued to prosper economically under the Pinochet government's usual efficiency, reaching an annual growth rate of 10 percent during the first half of 1989. For the purpose of preserving Chile's economic stability and progress, the government announced in October 1989 the creation of an autonomous central bank, to begin operation in early December. This bank would be free of control by the finance ministry and headed by an independent council of five members. It would serve to regulate the nation's financial system. The 1980 Constitution already contributed to Chile's fiscal stability with a provision that the central bank could not cover a deficit by printing new money. According to Andrés Bianchi, president of the new bank, its creation indicated that "as never before, there is very wide consensus in the country on the importance of keeping the economy in equilibrium."[52]

Contrary to some speculation that Pinochet might try to run for president in December 1989, although this would require a constitutional amendment, by February he had stated definitely that he did not consider himself eligible as a candidate and would turn over the presidency in March 1990 to his duly elected successor. He urged those who had voted for him in the plebiscite to join in supporting one candidate for president in the December election. By July Aylwin had been endorsed by most of the other parties in the Command for the No and was formally proclaimed the nominee of this coalition.

In the meantime, a group of proposed constitutional reforms was formulated to be submitted to the people in a plebiscite on July 30. Among other provisions, these reforms would reduce the length of future presidential terms from eight years to four, increase the number of elected members of the Senate from 26 to 38, and eliminate the constitutional provision outlawing the Communist Party. A proposed amendment reducing to three years the length of time after his departure from the presidency that Pinochet could remain as commander in chief of the army was rejected by his government. In the July 30 plebiscite 85.7 percent of those participating voted in favor of the amendments.

In August 1989 major parties of the Right and center Right agreed to support as their candidate for president Hernán Büchi, a political independent and former cabinet member in the Pinochet government. As minister of finance in recent years, Büchi was considered largely responsible for Chile's rapid economic growth and successful management of the foreign debt. According to the polls, Aylwin was supported by more than 50 percent of the voters, and Büchi was given only an outside chance of catching up. A third candidate was Francisco Javier Errázuriz, a prominent businessman.

In his last state-of-the-nation address on September 11, 1989, President Pinochet said the restoration of full democracy had always been the "final objective" of his administration. But he consistently refused to consider demands that he relinquish his army command along with the presidency. He insisted he wanted to retain his post as commander in chief to protect the army from possible political efforts to cut its budget or reduce its powers. He also was especially anxious to block any attempts to bring military officers to trial for alleged human rights violations.

Aylwin indicated that the government he would create would be dominated by Christian Democrats, Radical Party members, and the most moderate Socialists and would not make significant changes in the successful free-market economy promoted by the Pinochet government. Mindful of benefits demanded by the poorer classes, Alejandro Foxley, head of Aylwin's economic team and expected to become his minister of finance if he was elected, said, "We are going to produce change with stability."[53] According to an outline economic plan he had presented, the Aylwin government would follow an economic policy of low tariffs and no price controls.

DEMOCRACY AGAIN

December 14, 1989, witnessed a peaceful election in which more than 7 million people participated. Of these, 55.2 percent voted for a seventy-one-year-old former senator, Patricio Aylwin. Büchi received 29.4 percent and Errázuriz 15.4 percent.

"A mission has been completed," declared General Pinochet after he cast his ballot. He said his government had created "a society that is free, at peace and orderly."[54]

Aylwin, a leading Christian Democrat and strong advocate of free enterprise, who had been a dedicated opponent of Salvador Allende and had endorsed the 1973 coup, was supported by factions of the Socialist Party. This support provided interesting evidence of how far the Socialists had deviated from the Marxist policies of this party under Allende and how skillfully Aylwin had promoted their alliance with his Christian Democrats.

The results of congressional races also reflected how far voters had moved from their positions in 1973. Christian Democrats won 40 of the 120 seats in the Chamber of Deputies and 13 of 38 elected Senate seats. (In addition to these 38, there were 9 appointed senators.) Candidates of other pro-Aylwin parties won 30 seats in the Chamber of Deputies and 9 in the Senate. Rightist parties gained a total of 48 in the Chamber of Deputies and 16 Senate seats. Although a dozen Communist candidates ran as part of a coalition called the Broad Party of the Socialist Left, none was elected. Only two Broad Party candidates won, both from the leftist Socialist faction. The poor showing of candidates from the far Left was also indicative of the changed orientation of the public toward more moderate political representatives. This Congress was scheduled to occupy a new Congress building being completed in Valparaíso.

President-elect Aylwin was especially fortunate in inheriting a deficit-free government and a booming economy that had enjoyed five years of rapid growth, which reached 8.5 percent for 1989. Chile had profited considerably by impressive increases in exports of fruit, fish, and forestry products together with higher copper prices. The foreign debt, which amounted to about $21 billion in 1987, had been reduced to approximately $17 billion, and interest payments were met promptly. When Aylwin became president the exchange rate of the 1975 peso stood at 283.87 per U.S. dollar.

Aylwin selected a cabinet of twenty ministers, including nine Christian Democrats and six members of the recently reorganized Socialist Party. As expected, Alejandro Foxley was appointed minister of finance, considered the most significant economic post. Enrique Silva Cimma, leader of the Radical Party, was named foreign minister. Enrique Krauss, a Christian Democrat and close friend of Aylwin, was made interior minister. Another Christian Democrat, Patricio Rojas, became minister of defense. Gen. Fernando Matthei, air force commander, and Gen. Rodolfo Stange, commander of the carabineros, were asked by Aylwin to remain in their positions, as they were constitutionally entitled to do anyway, because they had played significant roles in the transition. Admiral Merino, navy commander, planned to retire. General Pinochet was asked by Aylwin to relinquish his army command, but he refused.

Before leaving the presidency in March 1990, Pinochet sought assurance from President-elect Aylwin that he and other military officers would not face prosecution for any alleged human rights abuses that may have occurred during the military regime. "It is not my intention to promote trials," Aylwin assured him.[55] At the same time, he indicated he would not prevent any investigation that might lead to a trial.

On March 11, 1990, Patricio Aylwin took the oath as president in the new Congress building in Valparaíso. He was sworn in by the newly elected president of the new Senate, fellow Christian Democrat Gabriel Valdés. International opposition to Pinochet appeared on this occasion when only three foreign presidents—those of Uruguay, Argentina, and Brazil—arrived while Pinochet was still in office. Eight other national leaders came a few hours after Aylwin took office to indicate their support of him but not Pinochet. Vice President Dan Quayle, heading the U.S. delegation, reached Santiago the day before and paid a courtesy call on Pinochet prior to the inaugural ceremony. After making the seventy-five-mile trip back to the capital following his inauguration, President Aylwin and his party were greeted by tens of thousands of cheering people lining the Alameda Bernardo O'Higgins, Santiago's main thoroughfare, along which they traveled to La Moneda, the presidential palace.

Not long after his inauguration, President Aylwin appointed a Truth and Reconciliation Commission to gather evidence regarding people believed to have disappeared since the 1973 coup. The report of this commission, issued in early March 1991, stated that 2,043 people had been killed by the military's secret police between 1973 and 1990. The discovery of mass gravesites in Santiago and other parts of Chile led to further diggings, discoveries of more bodies, and an increased awareness of the large number of "disappeared" persons.

Pinochet was highly critical of the commission's report and made clear his determination that neither he nor other military officers were to be prosecuted for human rights violations. Under the amnesty law approved during his regime, members of the armed forces were exempt from prosecution for torture and killings between 1973 and 1978 because this period was alleged to have been a time of civil war. In an address on the twentieth anniversary of the 1973 coup, Pinochet said, "We did not move against unarmed people, against unprepared or innocent people. Here in Chile there were 15,000 guerrillas."[56]

Although President Aylwin was under considerable pressure to bring to trial those responsible for any human rights abuses, he promised not to conduct a witch hunt against the military. As had been feared by some government officials, the release of this report led to an outburst of violence and a major confrontation between the armed forces and the Aylwin regime. The only military leader to express approval of the report was General Matthei. In March 1991 Aylwin made some progress in his reconciliation efforts when Congress approved a constitutional change that would permit the government to free as many as 195 political prisoners who had been held without bail by the Pinochet administration.

During the balance of Aylwin's term, friction continued between his government and the armed forces as he tried to broaden his control over the military against General Pinochet's determination to preserve its independence. Amnesty protection for military officers did not prevent the government from at least investigating cases of alleged human rights and other violations. General Pinochet was still commander of the army and had vowed never to permit one of his officers to go to prison. In reply to charges branding them human rights violators, Pinochet pointed to their record as the only occasion where a military force had taken over a country in chaos, restored stability, and established a progressive and prosperous economy.

Aylwin did not succeed in getting the Constitution amended to weaken the powers of the armed forces, and thus the privileges it granted General Pinochet and other officials were not reduced. Pinochet could remain as commander of the army until 1998 and the civilian government would not be able to remove him. He had appointed all but one of the sixteen members of the Supreme Court, and they could hold office for life. He also obtained a seat in the Senate for each of the armed services. In contrast to Argentina, where the military retired from power after losing prestige as a result of defeat in the Falklands War, when General Pinochet retired from the Chilean presidency the military was well organized and retained the prestige for which it long had been famous. When he stepped down from the presidency, General Pinochet acknowledged the authority of President Aylwin over him but refused to accept the authority of anyone else, including the minister of defense. As the end of his four-year term approached, Aylwin seemed disturbed by the fact that he would not see a complete return to democracy while he was in office because the 1980 Constitution was still there and he did not command enough votes in Congress to amend it sufficiently.

As president, Aylwin continued the free-enterprise economic policies of the Pinochet government, but he imposed large tax increases and applied the additional revenue to providing better medical care, education, and public housing. He also raised the minimum-wage level. Under his administration the economy continued to grow with greater foreign investments. After three years in office, he could boast that only 33 percent of Chile's people were living below the poverty line as compared with 40 percent when he took office. Unemployment had dropped to 4.4 percent, inflation had declined to 12.7 percent, and 1992 alone witnessed an economic growth of almost 10 percent. Under its public housing program, 105,000 homes per year were constructed by the Aylwin government compared with 40,000 annually during the Pinochet regime. High school scholarships covering textbooks and other expenses were estimated to have kept in school 100,000 students who otherwise would have dropped out. Foreign businessmen continued to be attracted to Chile by less corruption and greater administrative efficiency than they found in other parts of Latin America. By the end of Aylwin's term, the peso exchange rate was 420.35 per U.S. dollar.

In presidential and congressional elections on December 11, 1993, Chilean voters elected Eduardo Frei Ruiz-Tagle president, giving him and his center Left coalition the most impressive victory in Chile in more than sixty years. Frei received 58 percent of the approximately 8 million votes cast while his closest rival, conservative Arturo Alessandri, got only 24 percent.

"We will continue consolidating democracy," said Frei after his victory. "There is no way back—Chile has shown clear signs of its democratic will."[57]

Due to a constitutional revision during Aylwin's administration, Frei was elected for a six-year term extending to the year 2000. His margin of victory was a resounding confirmation of the social and economic programs that had produced the highest growth rate and one of the lowest levels of inflation in Latin America. Near the end of 1994, with the budget in balance, a surplus in the treasury, and inflation for the year at 12.2 percent, President Frei appeared to be maintaining a sound economic policy.

On September 11, 1994, thousands of people gathered outside the military academy in Santiago to celebrate the anniversary of the 1973 coup, which had brought General Pinochet to power. The crowd, composed of a large cross-section of society, chanted and cheered, "Pinochet, Pinochet, we want you, we want you another time!"[58] Many Chileans looked upon Pinochet as a villain; but thousands of others, mindful of the stability and economic progress he had brought and the contrast between Chile in 1973 and Chile in 1994, considered him the savior of the country.

During the trying decades through which Chile has recently passed, the strengths and weaknesses of the Chilean system became very clear. The people did not forget their long history of stable democracy. But when the abuse of this democracy allowed them to saddle themselves with a Marxist regime bent on destroying it, they were able to call upon a very professional, well-organized military to save them. Although not trained as political administrators, with the application of a realistic, no-nonsense approach, the armed forces not only freed Chile from the tentacles of Marxism but transformed a wild, inflationary economy into one very sound and progressive. In the opinion of many Chileans, Pinochet and his fellow officers overstayed their welcome; but when they relinquished power they left the nation able to resume life as it was before 1970. Now, after two free elections and the apparent return of sensible, democratic government, Chileans may enjoy their traditional democracy with the knowledge that, should they stumble again, the military will be standing by.

NOTES

1. *The Sunday Star* (Washington), September 27, 1964; *The Evening Star*, March 14, 1965.
2. *The New York Times*, November 4, 1964.
3. *The New York Times*, March 14, 1965.
4. *The Washington Post*, June 28, 1969.
5. *The New York Times*, October 4, 1970.
6. *The New York Times*, August 4, 1973.
7. *The New York Times*, August 26, 1973.
8. *Washington Star-News*, August 23, 1973.
9. *The New York Times*, August 26, 1973.
10. *The New York Times*, April 18, 1974.
11. *The New York Times*, October 18, 1973.
12. Address by V. Adm. Patricio Carvajal, Minister of Defense, at luncheon in Santiago for faculty and student members of the U.S. National War College Latin American trip group, April 29, 1974.
13. *The New York Times*, September 18, 1973.
14. Report of Navy Section, U.S. Military Group, Chile, October 1, 1973.
15. *The New York Times*, September 16, 1973.
16. *The Washington Star*, October 2, 1980.
17. *The New York Times*, September 18, 1973.
18. Ibid.
19. *The New York Times*, October 12, 1973.
20. *The New York Times*, October 7, 1973.
21. *The New York Times*, February 8, 1974.
22. Ibid.
23. *The New York Times*, September 13, 1974.
24. *The New York Times*, September 21, 1975.
25. *The New York Times*, May 3, 1977; September 12, 1977.
26. *The Washington Star*, July 11, 1977.
27. *The New York Times*, September 12, 1977.
28. *The Washington Star*, January 2, 1978.
29. *The New York Times*, January 9, 1978.
30. *The New York Times*, March 10, 1978.
31. *Washington Star-News*, September 18, 1973.
32. *The New York Times*, October 12, 1973.
33. *The New York Times*, May 18, 1974.
34. *The New York Times*, October 24, 1974.

35. *The Washington Star*, October 15, 1975.
36. *The New York Times*, December 14, 1975.
37. *The New York Times*, December 19, 1975.
38. *The Washington Star*, February 10, 1976.
39. *The Washington Star*, February 19, 1976.
40. *The New York Times*, June 5, 1976.
41. *The Washington Star*, June 5, 1976.
42. *The Washington Star*, June 9, 1978.
43. *The New York Times*, July 10, 1980.
44. *The Washington Star*, September 13, 1980.
45. *The New York Times*, July 9, 1981.
46. *The Washington Post*, September 12, 1985.
47. *The New York Times*, July 12, 1986.
48. *The New York Times*, April 2, 1987.
49. *The New York Times*, October 7, 1988.
50. *The New York Times*, October 15, 1988.
51. *The New York Times*, October 9, 1988.
52. *The New York Times*, December 11, 1989.
53. *The New York Times*, August 28, 1989.
54. *The New York Times*, December 15, 1989.
55. *The New York Times*, March 10, 1990.
56. *The New York Times*, September 12, 1993.
57. *The New York Times*, December 13, 1993.
58. *The New York Times*, October 6, 1994.

Chapter 5

Lessons from the Far South

From the foregoing it should be obvious that while blessed with many advantages, the nations of the Far South have encountered amazing difficulties. Although not beset by overpopulation, serious racial diversity, or widespread illiteracy, in recent decades the Uruguayans, Argentines, and Chileans, succumbing to human greed, destroyed much of the good life and many of the freedoms they formerly enjoyed. From firmly established democracies with long records of political stability, they degenerated into instability and military dictatorships. Rejecting sound economic policies, they engaged in unrealistic practices that led to exorbitant inflation and other critical problems. In contrast to traditional respect for individual freedoms, their military governments allegedly committed gross violations of human rights. The reasons for such unwise steps and the paths these countries have taken to their unenviable predicaments offer examples that should be avoided and warnings that should be heeded elsewhere.

In all three Far South republics the people sought democracy and found it. In Chile the process began early; and within a few years after independence, sound, stable, representative government was established. Throughout much of the nineteenth and well into the twentieth century a liberal trend brought enfranchisement of most adults and consequently a broad, democratic base. In Argentina the road to democracy was blocked for a time by regional conflicts; but after 1860 unification made possible progressive, representative government which, although controlled by the aristocracy, produced impressive benefits for the country as a whole. Electoral reforms of the early twentieth century extended Argentine democracy to the masses of people. In Uruguay internal division and external meddling retarded political developments in the nineteenth century, but in the early twentieth century a political revolution transformed this little nation into one of the world's most democratic republics and an extreme welfare state.

In these countries mass enfranchisement led to massive demands. In Chile rising expectations of an ever more vocal populace resulted over time in a considerable degree of welfarism. But not satisfied with the social security, extensive public housing, widespread educational facilities, realistic agrarian reforms, and other benefits which the government had provided, enough Chileans voted for Salvador Allende in 1970 to elect him president. In doing so they created a situation that destroyed their long-cherished democracy. In Argentina increasing demands of a greatly enlarged mass of voters—particularly the laboring classes—spawned military coups, the rise of Juan D. Perón, and dictatorship; while supernationalism encouraged unwise state ownership of public utilities and basic industries that proved very costly. In Uruguay political experimentation culminated in a very democratic administration by executive council; but along with it, socialistic experiments established a welfare state and led to expensive government operation of numerous commercial enterprises that suppressed private initiative. Socialism resulted in a ruinous financial drain on the national treasury that set off inflation which wiped out many welfare gains and temporarily stifled Uruguay's renowned democracy.

In Uruguay, Argentina, and Chile the people destroyed their democracy by abuse. They expected too much and demanded more than they were willing to pay for. They elected to public office too few statesmen and too many politicians. In each of these countries, as in the United States, politicians have found it easier—and politically more expedient—to spend money than to raise money. It is much easier to say yes than no to popular demands for various, often costly, benefits from the government. Influential pressure groups, with characteristically shortsighted views of what will serve their immediate interests and little thought or understanding of the long-range impact on the country, tend to demand more and more and expect the government to provide it. But they also resist increased taxes to furnish the necessary revenue. Thus the politician, ever seeking votes to gain or retain public office, has been prone to promise and try to provide public projects for the benefit of his constituents; but he has been very reluctant to impose sufficient taxes to pay for them. Consequently the people are granted more expensive social and economic concessions than the national treasury can stand.

A result is growing budget deficits. The government then resorts to borrowing, from domestic or foreign sources, to finance its increased commitments. But a government, like an individual or a family, can only go so far down this road. Its credit is not unlimited. The government, however, can legally take another step—it can print money. Without the restraint of a metallic monetary standard or other strict limitation, this practice can lead to continuing expansion of paper currency and consequent inflation. It was this ability to create currency that brought Uruguay, Argentina, and Chile, as well as many other countries, to economic ruin.

The actual value of inconvertible paper money is determined by its scarcity. A sharp increase in supply, such as the government's issuing a large amount of new currency to meet financial obligations, decreases its value accordingly. Nevertheless, it has been easier for a nation's leaders to resort to the printing presses for revenue to finance excessive public spending than to buck popular demand for such expenditures and resistance to increased taxation. Both leaders and their constituents have tried to ignore the consequences—cheapened currency and inevitable inflation. Obviously there can be other inflationary factors; but in these countries, as in many others, excessive government spending has been by far the principal one. Political leaders in Uruguay, Argentina, and Chile went so far in attempting to satisfy popular demands that they created wild inflation, which destroyed many of the benefits they had provided and led to destruction of the governments themselves.

The experiences of these republics show clearly how difficult it is for a nation to turn away from deficit spending and go back to sound fiscal policies. Having become accustomed to costly government handouts—be they subsidized public utilities, free health services, public educational facilities, social security, welfare payments of various sorts, or other benefits—the people tend to demand even more. Usually they elect to office candidates who promise more, not less. What they really want is more public spending and less inflation, but they refuse to see that excessive government outlays breed inflation. Attempts to reduce any services or remove from government payrolls unnecessary employees in order to balance the national budget encounter determined resistance.

Uruguay has demonstrated how difficult it is for a conservative democratic administration to reverse wild spending programs and return the country to a sound fiscal policy. The Blancos were elected to power in 1958 on a "save the peso" promise, but once in office they decided it was politically inexpedient to trim government spending enough to save the peso. They dared not abandon any of the elaborate and expensive welfare program, though inflation had rendered much of it worthless. In Chile the drastic reduction of inflation in the early years of the Jorge Alessandri regime shows what can be accomplished by a determined effort to reduce expenditures and balance the budget. But these gains were soon lost by a return to deficit financing.

Even the military rulers who assumed power in the Far South, although dictatorial and much less responsive to popular demands than the civilian administrators they replaced, hesitated to take the drastic steps necessary to balance their budgets. Because of the great influence of organized labor, Argentine military and civilian heads of state found it too difficult to impose meaningful austerity for sufficiently long periods to stabilize living costs until inflation became so severe that President Menem brought in Cavallo as economy minister and together they imposed economic realism. Under more favorable circumstances following the Allende orgy, Chile's Pinochet regime

succeeded in slowly reducing inflation and bringing the budget approximately into balance. In Uruguay, however, with strong resistance to change
retarding strenuous efforts to bring it down, inflation for 1994 stood at about
40 percent.

Eliminating or trimming virtually any appropriation adversely affects some
group, which often voices such strong objections that budgetary savings are
diminished or disappear. As the Far South experiences clearly show, eradicating the evils of excessive spending is extremely difficult even for an administration firmly dedicated to doing so.

What did the reckless policies pursued by Uruguayan, Argentine, and Chilean governments really accomplish? In each country excessive spending was
for different reasons; but in all of them the results were the same—plunging
currencies and extreme inflation. These states sank into quagmires because
year after year their treasury disbursements were considerably greater than
their income. In all three, from time to time, governments were able to reduce
inflation temporarily by such artificial means as price and wage controls; but
they were purely stopgap measures and did not bring lasting results because
deficit spending continued. Inflation tends to feed upon itself and produce
greater inflation, with annual deficits increasing rather than decreasing and
living costs rising accordingly. It mattered not how desirable such expenditures appeared to be. The fact that they resulted in perennial deficit financing
proved fatal.

Several times both the United States and the International Monetary Fund
provided financial assistance with the stipulation that these governments take
drastic measures to balance their budgets and thereby cut inflation. But while
preaching economy to them, the U.S. government itself was living on increasingly unbalanced budgets. Unfortunately Uruguay, Argentina, and Chile
followed our example rather than our advice.

A NATION THAT CONTINUALLY LIVES BEYOND ITS FINANCIAL MEANS
IS DOOMED. This lesson stands out above all others confirmed by the Far
South experiences. Practices in these countries clearly indicate that wage and
price controls and other artificial attempts to stop or retard inflation are only
temporary expedients. As long as a government spends more revenue than
it receives and prints additional currency to pay its bills, inflation will continue.

Ironically these advanced republics, with high percentages of literate people who can make themselves heard, have been more vulnerable to excessive spending and consequent inflation than some of the less democratic
states of Latin America. The same is true regarding their vulnerability to the
penetration of subversive influences. With firmer controls, many of the more
autocratic Latin American countries have avoided such calamities as have
befallen these three. But this fact should not be surprising. Individual freedoms, which existed in Uruguay, Argentina, and Chile for so long, confer
the right to blunder as well as to act wisely, to destroy as well as to construct.

With the freedom to search for more comforts and security, Uruguayans, Argentines, and Chileans went overboard. This is a very serious error that the people of several other democratic nations, including the United States, have committed in varying degrees.

Examples in the Far South confirm the ease with which "pie in the sky" can be sold to a gullible public. Early in this century Batlle y Ordóñez began selling his fellow Uruguayans on the fabulous mirage of welfarism. So prosperous was this little country then that for nearly fifty years it was able to support the ever growing benefits—and expenses—of its creeping socialism before the bubble burst. In Argentina, Perón's rise to power was based on his glowing promises of a great, new life for the urban laboring classes. With mass support, he and Peronism were able to coast along nearly a decade on the state's previous prosperity until the effects of his unrealistic practices caught up with him and the day of reckoning arrived. Even long after that the lure of his personality and propaganda campaign kept his name alive and enabled him to spend his last year back in the Casa Rosada. In Chile, predecessors from Arturo Alessandri to Eduardo Frei Montalva had sold the masses on assurances of a better life, before Allende, in a multiparty scramble, managed to grab the ball and start toward his Marxist goal. But by this time the nation's wealth had been so dissipated by several decades of overspending that the gross errors of his Socialist-Communist regime brought collapse in less than three years. These and some other highly literate nations have been disastrously shaken by voters who were misled into supporting a leader with the ability to sell "pie in the sky."

As the Uruguayan experience shows, people become tired of a certain way of life—no matter how good—and want a change. For many years in that pleasant land most people lived quite comfortably; but eventually they grew dissatisfied and threw away their comfortable life in search of a better one. There, as in Chile and Argentina, welfarism, aimed at raising living standards, actually lowered them by setting off extreme inflation. As these countries discovered, although salaries and wages go up in time of inflation, they usually do not rise as rapidly as the cost of living. Thus the standards of living go down. For people on fixed incomes, they go down much faster and farther.

In Uruguay too much welfarism not only destroyed the effectiveness of much of the welfare that had been provided—it did even more. Instead of satisfying public demands, various benefits granted by the government whetted an appetite for others. Also the ever increasing cost of living, resulting largely from expensive welfare schemes, brought economic discontent and social unrest. By the late 1960s these elements together with opposition to government austerity policies inspired violence. A result was Tupamaro terrorism, facilitated by relaxed law enforcement and the determination of many politicians to protect civil rights as they viewed them. This situation in turn led to military dictatorship.

Conflicts of NATIONALISM VERSUS REALISM loom large in the recent experiences of Uruguay, Argentina, and Chile. In all three, strongly nationalistic influences led to government ownership of public utilities and numerous other industries. Most of these endeavors demonstrated the general inefficiency of such operations. In Argentina, Perón, playing upon and magnifying the already strong spirit of nationalism, purchased the foreign-owned railroads and other utilities and turned the government to operating these and additional commercial ventures. In line with its socialistic experiments and following the now discredited theory that there was room for both public and private enterprise, the Uruguayan government became involved in various industries besides electric power, communication, and transportation facilities. In his attempt to convert Chile into a Marxist state, Allende seized many private businesses and took the country much farther down the road of nationalized industry than it had been previously.

Generally such operations have proved serious handicaps. As a result of influential politicians seeking jobs for constituents, these government-run companies, became overstaffed by incompetent employees. Due to popular opposition, the governments usually did not dare raise utility rates or prices of their other products sufficiently to compensate for increased operating costs. The result in most cases was inefficient operation and financial drain on the national treasury. While government-owned utilities often provided services at lower rates than would private companies, since these utilities lost money, which the government made up by printing more currency, the savings to consumers were offset by inflation. Industrial nationalization also discouraged much-needed foreign investment and, together with unfavorable political conditions, resulted in a flight of domestic capital.

Nevertheless, until 1989 attempts by Argentine governments to unload many of the state-owned enterprises were blocked by strong nationalist opposition; and for some forty years oil production there fluctuated as one administration after another succumbed to, or defied widespread protests against, participation of competent foreign companies in exploitation of Argentine petroleum resources. In Uruguay, due to widespread pressures against privatization, governments have continued to engage in various unprofitable businesses that could have been operated more efficiently by private companies. Shortly after the overthrow of Allende, Chile's military regime returned most expropriated commercial enterprises to their former owners, but it continued to be involved in copper mining and some other basic industries for which nationalization had strong support.

Uruguay, Argentina, and Chile furnish outstanding examples of how AN UNREALISTIC ADMINISTRATION THAT IGNORES A NATION'S RESOURCES AND LIMITATIONS CAN WRECK ITS ECONOMY AND DESTROY ITS PROSPERITY. Formerly all three countries were very productive and prosperous; but primarily because of unwise national administrative policies, their economies seriously deteriorated. While foreign-owned corporations continued to make it one of the world's leading copper producers, Chile, which long had been an exporter of farm products, underwent a serious agricultural decline. Its fertile lands were neglected and by mid-twentieth century had ceased to produce enough to feed its own people. Chile became an importer of food; and over the succeeding decades this importation proved an increasing financial burden on the nation, reaching catastrophic proportions under Allende. Realistically the Chilean military regime emphasized the agricultural potential and set a goal of getting Chileans back to where they would produce enough to feed themselves. This effort was so successful that by 1989 fresh fruit had become Chile's second largest export item.

Uruguay, which for many years had prospered under a sound economy geared to its fine agricultural resources, met with economic reverses under policies that favored its big urban center over rural areas of production. There and in Argentina unfavorable restrictions and tax structures retarded agriculture, while welfare programs and overly generous labor laws and decrees stifled achievement incentives among the urban laboring classes.

This result has been especially noticeable in Argentina, where highly organized industrial workers, spoiled by unearned raises and additional favors decreed by Perón, frequently have demanded and received increased wages and other benefits while actually decreasing their output. Beginning with Perón, the Argentine drive to industrialize was promoted at the expense of agriculture. Such a discriminatory policy was encouraged by the political weight of the predominantly urban population. Due to mismanagement begun by Perón, Argentina, formerly one of the world's greatest meat and grain producers, finally reached the point where it had to import beef and grain and decree beefless days and weeks in domestic consumption. It needed not necessarily impressive, new industrial development but a return to a sounder economic balance—along with its urban industries, a new emphasis on grain and meat by which it prospered before the Perón era. Fortunately the military government, after seizing power in 1976, reversed the Perón policy and impressively stimulated meat and grain production.

One of the greatest needs and demands throughout Latin America in recent decades has been agrarian reform. But by demanding too much too quickly, people in Chile turned their backs on realistic reform programs, such as those promoted by Jorge Alessandri and Frei, and instead brought in the extremist Allende, who tried to install a Cuban-type agrarian system with virtually all land under government control. There and in other countries, ultraconservative landholders, by resisting any change, actually encouraged changes.

In considerable measure the recent economic problems of Uruguay, Argentina, and Chile are political problems, resulting from extreme nationalism, excessive socialism, and preponderant influence of urban industrial sectors over rural areas. They also stem from reaction of the numerous members of the middle and lower classes against the privileged few in countries where political enfranchisement has enabled the formerly voiceless majorities to be heard for half a century or more. As the people became more educated and better organized, their demands grew dramatically and had increasing influence on political leaders. The theory that the state owes its people a living soared in popularity.

Uruguay and Argentina offer excellent examples of the DISTURBING EFFECTS OF TOO MUCH GOVERNMENT. In both countries large bureaucracies developed from the growing involvement of government in the lives of its people. More welfarism brought more welfare administrators, and more government economic ventures brought more bureaucrats to operate them. In turn bloated government payrolls resulted in increasingly severe financial burdens. The enlarged bureaucracies also reflected the encroachment of government on private enterprise as well as on individual freedoms.

In Argentina the rise of Perón and Peronism denied Marxist groups an opportunity to gain a significant foothold, but Uruguay and Chile present interesting contrasts regarding MARXIST INFLUENCES. In both of them traditional dedication to democracy and individual rights facilitated the rise of Communist and other far Left groups, but their degree of success was due to other political factors. In Uruguay, although minor parties existed, none could seriously challenge the big Colorado and Blanco organizations. Until very recently, even the leftist Broad Front coalition was unable to make an impressive showing against these two major bodies, although a few left-wing members in the General Assembly from time to time did wield considerable influence as a balance in the close division of power between the Blancos and Colorados.

In Chile, however, where the two-party system long ago had split into a multiplicity of parties, it was a different story. Here well-organized Socialist and Communist groups found their opportunity in an effective coalition operating in an extremely factionalized environment. But although Allende, backed by the Socialist-Communist-controlled Popular Unity, acquired a slight plurality in the 1970 election and won the presidency, he was unable to transform Chile into a Marxist state because of the political cards stacked against him. Here the democratic tradition was so strong and the people so capable of making themselves heard, either through the powerful Congress or in well-organized public demonstrations, that Allende could not seize absolute power, as Fidel Castro advised him to do, and he failed in his attempt to create a Marxist dictatorship through constitutional channels. Chile also had the advantage of a very effective military organization capable of protecting it from Allende and the Soviet attempt to gain control of the country.

As the world's first freely elected Marxist government, the Allende regime offers some interesting insights into the thinking and reaction of a democratic nation. For several decades before 1970 so many Chileans, in their quest for a more rewarding life, had flirted with the far Left that in 1958 and 1964 there was great fear among more moderate elements that Allende might win. Although forewarned by the examples of other Communist-ruled countries, numerous Chileans, oblivious of the dangers, adopted the false hopes of many Cubans during early months of the Castro regime—that they could gain certain advantages from a Marxist government without losing their freedoms and being taken over by it. Under such unrealistic assumptions, approximately 36 percent of the Chileans who went to the polls in September 1970 were so anxious for more drastic reforms and more generous handouts that they took a chance and voted for Allende. Even his Christian Democrat colleagues in Congress, many of whom had been closely associated with him for years, were sufficiently swayed by his promises to respect the constitutional system that they voted for congressional confirmation of his election. But Allende was a minority president and never was able to muster a majority support. He had been elected because of a divided majority. When his mistakes and misdeeds wrought such havoc and the threat to survival of Chilean democracy became so obvious, the majority united and sought to oust him. Since by this time it was too late to save the democracy, they opted for a military takeover and what they believed would be a temporary loss of their constitutional system rather than the more permanent loss that Allende's policies seemed to threaten.

NO MATTER HOW WELL ESTABLISHED AND PERMANENT A DEMOCRACY MAY APPEAR TO BE, DICTATORSHIP—EITHER CIVILIAN OR MILITARY—IS ALWAYS A POSSIBILITY. This is another of the important lessons substantiated by the Far South experiences. As recent events in these republics unmistakably show, a country can change quickly from a longtime democracy, where human rights have been carefully respected, into an oppressive dictatorship.

While there have been many cases of a nation unwittingly electing an undesirable head of state, there are others where it has done so after clear warnings of the probable consequences. The search for political leaders who would satisfy their ever increasing desires caused voters in Argentina and Chile to elect Perón and Allende. Having saddled themselves with such a regime, after its misguided policies created disaster, the people were faced with the problem of how to get rid of the now unpopular administration which appeared determined to perpetuate itself in power. With military takeover the only apparent salvation, these governments were set aside by coups that brought the armed forces into complete control. Thus in Argentina the rise and influence of a Peronist Party, backed by mass support, led to renewed and intensified military dictatorship. In Chile the threat of a Marxist dictatorship under the coalition that had elected Allende, together with the chaotic economic consequences of his administrative mismanagement, brought the military to power by popular demand.

In Uruguay the process was somewhat different, but the results were about the same. There the armed forces were called in by a democratic government to put down left-wing terrorism that, facilitated by Uruguayan dedication to democracy and individual freedoms, had developed amid the nation's abundant welfarism and inflation. Having accomplished this mission, the military assumed complete control for the purpose of solving the serious economic problems that socialism had inflicted.

Chile and Uruguay experienced rapid transitions from democracy to military dictatorship. In neither one did the attempts of politicians to curry favor with their constituents by supporting costly and unwise government handouts bring lasting benefits to themselves or their nation. On the contrary, in both of them the democracy that had been carefully constructed over a period of many years evaporated in the heat generated by excessive public spending, corruption, and subversive activities. Argentina's transition was slower, with military and civilian administrations interspersed; but there also political rivalries, unbalanced budgets, and increasing inflation amid popular clamor for more favors from the government carried the nation to complete military rule. In all three countries the people, through their political leaders, destroyed their democracy by creating situations that invited military takeover.

In these states the military establishments were traditionally nonpolitical. They became involved in political affairs due to civilian mismanagement. In Argentina before the Perón era the armed forces had been brought gradually into the political scene because of administrative corruption and the rivalries of political leaders; but in Chile and Uruguay for several decades prior to the 1970s crises the military had remained aloof from political administration. Nevertheless, in all three, conditions became so bad that military chiefs found the need—or excuse—to intervene and stay in power for the purpose of cleaning up the mess.

Several years ago, under military guidance, Uruguay, Argentina, and Chile began trying to find their way back to a better life such as they had once known. But it was not easy; and for each one the journey has been torturous and slow. As political administrators, the military heads of state encountered many serious problems. Handicapped by lack of training or experience in political administration, they undertook extremely difficult tasks. In all three countries the military governments attempted to do what their civilian predecessors failed to accomplish—drastically reduce inflation, restore a sound and productive economy, and at the same time, suppress and keep in check subversive activities. Although Uruguayans, Argentines, and Chileans complained bitterly about the extreme inflation from which they suffered, they also opposed austerity and voiced loud objections to the loss of any amenities they formerly enjoyed.

Events of recent decades in the Far South reveal clearly WHY MANY PEOPLE ACCEPT MILITARY GOVERNMENT. There in democratic countries where militarism was not traditional, Uruguayans, Argentines, and Chileans became so disillusioned with corrupt democracy that they turned in desperation to the armed forces to save them from subversive dangers and the effects of their political and economic blunders. Many Chileans who had lost business establishments or land in the Allende regime welcomed the succeeding military government because it returned their property. They and others who saw their fortunes as well as their freedoms slipping away under Allende were willing to tolerate a military dictatorship for a while in the hope of eventually regaining economic sanity and their democratic political system. Economic prosperity under Pinochet brought greater toleration of his government than was true of military dictatorships in Argentina and Uruguay. In Argentina political mismanagement and sudden changes of government over the past several decades produced such a widespread lethargy regarding the political system that most people appeared unconcerned over another coup or whether the heads of state were civilian or military. In Uruguay, where the military rulers respected the democratic tradition at least to the extent of keeping a civilian in the presidency until 1981, this administration was accepted temporarily because of the internal security and economic improvements it seemed to provide.

Nevertheless, recent events in these republics also confirm that the people have considerably more control over a democratic government, no matter how bad it may be, than they do over military dictators. In the Far South the democratic tradition remains strong and the people cannot be expected to tolerate military rule indefinitely. Especially is this true in Chile and Uruguay. But DEVELOPMENTS IN ALL THREE STATES ILLUSTRATE HOW MUCH EASIER IT IS TO BRING THE ARMED FORCES INTO POLITICS THAN IT IS TO GET THEM OUT. The road back to civilian, representative government has been long and difficult; and the democracies that have appeared are more restricted than their democratic predecessors.

Much has been said and many complaints have been issued regarding alleged VIOLATIONS OF HUMAN RIGHTS by the recent military regimes in these countries. But officials of the accused governments have claimed that human rights advocates do not understand the situations existing there and the serious problems they faced in trying to control subversive actions. It should be expected that military rulers are going to treat suspected terrorists and others who pose a threat to the established order with less humanitarianism than would the liberal, civilian administrators they replaced. All three countries reveal the extremes to which military leaders may go in dealing with leftist-inspired subversion and other problems. As they saw it, subversives flourished because of administrative leniency, and harsh methods were necessary to confront harsh realities. Nevertheless, the military governments do appear to have exceeded reasonable limits and engaged in more drastic practices than necessary to cope with the dangerous crises they faced. Moreover, wholesale arrests, torture, and other violations of human rights, which were begun for the purpose of suppressing leftist subversive activities, apparently were extended to include many people who simply disagreed with the military administration.

By way of summary, it should be borne in mind that the economic difficulties, subversive disturbances, and political problems the Far South has
experienced in recent decades were caused primarily by the Uruguayans,
Argentines, and Chileans themselves. Their unrealistic political and economic experiments created the environment and set the stage for unbelievable inflation with which they found it very difficult to cope; for destructive
guerrilla operations that only firm, military actions could subdue; and for
military dictatorships that temporarily supplanted their democratic governments. These experiments inspired illusions of a better life, but they did not
bring lasting solutions to old problems such as unemployment and economic
and social disparities. Indeed, they produced some momentous new problems.

The mistakes these republics have made are ones to which any free society
is vulnerable. Unfortunately, other democratic nations have blundered into
similar errors.

CONSEQUENCES SUCH AS THOSE EXPERIENCED BY URUGUAY, AR-
GENTINA, AND CHILE MAY BE EXPECTED IN ANY COUNTRY THAT FOR
A LENGTHY PERIOD OF TIME IGNORES REALITY—EVEN THE UNITED
STATES OF AMERICA!

Selected Bibliography

URUGUAY

Amnesty International. *Amnesty International Report on Human Rights Violations in Uruguay*. London: Amnesty International Publications, 1983.

————. *Political Imprisonment in Uruguay*. London: Amnesty International, 1979.

————. *Uruguay Deaths Under Torture, 1975–77*. London: Amnesty International Publications, 1978.

Arena, Domingo. *Batlle y los problemas sociales del Uruguay*. Montevideo: Claudio García y Cía., 1939.

Bizzozero, Lincoln. *Los inicios del Mercosur y el ingreso de Uruguay*. Montevideo: Facultad de Ciencias Sociales, Unidad Multidisciplinaria, 1993.

Blanco Acevedo, Pablo. *Estudios constitucionales*. Montevideo: Impresora Uruguaya, 1939.

Brannon, Russell H. *The Agricultural Development of Uruguay: Problems of Government Policy*. New York: Praeger, 1968.

Chiarino, Juan Vicente, and Miguel Saralegui. *Detrás de la ciudad: Ensayo de síntesis de los olvidados problemas campesinos*. Montevideo: Impresora Uruguaya, 1944.

Contemporary Uruguay: Problems and Prospects. Liverpool: University of Liverpool, Institute of Latin American Studies, 1989.

DeMelo, Jaime. *How the Financial Statements of Uruguayan Firms in 1973–81 Reflected Stabilization and Reform Attempts*. Washington, DC: World Bank, 1985.

Dobler, Lavinia G. *The Land and People of Uruguay*. Rev. ed. Philadelphia: Lippincott, 1972.

Erserguer, Enrique V. *Cosas del Uruguay*. Montevideo: A. Monteverde, 1943.

Fernández Artucio, Hugo. *The Nazi Underground in South America*. New York: Farrar and Rinehart, 1942.

Finch, Elizabeth A. *The Politics of Regional Integration: A Study of Uruguay's Decision to Join LAFTA*. Liverpool: University of Liverpool, Centre for Latin American Studies, 1973.

Finch, Martin H. J. *A Political Economy of Uruguay Since 1870*. New York: St. Martin's Press, 1982.

Fitzgibbon, Russell H. *Uruguay: Portrait of a Democracy*. London: George Allen and Unwin, 1956.

Gallinal, Gustavo. *El Uruguay hacia la dictadura*. Montevideo: Editorial Nueva América, 1942.

Generals and Tupamaros: The Struggle for Power in Uruguay, 1969–1973. London: Latin America Review of Books, 1974.

The Generals Give Back Uruguay: A Report on Human Rights. New York: Lawyers Committee for International Human Rights, 1985.

Gilio, Maria Esther. *The Tupamaro Guerrillas*. New York: Saturday Review Press, 1972.

Giudici, Roberto B. *Batlle y el batllismo*. Montevideo: Imprenta Nacional Colorada, 1928.

Giuffra, Elzear S. *La República del Uruguay: Explicación geográfica del territorio nacional*. Montevideo: A Monteverde y Cía., 1935.

González, Luis E. *Political Parties and Redemocratization in Uruguay*. Montevideo: Centro de Informaciones y Estudios del Uruguay, 1984.

———. *Political Structures and Democracy in Uruguay*. Notre Dame, IN: University of Notre Dame Press, 1991.

González Lapeyre, Edison. *Los límites de la República Oriental del Uruguay*. Montevideo: A. M. Fernández, 1992.

Handelman, Howard. *Military Authoritarianism and Political Change in Uruguay*. Hanover, NH: AUFS, 1978.

Hanson, Simon G. *Utopia in Uruguay: Chapters in the Economic History of Uruguay*. New York: Oxford University Press, 1938.

Human Rights in Uruguay. Montevideo: República Oriental del Uruguay, Palacio Legislativo, 1978.

Institucionalidad laboral y crecimiento económico en el Uruguay. Montevideo: Academia Nacional de Economía, 1993.

Inter-American Commission on Human Rights. *Report on the Situation of Human Rights in Uruguay*. Washington, DC: Inter-American Commission on Human Rights, 1978.

Jackson, Geoffrey. *People's Prison*. London: Faber, 1973.

———. *Surviving the Long Night: An Autobiographical Account of a Political Kidnapping*. New York: Vanguard Press, 1974.

Jellinek, Sergio. *Uruguay, a Pilot Study of Transition from Representative Democracy to Dictatorship*. Stockholm: Institute of Latin American Studies, 1980.

Juega Farrulla, Arturo. *Las tres constituciones de la República Oriental del Uruguay, 1917–1930–1934*. Montevideo: Librería Perkin, 1941.

Kaufman, Edy. *Uruguay in Transition: From Civilian to Military Rule*. New Brunswick, NJ: Transaction Books, 1979.

Labrousse, Alain. *The Tupamaros: Urban Guerrillas in Uruguay*. Harmondsworth, England: Penguin, 1973.

Llana Barrios, Mario. *El juicio político: Estudio constitucional histórico-político*. Montevideo: Impresora Moderna, 1942.

Martínez Lamas, Julio. *Economía uruguaya*. Montevideo: Claudio García y Cía., 1943.

————. *Riqueza y pobreza del Uruguay: Estudio de las causas que retardan el progreso nacional.* 2d ed. Montevideo: Tipografía Atlántida, 1946.

Martorelli, Horacio. *La sociedad rural uruguaya.* Montevideo: Fundación de Cultura Universitaria, 1982.

Moss, Robert. *Uruguay: Terrorism versus Democracy.* London: Institute for the Study of Conflict, 1971.

O'Neill Cuesta, Fernando. *Anarquistas de acción en Montevideo, 1927–1937.* Montevideo: Editorial Recortes, 1993.

Pendle, George. *Uruguay: South America's First Welfare State.* New York: Royal Institute of International Affairs, 1952.

Pérez, Silvestre. *Filosofía del federalismo en el Río de la Plata.* Montevideo: Tipografía Atlántida, 1948.

Pintos, Francisco R. *Batlle y el proceso histórico del Uruguay.* Montevideo: Claudio García y Cía., 1938.

Pivel Devoto, Juan E. *Historia de los partidos políticos en el Uruguay.* Montevideo: Claudio García y Cía., 1942.

Pivel Devoto, Juan E., and Alcira Ranieri de Pivel Devoto. *Historia de la República Oriental del Uruguay.* Montevideo: R. Artagaveytia, 1945.

Porzecanski, Arturo C. *Uruguay's Tupamaros: The Urban Guerrillas.* New York: Praeger, 1973.

Rial Roade, Juan. *The Political Conjuncture in Uruguay.* Montevideo: Centro de Informaciones y Estudios del Uruguay, 1984.

Rodríguez Fabregat, Enrique. *Batlle y Ordóñez, el reformador.* Buenos Aires: Editorial Claridad, 1942.

Salom, Miguel. *Seguro obligatorio social.* Montevideo: Editorial La Casa del Estudiante, 1943.

Salterain Herrera, Eduardo de. *Enseñanza secundaria uruguaya.* Montevideo: Casa A. Barreiro, 1942.

Sanguinetti Freire, Alberto. *Legislación social del Uruguay.* 2d. ed. 2 vols. Montevideo: A. Barreiro y Ramos, 1949.

Seppa, Dale A. *Uruguayan Paper Money.* Chicago: Obol International, 1974.

Taylor, Philip B. *Government and Politics of Uruguay.* Westport, CT: Greenwood Press, 1984.

Uruguay, the End of a Nightmare? New York: Lawyers Committee for International Human Rights, 1984.

Uruguay and the United Nations. Westport, CT: Greenwood Press, 1974.

Uruguay: Generals Rule. London: Latin American Bureau, 1980.

Uruguay nunca más: Human Rights Violations, 1972–1985. Philadelphia: Temple University Press, 1992.

Vanger, Milton I. *José Batlle y Ordóñez of Uruguay, the Creator of His Times, 1902–1907.* Waltham, MA: Brandeis University Press, 1980.

————. *The Model Country: José Batlle y Ordóñez of Uruguay, 1907–1915.* Hanover, NH: University Press of New England, 1980.

Veiga, Danilo. *Regional Development and Population Distribution in Uruguay.* Montevideo: Centro de Informaciones y Estudios del Uruguay, 1979.

Violations of Human Rights in Uruguay (1972–1976). Toronto: Inter-Church Committee on Human Rights in Latin America, 1978.

Weinstein, Martin. *Uruguay, Democracy at the Crossroads*. Boulder, CO: Westview Press, 1988.

————. *Uruguay: The Politics of Failure*. Westport, CT: Greenwood Press, 1975.

Wettstein, Germán, ed. *El Frente Amplio en el umbral del gobierno nacional*. Montevideo: La República, 1993.

Williman, José Claudio. *Una comedia política, 1937–1943*. Montevideo: Impresora Moderna, 1943.

Zavala Muniz, Justino. *Batlle, héroe civil*. Mexico: Fondo de Cultura Económica, 1945.

Zum Felde, Alberto. *Evolución histórica del Uruguay*. 3rd ed. Montevideo: M. García, 1945.

————. *Proceso intelectual del Uruguay y crítica de su literatura*. Montevideo: Imprenta Nacional Colorada, 1930.

ARGENTINA

Alexander, Robert J. *Juan Domingo Perón*. Boulder, CO: Westview Press, 1979.

————. *The Perón Era*. New York: Columbia University Press, 1951.

Argentine National Commission on the Disappeared. *Nunca más*. New York: Farrar, Straus, Giroux, 1986.

Baily, Samuel L. *Labor, Nationalism, and Politics in Argentina*. New Brunswick, NJ: Rutgers University Press, 1967.

Blankstein, George I. *Perón's Argentina*. Chicago: University of Chicago Press, 1953.

Borroni, J. Otelo, and Roberto Vacca. *Eva Perón*. Buenos Aires: Centro Editor de America Latina, 1971.

Braun, Oscar. *El desarrollo de la capital monopolista en la Argentina*. Buenos Aires: Tiempo Contemporáneo, 1970.

Bruno, Cayetano. *Historia de la iglesia en la Argentina*. 7 vols. Buenos Aires: Don Bosco, 1966–1971.

Cámpora, Héctor J. *La revolución peronista*. Buenos Aires: Editorial de la Universidad de Buenos Aires, 1973.

Cantón, Darío. *Elecciones y partidos políticos en la Argentina*. Buenos Aires: Siglo XXI, 1973.

————. *El Parlamento Argentino en épocas de cambio: 1890, 1916, y 1946*. Buenos Aires: Editorial de Instituto, 1965.

————. *Military Interventions in Argentina: 1900–1906*. Buenos Aires: Centro de Investigaciones Sociales, 1967.

Ciria, Alberto. *Perón y el justicialismo*. Buenos Aires: Siglo XXI, 1972.

Comisión Nacional sobre la Desaparición de Personas. *Nunca más*. Buenos Aires: Editorial Universitaria de Buenos Aires, 1984.

Concatti, Rolando. *Nuestra opción por el peronismo*. Mendoza: Publicaciones del Movimiento Sacerdotes para el Tercer Mundo, 1972.

Consultation Among the American Republics with Respect to the Argentine Situation. Washington, DC: Memorandum of the United States Government, 1946.

Díaz Alejandro, Carlos F. *Essays on the Economic History of the Argentine Republic*. New Haven: Yale University Press, 1970.

Di Tella, Guido. *Perón-Perón, 1973–1976*. Buenos Aires: Sudamericana, 1983.

Editors of *La Prensa*. *Defense of Freedom*. New York: John Day, 1952.

Estevey, Luis Adolfo. *¿Liberalismo o nacionalismo?* Buenos Aires: Editorial Difusión, 1941.

Falcoff, Mark, and Ronald H. Dolkart. *Prologue to Perón: Argentina in Depression and War.* Berkeley: University of California Press, 1975.

Filippo, Virgilio. *El Plan Quinquenal, Perón y los Comunistas.* Buenos Aires: El Ateneo, 1948.

Fillol, Tomás Roberto. *Social Factors in Economic Development: The Argentine Case.* Cambridge, MA: MIT Press, 1961.

Floren, María. *The Woman with the Whip: Eva Perón.* New York: Doubleday, 1952.

Fraser, Nicolas, and Marysa Navarro. *Eva Perón.* New York: Norton, 1980.

Frondizi, Arturo. *La Argentina: ¿Es un país subdesarrollado?* Buenos Aires: Ediciones CEN, 1964.

Gambini, Hugo. *El peronismo y la iglesia.* Buenos Aires: Brújula, 1971.

Godio, Julio. *La caída de Perón: De junio a septiembre de 1955.* Buenos Aires: Gránica, 1973.

Goldwert, Marvin. *Democracy, Militarism, and Nationalism in Argentina, 1930–1966.* Austin: University of Texas Press, 1972.

Gómez Morales, Alfredo. *Política económica peronista.* Buenos Aires: Escuela Superior Peronista, 1951.

Greenup, Ruth, and Leonard Greenup. *Revolution Before Breakfast: Argentina, 1941–1946.* Chapel Hill: University of North Carolina Press, 1947.

Hodges, Donald C. *Argentina, 1943–1976: The National Revolution and Resistance.* Albuquerque: University of New Mexico Press, 1976.

Imaz, José Luis de. *Los que mandan (Those Who Rule).* Albany: State University of New York Press, 1970.

Josephs, Ray. *Argentine Diary.* New York: Random House, 1944.

Kennedy, John J. *Catholicism, Nationalism, and Democracy in Argentina.* Notre Dame: University of Notre Dame Press, 1958.

Kohl, James, and John Litt. *Urban Guerrilla Warfare in Latin America.* Cambridge, MA: MIT Press, 1974.

Lieuwen, Edwin. *Generals vs. Presidents: Neomilitarism in Latin America.* New York: Praeger, 1964.

Mende, Raúl A. *El Justicialismo: Doctrina y realidad peronista.* Buenos Aires: Alea, 1950.

Organization of American States, Inter-American Commission on Human Rights. *Report on the Situation of Human Rights in Argentina.* Washington, DC: General Secretariat OAS, 1980.

Owen, Frank. *Perón: His Rise and Fall.* London: Cresset, 1957.

Page, Joseph A. *Perón: A Biography.* New York: Random House, 1983.

Parera, Ricardo. *Democracia cristiana en la Argentina.* Buenos Aires: Editorial Nahuel, 1967.

Peralta Ramos, Monica. *The Political Economy of Argentina.* Boulder, CO: Westview Press, 1992.

Peralta Ramos, Monica, and Carlos Waisman, eds. *From Military Rule to Liberal Democracy in Argentina.* Boulder, CO: Westview Press, 1987.

Perón, Eva. *La razón de mi vida.* Buenos Aires: Peuser, 1951.

Perón, Juan Domingo. *Conducción política.* Buenos Aires: Freeland, 1971.

Poneman, Daniel. *Argentina: Democracy on Trial.* New York: Paragon, 1987.

Potash, Robert A. *The Army and Politics in Argentina, 1928–1945: Yrigoyen to Perón.* Stanford: Stanford University Press, 1969.

———. *The Army and Politics in Argentina, 1945–1962: Perón to Frondizi.* Stanford: Stanford University Press, 1980.

———. *The Impact of Professionalism on the Twentieth-Century Argentine Military.* Amherst: University of Massachusetts Program in Latin American Studies, 1977.

Rennie, Ysabel. *The Argentine Republic.* New York: Macmillan, 1945.

Richmond, Leonard T. *Argentina's Third Position and Other Systems Compared.* Buenos Aires: Acme Agency, 1949.

Rock, David. *Argentina, 1516–1987: From Spanish Colonization to Alfonsín.* Berkeley: University of California Press, 1987.

———. *Politics in Argentina, 1890–1930: The Rise and Fall of Radicalism.* Cambridge: Cambridge University Press, 1975.

Scobie, James R. *Argentina: A City and a Nation.* 2d ed. New York: Oxford University Press, 1971.

Smith, Peter H. *Argentina and the Failure of Democracy: Conflict Among Political Elites, 1904–1955.* Madison: University of Wisconsin Press, 1974.

Smith, William. *Authoritarianism and the Crisis of the Argentine Political Economy.* Stanford: Stanford University Press, 1989.

Snow, Peter G., and Luigi Manzetti. *Political Forces in Argentina.* 3d ed. Westport, CT: Praeger, 1993.

Timerman, Jacobo. *Prisoner Without a Name, Cell Without a Number.* New York: Alfred A. Knopf, 1981.

Toer, Mario, ed. *El movimiento estudiantil de Perón a Alfonsín.* Buenos Aires: Centro Editor de América Latina, 1988.

Troncoso, Oscar A. *Los nacionalistas argentinas.* Buenos Aires: Ediciones S.A.G.A., 1957.

United Nations Economic Commission for Latin America. *Economic Development and Income Distribution in Argentina.* New York: United Nations, 1969.

Waisman, Carlos. *Reversal of Development in Argentina: Postwar Counterrevolutionary Policies and Their Structural Consequences.* Princeton, NJ: Princeton University Press, 1987.

Waldmann, Peter. *El peronismo, 1943–1955.* Buenos Aires: Sudamericana, 1981.

Whitaker, Arthur P. *Argentina.* Englewood Cliffs, NJ: Prentice-Hall, 1964.

———. *Argentine Upheaval: Perón's Fall and the New Regime.* London: Atlantic Press, 1956.

World Bank. *Argentina: Reforms for Price Stability and Growth.* Washington, DC: World Bank, 1990.

Wynia, Gary W. *Argentina in the Postwar Era: Politics and Economic Policy Making in a Divided Society.* Albuquerque: University of New Mexico Press, 1978.

Zalduendo, Eduardo. *Geografía electoral de la Argentina.* Buenos Aires: Ediciones Ancora, 1958.

Zuccotti, Juan Carlos. *La emigración argentina contemporánea.* Buenos Aires: Plus Ultra, 1986.

CHILE

Alexander, Robert J. *The Tragedy of Chile*. Westport, CT: Greenwood Press, 1978.

Allende, Salvador. *Allende: Su pensamiento político*. Santiago: Editorial Quimantú, 1972.

Angell, Alan. *Politics and the Labour Movement in Chile*. London: Oxford University Press, 1972.

Arellano, José Pablo. *Políticas sociales y desarrollo, Chile: 1924–1984*. Santiago: CIEPLAN, 1985.

Arriagada, Génaro. *The Politics of Power: Pinochet*. New York: Unwin Hyman, 1988.

Bascuñan Edwards, Carlos. *La izquierda sin Allende*. Santiago: Editorial Planeta, 1990.

Bauer, Arnold J. *Chilean Rural Society from the Spanish Conquest to 1930*. Cambridge: Cambridge University Press, 1975.

Bitar, Sergio. *Chile: Experiment in Democracy*. Philadelphia: Institute for the Study of Human Issues, 1986.

Bouvier, Virginia Marie. *Alliance or Compromise: Implications of the Chilean Experience for the Catholic Church in Latin America*. Syracuse, NY: Maxwell School at Syracuse University, 1983.

Castillo, Jaime. *Las fuentes de la Democracia Cristiana*. Santiago: Editorial del Pacífico, 1963.

Cavallo Castro, Ascanio, Manuel Salazar Salvo, and Oscar Sepúlveda Pacheco. *La historia oculta del régimen militar, Chile 1973–1988*. Santiago: Editorial Antárctica, 1990.

Caviedes, César. *Elections in Chile: The Road to Redemocratization*. Boulder, CO: Lynne Rienner, 1991.

———. *The Politics of Chile: A Sociogeographical Assessment*. Boulder, CO: Westview Press, 1979.

Chelén Rojas, Alejandro. *Trayectoria del socialismo*. Santiago: Editorial Austral, 1966.

Cruz Coke, Ricardo. *Geografía electoral de Chile*. Santiago: Editorial del Pacífico, 1952.

Davis, William Columbus. *The Last Conquistadores: The Spanish Intervention in Peru and Chile, 1863–1866*. Athens: University of Georgia Press, 1950.

Debray, Regis. *The Chilean Revolution: Conversations with Allende*. New York: Vintage Press, 1971.

Delano, Manuel, and Hugo Traslaviña. *La herencia de los Chicago Boys*. Santiago: Las Ediciones del Ornitorrinco, 1989.

De Vylder, Stefan. *Allende's Chile: The Political Economy of the Rise and Fall of the Unidad Popular*. Cambridge: Cambridge University Press, 1976.

Drake, Paul, and Iván Jaksic. *The Struggle for Democracy in Chile, 1982–1990*. Lincoln: University of Nebraska Press, 1991.

Echaiz, Rene León. *Evolución histórica de los partidos políticos chilenos*. Santiago: Editorial Francisco de Aguirre, 1971.

Espinosa, Juan, and Andrew Zimbalist. *Economic Democracy: Workers' Participation in Chilean Industry, 1970–1973*. New York: Academic Press, 1978.

Falcoff, Mark. *Modern Chile: 1970–1989*. New Brunswick, NJ: Transaction Books, 1989.

Farrell, Joseph. *The National Unified School in Allende's Chile*. Vancouver: University of British Columbia Press, 1986.

Faúndez, Julio. *Marxism and Democracy in Chile: From 1932 to the Fall of Allende.* New Haven: Yale University Press, 1988.

Fermandois, Joaquin. *Chile y el mundo 1970–1973: La política exterior del gobierno de la Unidad Popular y el sistema internacional.* Santiago: Ediciones Universidad Católica de Chile, 1985.

Fleet, Michael. *The Rise and Fall of Chilean Christian Democracy.* Princeton, NJ: Princeton University Press, 1985.

Foxley, Alejandro. *Latin American Experiments in Neoconservative Economics.* Berkeley: University of California Press, 1983.

Furci, Carmelo. *The Chilean Communist Party and the Road to Socialism.* London: Zed Press, 1984.

Galdames, Luis. *A History of Chile.* Tr. and ed. by Isaac J. Cox. Chapel Hill: University of North Carolina Press, 1941.

Garcés, Joan. *Allende y la experiencia Chilena.* Barcelona: Editorial Ariel, 1976.

———. *El estado y los problemas tácticas en el gobierno de Allende.* Madrid: Siglo XXI, 1974.

Garretón, Manuel Antonio, and Tomas Moulian. *La Unidad Popular y el conflicto político en Chile.* Santiago: Ediciones Minga, 1983.

Geisse, Francisco, and José Antonio Ramírez Arrayas. *La reforma constitucional.* Santiago: CESOC, 1989.

Gil, Federico, Ricardo Lagos, and Henry Landsberger, eds. *Chile at the Turning Point: Lessons of the Socialist Years, 1970–1973.* Philadelphia: Institute for the Study of Human Issues, 1979.

Hojman, David, ed. *Chile After 1973: Elements for the Analysis of Military Rule.* Liverpool: University of Liverpool, Centre for Latin American Studies, 1985.

Jobet, Julio César, and Alejandro Chelén Rojas, eds. *Pensamiento teórico y político del Partido Socialista.* Santiago: Editorial Quimantú, 1972.

Johnson, Dale. *The Chilean Road to Socialism.* New York: Anchor Press, 1973.

Junta de Gobierno. *Libro blanco del cambio de gobierno en Chile.* Santiago: Editorial Lord Cochrane, 1973.

Kaufman, Edy. *Crisis in Allende's Chile: New Perspectives.* New York, Praeger, 1988.

Lagos, Ricardo. *Hacia la democracia: Los socialistas en el Chile de hoy.* Santiago: Ediciones Documentas, 1987.

Loveman, Brian. *Chile: The Legacy of Hispanic Capitalism.* New York: Oxford University Press, 1988.

———. *Struggle in the Countryside: Politics and Rural Labor in Chile, 1919–1973.* Bloomington: University of Indiana Press, 1976.

Maira, Luis. *Dos años de Unidad Popular.* Santiago: Editorial Quimantú, 1973.

Mamalakis, Markos J. *The Growth and Structure of the Chilean Economy: From Independence to Allende.* New Haven: Yale University Press, 1976.

Martínez, Javier, and Eugenio Tironi. *Las clases sociales en Chile: Cambio y estratificación, 1970–1980.* Santiago: Ediciones SUR, 1985.

Medhurst, Kenneth, ed. *Allende's Chile.* New York: St. Martin's Press, 1972.

Merino Darrouy, Luis. *Evolución del poder executivo en Chile.* Santiago: Editorial Universitaria, 1949.

Moran, Theodore H. *Multinational Corporations and the Politics of Dependence: Copper in Chile.* Princeton, NJ: Princeton University Press, 1974.

Nunn, Frederick M. *Chilean Politics 1920–1931: The Honorable Mission of the Armed Forces.* Albuquerque: University of New Mexico Press, 1970.

————. *The Military in Chilean History: Essays on Civil-Military Relations, 1810–1973.* Albuquerque: University of New Mexico Press, 1976.

O'Brien, Philip. *Allende's Chile.* New York: Praeger, 1976.

O'Brien, Philip, and Jackie Roddick. *Chile: The Pinochet Decade.* London: Latin American Bureau, 1983.

Oppenheim, Lois H. *Politics in Chile.* Boulder, CO: Westview Press, 1993.

Orrego Vicuña, Claudio. *Chile: The Balanced View.* Santiago: Editora Gabriela Mistral, 1975.

Petras, James. *Politics and Social Forces in Chilean Development.* Berkeley: University of California Press, 1969.

Pinochet, Augusto. *El día decisivo: Il de septiembre de 1973.* Santiago: Editorial Andrés Bello, 1979.

Pollack, Benny. *Mobilization and Socialist Politics in Chile.* Liverpool: Latin American Centre of the University of Liverpool, 1980.

Prats, Carlos. *Memorias: Testimonio de un soldado.* Santiago: Ediciones Pehuén, 1985.

Roxborough, Ian, Philip O'Brien, and Jackie Roddick. *Chile: The State and Revolution.* London: Macmillan, 1977.

Smith, Brian H. *The Church and Politics in Chile: Challenges to Modern Catholicism.* Princeton, NJ: Princeton University Press, 1982.

Steenland, Kyle. *Agrarian Reform Under Allende: Peasant Revolt in the South.* Albuquerque: University of New Mexico Press, 1977.

Stevenson, John R. *The Chilean Popular Front.* Philadelphia: University of Pennsylvania Press, 1942.

Tomic, Radomiro. *Tomic: Testimonios.* Santiago: Editorial Emisión, 1988.

Valenzuela, Arturo. *The Breakdown of Democratic Regimes: Chile.* Baltimore: Johns Hopkins University Press, 1978.

Valenzuela, Arturo, and J. Samuel Valenzuela, eds. *Chile: Politics and Society.* New Brunswick, NJ: Transaction Books, 1976.

Valenzuela, J. Samuel, and Arturo Valenzuela, eds. *Military Rule in Chile: Dictatorship and Oppositions.* Baltimore: Johns Hopkins University Press, 1986.

Walton, Gary. *The National Economic Policies of Chile.* Greenwich, CT: Jai Press, 1985.

Zammit, J. Ann. *The Chilean Road to Socialism.* Sussex, England: University of Sussex, Institute of Development Studies, 1973.

Zeitlin, Maurice. *The Civil Wars in Chile.* Princeton, NJ: Princeton University Press, 1984.

Index

About the Author

WILLIAM COLUMBUS DAVIS' academic career spans more than a quarter of a century and includes positions with the University of Georgia, George Washington University, and most recently the National War College, where he served as Professor of International Affairs. Director of Latin American Studies at all three institutions, Dr. Davis earned his Ph.D. from Harvard.

ISBN 0-275-95021-2

90000>

EAN

9 780275 950217

HARDCOVER BAR CODE